# PRIYANKA CHOPRA

# PRIYANKA CHOPRA

### THE INCREDIBLE STORY OF
### A GLOBAL BOLLYWOOD STAR

## ASEEM CHHABRA

RUPA

Published by
Rupa Publications India Pvt. Ltd 2018
7/16, Ansari Road, Daryaganj
New Delhi 110002

*Sales centres*:
Allahabad Bengaluru Chennai
Hyderabad Jaipur Kathmandu
Kolkata Mumbai

ISBN: 978-93-5304-116-8

First impression 2018

10 9 8 7 6 5 4 3 2 1

*To Ishan, who saw* Bluffmaster!
*with me, and we finally discovered Priyanka Chopra*

# CONTENTS

# INTRODUCTION

'Does Priyanka Chopra deserve a book?' I was asked this question last year by a British film festival programmer friend, who follows Indian cinema keenly.

'Yes,' I told him.

Priyanka Chopra certainly deserves a book. There is a long line of Indian actors who have tried to work in the West, especially in Hollywood. Some like Shashi Kapoor and Om Puri succeeded in getting interesting films that satisfied their creative impulses while also working in mainstream Bollywood films. Today, Irrfan Khan happily straddles between Bollywood and Hollywood. However, many failed and moved back to their comfort zone as well. Priyanka is perhaps the only other major crossover success story after Irrfan Khan.

But Priyanka took a huge risk. She put her life on hold in India (although she did not actually quit Bollywood), jumped out of her safety net, first tried her luck as a singer in the US—exploring a talent that until then she was secretive about—to break into an extremely competitive market to later transition into an actress. Did she succeed in her endeavours? Yes, she did, although the final jury verdict is yet to be delivered. But the important thing to note is that she never gave up and kept on pushing ahead. It is not a surprise, especially since she has often said in interviews that she hates failures.

'She doesn't have that in her DNA to give up,' says her Bollywood friend, director and producer Karan Johar, who has keenly observed her career from its very beginning. 'She's an active doer. She just knows how to combat any pitfalls in her destiny chart and emerge victoriously. That's just the way she is.'

Another Priyanka admirer and observer is her Miss India co-contestant and actress Dia Mirza. Dia was crowned Miss Asia Pacific in December 2000 a few days after Priyanka became Miss World at the ceremony in London. The two have stayed friends since that momentous year in their lives.

'Over the years my affection and respect for Priyanka has grown, more so now, the way she has conducted herself and the choices she has made and pushed the boundaries,' Dia says. 'As a country, especially as an industry, we are so quick to contain individuals. We want to put them in these boxes. And she (Priyanka) is so consistent and persistent in breaking those boxes and saying, "I am much more than this. You cannot confine me. I cannot be contained".'

⁀

It was in the fall of 1999, when Priyanka Chopra—just 17 years old—travelled to Mumbai from Bareilly. She was accompanied by her mother, Dr Madhu Chopra. Priyanka had been invited to participate in the Miss India contest sponsored by *Femina* magazine and *The Times of India.*

In Mumbai, Priyanka met her co-contestants at the Ambassador Hotel. Later, Dia Mirza would recall the confidence with which Priyanka spoke and her American accent, because of the two years she had spent in the US. But she was just a regular Indian teenager. Since she was the daughter of a doctor-couple who was employed by the army, she had lived in many cities across India.

Priyanka Chopra has travelled an incredible journey in less than two decades. Today, she is considered one of the biggest stars in Bollywood, even though her last Indian film—Prakash Jha's *Jai Gangaajal*—was released in March 2016. The same year she was awarded the Padma Shri for her contribution to the arts. While she has not shot any other film in India since then, her every move in the US or elsewhere in the world is tracked by the media and her fans.

A lot of that has to do with social media. Priyanka is extremely active on social media platforms like Twitter and Instagram. She knows how to use social media to her advantage—reporting everything she eats, where she parties or who she meets, whether it is at a UN conference, in a refugee camp in the Middle East or at a gala event at the Metropolitan Museum of Art. Even what she sees from her high-rise New York City apartment—falling snow or the night view of Manhattan is shared with her fans. Priyanka was also one of the first Indian celebrities to create a Twitter account.

Towards the end of 2017, a *Forbes* magazine list—100 top Indian celebrities according to their annual earnings—placed Priyanka Chopra at number seven and she was the only female in the 'Top 10' list. Her earnings at that time was ₹68 crore.[1] Her male competitors—the top six in the list—were actors Salman Khan, Shah Rukh Khan, Akshay Kumar and Aamir Khan, and cricketers Virat Kohli and Sachin Tendulkar.

In December 2017, Priyanka delivered the Penguin Annual Lecture in Delhi's Siri Fort Auditorium. The title of her talk was, 'Breaking The Glass Ceiling: Chasing A Dream.' The hall was packed with Priyanka's fans who cheered at her every joke and listened attentively as she shared a step-by-step guide to becoming a successful celebrity. When she sat down for a conversation with the moderator of the evening—Sonia Singh of NDTV—she was asked if the zeroes on her pay cheque mattered.

'Definitely they do,' Priyanka responded. 'I was not born with a silver spoon and I worked really hard to be where I am today.' And then she emphasized on something that bothered her. 'There are many people who talk about the kind of numbers apparently I get for certain minutes of my time. But has anyone ever asked the boys about the zeroes on their cheques? I mean they get a ridiculous amount of zeroes.'

It should be noted that Priyanka has been working full-time since she was 17. But she never lost sight of her goals and her aspirations to be the best in her field. She always channelled her energy in that direction. As the years passed, she evolved from the teenager from Bareilly who became Miss India in 2000 to one of the finest Indian actresses in the mainstream, commercial film space. Perhaps that is what sets her apart from other Bollywood actresses.

Then, there is also the fact that she works very hard. As Dia Mirza says, 'She just never stops working hard. She works non-stop. I don't think she sleeps.' In fact, Priyanka Chopra works a lot harder than any of her peers in India, and because of all her efforts (and definitely some really smart advisers who sincerely believe in her), she has become a celebrity in the US as well, whose face many (I hesitate to say most) Americans recognize. And all this happened just a few years ago.

⌁

In the early December of 2016, I went to meet actor, writer and director Manav Kaul at a café in the Versova neighbourhood of Mumbai. He had suggested we could meet at Leaping Windows, a corner café off Yari Road. I had known Manav for a few years and he was the first person I contacted to talk about working with Priyanka Chopra. The two had appeared together in *Jai Gangaajal*, released earlier that year in March.

As I got off the cab, I noticed that the café was actually located on Dr Ashok Chopra Marg. On reading the name, I immediately recalled the controversy when Priyanka had been criticized for using her influence to get the road named after her late father. But I also saw this as a sign, a good omen, a blessing perhaps, as I was beginning work on a book on Priyanka Chopra. I had somehow landed on Dr Ashok Chopra Marg—a road that led to the apartment-building where the Bollywood star lived when she was in India. And all this was completely unplanned.

I was late in becoming Priyanka Chopra's fan. In fact, the first film of hers that I watched in a theatre in New York was *Bluffmaster!* and that was in 2005. She had acted in thirteen films before that, including *Thamizhan* (2002)—a Tamil film—which was also her first appearance on the screen. Of course I knew about her existence in Bollywood and I would later watch many of her early films—from *Andaaz* (2003) to *Aitraaz* (2004) and *Mujhse Shaadi Karogi* (2004).

I thought Priyanka was attractive, rather sexy, in *Bluffmaster!* (2005). But the film belonged to Abhishek Bachchan, who back then was a star. I also remember discovering Riteish Deshmukh in that film. The next day at work—I was at that time the editorial business manager of a few celebrity tabloids, including *National Enquirer* and *Star*—I told the only other Indian employee in the company that I had seen *Bluffmaster!* that weekend.

'She's so pretty,' my colleague said, referring to Priyanka Chopra. 'I guess she is,' I responded. I am never drawn to actors just because of their good looks. 'She's so pretty,' my colleague repeated. 'Okay, fine, she is pretty,' I said, trying to shut him up.

I remember thinking Priyanka was likeable in *Don* (2006) and

*Krrish* (2006). But it was not until I saw *Fashion* (2008), *Dostana* (2008) and *Kaminey* (2009) on the opening night in a packed theatre in the East Village in Manhattan that I began to take her seriously as an actress and see beyond her obvious good looks and sex appeal. By the time I saw her in *Barfi!* (2012), *Dil Dhadakne Do* (DDD) (2015) and *Bajirao Mastani* (2015), I had become an admirer of Priyanka, her acting (although I always felt she needed good directors to push her) and her projects—especially in the US. For the past five-six years, as I followed and wrote about Priyanka's 'move' to the US, I was amazed at how dedicated she was, putting her heart and soul into every new project, even when some did not succeed.

Priyanka is in news all the time now. The press in India and even the tabloids in the US cover even the minor details of her life—when she cuts her hair to give a new look to her *Quantico* character Alex Parrish or when she meets Prime Minister Narendra Modi in Berlin wearing a dress, showing a lot of legs. When she got trolled on Twitter for showing skin while she sat with the prime minister, she responded by posting a picture on Instagram where both she and her mother were exposing their legs—her mother was wearing a miniskirt.

But Priyanka is in news for other things as well. In the fall of 2017, her name appeared in *Variety*'s 'Power of Women' honoree list. She shared the honour with Oscar-winner Octavia Spencer, actress Michelle Pfeiffer and singer Kelly Clarkson. These powerful women were recognized for their philanthropic work. Priyanka has been the global UNICEF Goodwill Ambassador since 2016. Before that, she was the UNICEF Goodwill Ambassador for India for nearly a decade. A year after being appointed the global ambassador at a ceremony in New York, Priyanka travelled to Amman, Jordan, where she spent time at UNICEF's Makani Centre with Syrian refugees, especially children and teenagers.

The press and her social media accounts were full of images of the star, sometimes with her head covered in what looked like a regular dupatta, surrounded by smiling refugee children.

'Philanthropy has been something that is inherently a part of my life from when I was growing up,' Priyanka told *Variety* while speaking for the magazine's special October 2017 issue.[2] She added that even as an 18-year-old Miss World pageant winner, she had realized that while she could not change the world herself, she could work towards making a difference in people's lives. 'One person cannot eradicate poverty, but I realized that (with) the platform that I had, whatever I said would be spoken about, would be written about.'

In November 2017, Priyanka's name appeared in the *Forbes* list of the 100 Most Powerful Women in 2017.[3] Priyanka was number 97 on the list. Other women of Indian origin on the list included Indra Nooyi, Chairperson and CEO of PepsiCo (#11), Chanda Kochhar, CEO of ICICI Bank (#32), Nikki Haley, US Ambassador to the UN (#43), Roshni Nadar Malhotra, CEO of HCL Corporation (#57), Kiran Majumdar-Shaw, Founder-Chair, Biocon Ltd. (#71) and Shobhana Bhartia, Chair, HT Media (#92). It was a remarkable honour for Priyanka. The brief write-up on Priyanka read:

> Chopra is arguably the most successful Bollywood actor to cross over to Hollywood... As the star of ABC's *Quantico*, she's one of TV's highest-earning actresses and the first Indian actor to lead a drama series on American television.

It then went on to list her achievements as a film producer in India, her UNICEF appointment, her participation in United Nations Foundation's Girl Up campaign and her non-profit organization—The Priyanka Chopra Foundation for Health and Education—that provides schooling and medical care for over seventy girls.[4]

Another *Forbes* listing stated that from 1 July 2016 to 30 June 2017, Priyanka Chopra made $10 million, nearly half of which came from her endorsements—from Pantene to Nirav Modi's jewellery (which she quit in early 2018, in the wake of the financial scandals associated with the company) and at least $1 million for representing Lyf Mobile, 'proving her dominance in India remains strong, despite her growing U.S. presence.'[5] The *Forbes* piece acknowledged the risks Priyanka took when she entered the US market. 'Becoming a movie star isn't easy—just look at all the aspiring actors waiting tables in Los Angeles,' the article stated. And it gave Priyanka credit for becoming a star in the US. 'What's tougher? Becoming a movie star twice over.'

ᔕ

Priyanka did not collaborate with me in writing this book. I wish that had happened and believe me, I did try, but there are things beyond my control. As I set out to research for this book, I wanted to understand who the real Priyanka Chopra is and how did she get to where she is today. In early October 2017, I took a long subway ride deep into Queens, New York—one stop before that end of the F Line—and then hopped on a bus to go to the Robert F. Kennedy Community High School, just to imagine the world when Priyanka Chopra was a student there. I sat across the school in a bus shelter, thinking of her life in the immigrant-rich, working-class neighbourhoods of Queens. And I thought about the different aspects of her personality—the many Priyanka Chopras that we know today.

There is a movie star in Priyanka Chopra that we all admire. We are connected with her on social media, following her tweets and her Instagram posts while her aura and charm continue to shine over her, besides her beauty. This is what the *Quantico* creator Joshua Safron said about her to *Complex* magazine: 'It is that superstar quality. That Julia Roberts quality, that Meg Ryan quality, that thing of Sandra Bullock. You feel like you could actually know them, but you also know that you could never know them. She's living on two different levels at once. That's what I like so much about her. She's not untouchable in any way even though she looks like a goddess. I think that's really rare. It's like lightning in a bottle.'[6]

And this is what *Complex* reporter Franzier Tharpe said after he watched her up close. 'She's based her career on an inborn, screen-queen magnetism, the wildly unattainable beauty wedded to the girl next door. I can feel it as I sit next to her in her trailer, and later on set between takes. As she speaks to her assistants, her husky voice (MarieClaire.com referred to her voice as "marvel of postcoital huskiness"[7]) seamlessly oscillating between alluring and respectfully commanding, she pushes her thick, wavy brown hair to the side while her lips part into a beaming wide smile.'

And yes, there is a down-to-earth quality Priyanka has—the small-town girl who still holds on to some of the simple values that she acquired as a child growing up in a middle-class family. 'My parents were doctors,' she told MarieClaire.com. 'We were real people. In India, real people don't become movie stars.'[8]

And as Karan Johar says, she has a heart of gold. 'She is very positive about her colleagues,' Karan adds. 'I have never sensed any competition. She is always appreciative, sending flowers for anyone if their performance has been good. *Woh bade dilwali hai* (She has a big heart). In this industry, sometimes it takes a lot to compliment someone else, but she has the confidence that she can do well also. She is sorted.'

Then, there is Priyanka, the foodie, who loves to eat junk food. *Quantico*'s Safran was truly surprised to find this quality in her, given that she is such a big star. 'She's famous and glamorous…' says Joshua Safran. 'She can't walk anywhere in

New York without being mobbed. But she's also the kind of a person who will very happily have Domino's delivered to the set for lunch. Domino's.'[9]And on a *Koffee With Karan* episode in 2007, Priyanka and Hrithik Roshan argued over who had more burgers at Burger King when the two were at the Singapore airport.

While writing this book, I set out to fathom how Priyanka became a celebrity first in India, and soon after she arrived in the US. But I also believe it is important to understand where Priyanka started from. Hence, I have also attempted to explore the story of the young girl from a middle-class army family in Bareilly who evolved into such a fine actress and a star. And how she continues to remain sorted.

In 2014, Priyanka was shooting for director Zoya Akhtar's *Dil Dhadakne Do* (2015) on a cruise ship and she responded to a set of questions I had sent her via email. 'There are so many personas of Priyanka Chopra. But who is the real Priyanka Chopra?' I asked.

Her response was:

With regard to the 'real' Priyanka Chopra... LOL!! You're looking at her...what you see is what you get. 100 per cent. I have good days and bad days like most people, but I have always been true to God and myself and that's how I keep living!

# 1

# WONDER YEARS:
# JAMSHEDPUR, NEW YORK
# AND BAREILLY

*I*t was a regular life with a heavy emphasis on education. Priyanka Chopra's parents were a middle-class couple—both doctors in the Indian Army. Dr Ashok Chopra, a surgeon, was from Ambala. His wife Dr Madhu Chopra—a double PhD, a gynaecologist and ENT specialist—was from Jamshedpur (once a part of Bihar and now in Jharkhand). She was the daughter of Congress leader Dr Manohar Kishan Akhouri and Madhu Jyotsna Akhouri (a Syrian Christian by birth, her original name was Mary John), a one-time member of the Bihar Legislative Assembly.

As is common practice in India, Madhu Chopra went to her parents' home to deliver her first child. She gave birth to a baby girl on 18 July 1982. Priyanka was born in Jamshedpur's Tata Main Hospital, located in the city's Bistupur area. Her maternal grandmother was once a nurse trainee in the hospital after she came to Bihar from Kerala. Her grandfather lived in Adityapur, the sister-city of Jamshedpur, separated by Kharkai River.

As her parents were with the army, they would often get transferred. Dr Madhu Chopra also continued with her studies after Priyanka was born. So, young Priyanka spent a very little part of her childhood with her mother. 'She was probably a year old when she began living with my parents,' Dr Madhu Chopra said in an interview.[10] 'They sent her to me when she was six years old because I was doing my post-graduation.' In reality, Dr Chopra believes she hardly raised her firstborn. 'I can't take that credit from her. She barely stayed with me so she has very little influence from me. She was brought up by most of my family all her life.'

Like some parts of Priyanka's early life, the details here are a bit fuzzy. While her mother stated that the young girl did not live with her for a long while, often in interviews, Priyanka has suggested that she was staying with her parents. Surely, she visited her parents during holidays. It is also possible that her parents' postings to different locations jumbled up minor details in her young mind.

Some children find it unsettling when they barely see their parents during their early childhood, shift schools, make new friends, lose touch with old ones and get used to new homes. It makes them introverts. Others make the most of it. Given Priyanka's exuberant personality, evident on talk shows in the US, and the ease with which she transitioned first to Bollywood and later adjusted to her new life in America, it appears that she actually thrived in that unsettled, constantly changing way of living.

In an interview in 2008, she said she did not mind the moves even during the school year. 'Shifting schools often meant I could be as naughty at school as I wanted to be because I knew that I'd be somewhere else soon,' she said. 'But importantly, I welcomed it as a new experience. I think that's what made me adaptable, which helps me even today.'[11]

One of the small towns the Chopra family lived in was Leh. It was in the early 1990s and Priyanka was about nine at that time. In August 2010, a cloudburst resulted in a lot of destruction in Leh. While speaking to her fans and Twitter followers to support the efforts to rebuild Leh, Priyanka recalled her childhood memories of living in Ladakh. 'We were all army kids there,' she remembered. 'We weren't living in houses, we were in bunkers in the valley and there was a stupa right on top of a hill which used to overlook our valley. We used to race up to the top of the stupa and that too *nange paon* (barefoot).'[12]

Talking about her childhood on Anupam Kher's talk show, Priyanka said that she was always very competitive as a child. '*Mujhe* first *anna bahut accha lagta tha* (I always liked to come first).'[13] And then, she added that she does not know how to handle failure. '*Main depression mein chalee jatee hoon. Main sotee rehtee hoon. Apne blanket main rehtee hoon, apne room main rehtee hoon. Badee moody ho jatee hoon.* (I go into depression. I keep sleeping. I stay under my blanket, in my room. I get very moody.)'

As a child—like many kids—she loved the word 'No'. So her mother would try reverse psychology on her by suggesting to her that maybe she should not go to school on a particular day. Then, she would question her mother, '*Kyon, aap kaun hote ho mujhe bolne wale* (Why, who are you to tell me not to go to school)?' There was a sense of rebelliousness in her. She felt powerful in saying 'No'. She believes, as a punishment, she was sent to a boarding school at the age of seven. She spent the third, fourth and fifth standards at La Martiniere Girls' School in Lucknow. '*Main kafee sudhar kar wahan se wapis aayee* (I was quite well-reformed by the time I came back from there),' she said, laughing. 'I was the only child *saat saal tak. And pehli beti* in my entire *khandaan* (I was the only child for seven years. And I was the first girl child in my entire family).'

The happier memories of her childhood include celebrating Diwali, as she looked forward to getting new clothes, gifts and school vacations. And then there is the memory of lighting diyas, which always became her responsibility. 'Even today, it is my responsibility to light up the diyas at home, unless I'm shooting abroad,' she said in an interview.[14] 'But if in town, I love to follow the ritual. Not that I have a choice, my mother starts grumbling otherwise.'

And on Christmas Eve, little Priyanka would pray that somehow Santa Claus would overlook all the mischievous things that she had done. Like all children who are told about Santa Claus, Priyanka also wanted gifts, and that one day of the year, she would hope that all her bad deeds were forgotten. 'I was like Santa *ko toh pata nahi chalega na ki maine yeh kiya tha to woh kiya tha* (Santa would not know that I had done this or I had done that),' she told a reporter[15]. As it would happen, every year her parents left gifts for her. Her belief in Santa stayed firm. 'I believed that I was a good girl. Good enough for Santa.'

∽

She was a chatterbox and would often imitate people. Hence, her parents gave her the nickname Mithoo. '*Mithoo kaun naam rakhta hai apne bachhe ka?* (Who names their child Mithoo?)' she asked Kher, while his audience laughed. Even young Priyanka was not too happy with that name. 'Of course I thought that was a very tacky name and I changed my name to Mimi,' she later told journalist and critic Anupama Chopra[16]. So in preschool, one day, she came home and announced she wanted to be called Mimi. And her mother actually convinced herself that this was some sort of premonition and that her daughter would one day become an elegant star like a French actress. 'It's my nickname. Punjabis have funny nicknames,' Priyanka added.

At the age of 13, Priyanka visited the US for the first time, accompanied by her mother and brother. Her mother's sister was staying in Cedar Rapids, Iowa, at that time. She visited her cousin's school and was surprised to see kids dressed in casual clothes. In India, practically all schoolchildren have to wear uniforms even today. She attended her cousin's class. That day, the school kids had to take an aptitude test. Priyanka scored high and the school asked if she would like to study there. The school even offered to arrange for her student visa. Having lived on and off with other relatives, Priyanka was excited about this change. And that is how 13-year-old Priyanka Chopra joined the John F. Kennedy High School in Cedar Rapids. In 2013, JFK High School was ranked as the best school in Iowa in the annual survey conducted by *U.S. News and World Report*. The school's Wikipedia page lists

Priyanka as a top notable alumna, although it does not mention that she left the school before she graduated.

Iowa is a cold state located in the middle of America. Winters drag on for months and the summers are short and mild. The average winter temperature is about 4° Celsius and the highest in the summer goes up to 30° Celsius. Coming from India, Priyanka probably struggled with Cedar Rapids weather. But perhaps it hardened her and prepared her for the future. Years later in 2015, Priyanka ended up spending substantial time in the cold city of Montreal, Canada, while shooting for the first season of her television show *Quantico*. On the television talk show, *Live With Kelly and Michael* on 4 March 2016, this is what Priyanka said about Montreal: 'Lovely people, lovely food, terrible weather.'[17]

Priyanka's aunt and her family moved around in the US. The next stop for the family was Queens—the working class borough of New York City, rich with immigrants from all over the world. In Queens, Priyanka attended the Robert F. Kennedy Community High School, located on the edge of the upscale Kew Gardens area, but more in the working class Flushing part of the borough, with large Asian (Chinese, Korean, Vietnamese and some South Asian), Arab, African American and Hispanic populations. White kids are usually in a minority in such neighbourhoods.

The school is located on Parsons Boulevard, a 10-minute bus ride away from the F subway train, so Priyanka would ride the subway every day on a student train and bus pass. In the fall of 2015, when she appeared on *Live with Kelly and Michael* to promote the first season of *Quantico*, Priyanka revealed that she had taken the subway to come to the show. The show even projected two images of Priyanka sitting in the subway, smiling for the camera, with co-passengers oblivious to the presence of a big star in their midst (*Quantico* had yet to air on television, so Priyanka's stardom then was limited to India and the Indian diaspora). But then again, New Yorkers are used to celebrities riding subway trains. Hollywood actors Jake Gyllenhaal and Katie Holmes are often seen riding the city's subways.

'It's so fun,' she said about riding the subway. 'I used to take the subway when I was in school in Queens. Me and my cousins used to come to Manhattan (a half-hour ride by the express subway train) almost every weekend just to look at Fifth Avenue and Saks (the upscale department store called Saks Fifth Avenue) and beautiful people. And just a few days ago, shooting on Fifth Avenue (for *Quantico*), it felt like a...' (She made the gesture of a full circle.)[18]

In the email interview she did with me while she was shooting for *Dil Dhadakne Do*, she reflected on her teenage years in the US. 'I really miss going clothes shopping with my cousin and hunting for bargains!' she wrote. 'We had so much fun. I think I mostly miss having a simple life... I was quite a carefree girl. During most of my impressionable years I was in America, so I had a very normal "American Teenager" experience.'

In her childhood in Queens, Priyanka experienced the rich mosaic of American immigrant lives—with women in hijabs sitting in buses next to Korean and Latino grandmothers. She was obsessed with food even at that age and would stop for a New York-style pizza or even a Caribbean sandwich at a store next to her school. 'My favourite thing about New York was its food,'[19] she would say many years later in 2016 on *The Tonight Show Starring Jimmy Fallon*. 'The pizza,' she said with absolute delight. 'Today, again I landed from Miami to come for this show and the first thing I did was to have a hot dog at a hot dog stand.'

These days, Priyanka enjoys the high-profile life of five-star hotels and flies first class. Her current Manhattan apartment is located in the pricey Tribeca neighbourhood. But living in Queens introduced her to a different facet of New York City. Through her classmates, Priyanka was exposed to American hip-hop and R&B music. It was here that she also developed a crush on one of her classmates. Priyanka was 14 and in ninth grade when she attended the junior prom hoping to impress the guy she had a crush on. It all sounds like a joke now, but this is what Priyanka told Kelly Ripa and Michael Strahan on their show on 4 March 2016: 'It is terrible. I had a crush on this guy who was a junior. And then there was another guy who had a crush on me. He asked me to the prom and I agreed only so that I would get to meet my crush at the prom. I was mean, but now I know better.'[20]

In early February 2017, Priyanka appeared on *The Late Show with Stephen Colbert* where she mentioned that she attended school in Flushing, Queens, and she had picked up a New York accent by the time she returned to India. 'Please it's so embarrassing,' she said to Colbert, as she continued with her story. 'I would say, "Can I have some cawfee?"'[21]

Sometime after she was in New York, her aunt's family moved to Massachusetts. This time, Priyanka joined a school in Newton, a suburb of Boston. There, she attended the Newton North High School. Like her schools in Cedar Rapids and Queens, Newton North was also a public school—which, in the US, means a school funded by the local government, where education is free, class sizes are big and, depending on the neighbourhood, there are often students from low-income families. In many of these neighbourhoods, students tend to come from single-parent families—usually headed by mothers and absent fathers. There is a culture of drugs and crime, often leading to the kids dropping out of schools. But while many students struggle in such environments, a few turn out to be high achievers.

One of Newton North's celebrity alumni is Matt Le Blanc, the star of the hit TV sitcom *Friends*. But Le Blanc is 15 years older than Priyanka and so he attended the school long before she did.

Priyanka engaged in theatre and music activities in the school, and led the life of a regular American teenager—including joining football games and pep rallies to support the school team. But at the same time, she also experienced the worst kind of racism there. In particular, as Priyanka revealed to *Complex* magazine, her nemesis in the school was an African-American freshman called Jeanine.

'She was black, and supremely racist,' Priyanka recounted the experience that has stayed with her since her teenage years. 'Jeanine used to say, "Brownie, go back to your country, you smell of curry," or "Do you smell curry coming?" You know when you're a kid, and you're made to feel bad about where your roots are, or what you look like? You don't understand it, you just feel bad about who you are.'[22]

Priyanka's story created a lot of ripples, especially in India where there is a common misconception about racism being rampant in the US. Many people were unclear regarding the reason she was treated badly by a non-white student. Even Anupam Kher seemed confused by the idea of black on brown racism. To that, Priyanka said, '*Pata nahin, shayed unko main pasand nahin thee* (I don't know, perhaps they didn't like me). It really affected me. *Confidence apka poora toot jaata hai. Main early jatee thee school, taakee pehle class main pahunch jaaon. Mujhe woh ladkiyan milen nahin* (One loses confidence. I would go to school early, so that I could get to class first. I hoped I would not encounter those girls). I used to leave late.'

In another interview with journalist Rajeev Masand, Priyanka said that she got into a catfight in school in tenth grade. She might have been talking about one of her tormentors at Newton High. 'She accused me of some really stupid things. And it was quite racist actually at that point. I got really angry with her and she said, "Let's talk it outside..." We actually fought on the basketball court and it was good fun.' During the fight, Priyanka broke the other girl's nose and later felt bad about it. And so she went to the hospital to see her. 'I was still scared of her when I went to meet her. I thought she would just get up from her bed and punch me. But it was all right, she was fine later.'[23]

Priyanka did find a way to stand up against these negative voices. In Newton North, she was a disciplined student, good at everything in school, studies, as well as in extracurricular activities. She would sing and act in plays too. Around that time, her mother came to visit her and Priyanka insisted that she wanted to come back home. Life in America had not been easy for Priyanka Chopra. 'I just needed a break,' she told Rajeev Masand. 'I wanted to feel I belong somewhere.'

There were other childhood traumas that Priyanka has recalled over the years. She told Anupam Kher that she had low self-esteem, as her family would often comment on her dark complexion. 'As a joke. You know Punjabi families *main* dusky skin *ko zyada* appreciate *nahin karte. Meri poori* family *gori-chitee hai, aur main aur mere* dad dusky *nikle.* "*Bechari ka kya hoga. Koi shadi nahin karega us se*"—*aisa sab sunne ko milta tha,* when I was growing up (You know how Punjabi families do not appreciate dusky skin tones. My entire family is fair-skinned, but my dad and I turned out to be dusky. "Poor thing, what will happen to her? Who will marry her?"—I would have to listen to such things when I was growing up). All these things really affected me that time.'

That constant sense of being reminded that she was dark stayed with her even in her early years of adulthood, when one of the first brands she endorsed was a skin-lightening cream. Later, she regretted her decision, but was not embarrassed to speak about it. She admitted so to a Pakistani-British journalist in an interview for *The Guardian*. 'I got swayed into doing it,' she said, 'but then I realized it made me feel like I did as a kid—I used to try all those products until I became Miss India.'[24]

The memories of being taunted by her family members haunted her for a long time. 'It really works on your psyche, man. We don't realize it, but it does. I never really understood how much that affected me until I was a teenager.'

As she revisits the tough moments of her childhood and teenage years one cannot help observe how honest Priyanka is when she speaks to the press about the life she has led, or where she has come from. It is a sign of a good middle-class upbringing and has always been one of her greatest strengths.

Despite her struggles in the US and the pressures from some of her family members, Priyanka developed a sense of confidence from an early age. She always kept the bar high for herself. Success was then just a sweet aftertaste.

On returning to Bareilly where her father was posted when she asked her mother to take her to India, Priyanka joined the city's Army Public School. The family lived in the cantonment area. It was an experience that taught her the value of discipline, she told a *Vogue* reporter in a video interview.[25]

There were other challenges Priyanka faced when she returned to India as she had acquired a heavy American accent. She had to quickly adjust to the India she had returned to. It was difficult for her to wear jeans and other western outfits in a small conservative town like Bareilly. The US-returned teenager had to tone down the Americanisms she had acquired. But some habits were harder to lose. In Army School, for instance, Priyanka would be seen wearing shorter skirts, her nails would be painted and she had more stylish hair as compared to the other girls. 'She seemed cut out for her profession right from the start,' says Pushpa Kanyal, the teacher in-charge of discipline at the Army Public School.[26]

In 1999, Priyanka entered the May Ball Queen contest organized by the Bareilly Club. She was hesitant at first and even made an excuse that she was not prepared. But she won the title, which brought a lot of attention to the America-returned Priyanka Chopra who by her own admission had grown into an attractive young woman. In a small town like Bareilly, that caused a commotion of sorts.

Finally, Priyanka's father took a drastic step to control the attention his daughter was getting. '*Mere* dad *ne mere sare* western clothes confiscate *kar diye* (My dad confiscated all my western clothes),' she told Anupam Kher. 'And I had also grown up.' Thus, new sets of salwar kameez were stitched for her.

As a young child, Priyanka used to accompany her parents to medical camps they would hold in villages. 'My job was to help the pharmacist hand out pills to the patients. I took my job very seriously,' she said.[27] She found the work rewarding. Like her parents with multiple degrees, she wanted to pursue further education, although it was clear that she did not want to become a doctor. 'I knew since I was five,' she told *Glamour* magazine.[28] 'I was practically raised in a hospital, (but with) the level of formaldehyde and the sight of blood, I knew I couldn't be a doctor!'

Fate anyway had other plans for her and her focused vision led her to follow a different path. The America-returned teenager from Bareilly was about to become a beauty queen, and subsequently an actress, a singer and a superstar.

# 2

# THE TITLE QUEEN: MISS INDIA, MISS WORLD

*I*n 1999, Dr Ashok Chopra brought the 17-year-old Priyanka to Rajiv Suri's photo studio in Bareilly. Almost twenty years later, Suri Colour Labs Private Limited is still located in Bareilly's Butler Plaza Complex with its strip malls in the Civil Lines area.

As Suri recalls, Dr Chopra wanted a few pictures to be taken so his daughter could enter the *Femina* Miss India contest. But Priyanka has often told a slightly different story. She claims that it was her brother Siddharth who had insisted those pictures be sent to the Miss India contest.[29]

'*Didi to itni pretty hai. Didi itni lambi hai* (Didi is so pretty, Didi is so tall),' she quoted her brother, suggesting that he talked his mother into sending the pictures. And Priyanka's mother, Dr Madhu Chopra, added to the family lore, 'My son...found them (the photographs) and brought them to me. He was just 10 years old. *Aur usko chup karane ke liye* (*in order to stop his incessant requests*), I sent it.'[30] The mother and daughter failed to mention that Priyanka had been crowned the 1999 May Queen Ball at the Bareilly Club. The family was already charting out her future for international beauty pageants.

According to Priyanka, the photos her father wanted photographer Rajiv Suri to take were for a college scholarship application to Australia. 'They were formal pictures,' she said. Then she added, 'The photographer said, "You are very pretty, so let me take some more pictures," so I got a bit excited and said, "*Le lijiye* (go ahead), alright".'[31]

However, a different story surfaced when Priyanka was promoting the first season of *Quantico*. Reporting from Montreal where Priyanka was shooting for the show, *The New York Times*' Kathryn Shatuck wrote: 'Returning to Bareilly, India, the end of her junior year, she was studying for her university boards when her mother, pleased by Ms. Chopra's swanlike transformation, sent photos to the Miss India pageant.'[32]

As is often in the case of celebrities—and it definitely happens again and again in Priyanka Chopra's life stories—minor details tend to be embellished, added on, like a touch of masala to make the narrative seem more palpable and believable for the fans. This is not to say that she speaks untruth, but the real truth is never clearly revealed.

The pictures Suri took are all in soft focus. Priyanka looks like the young Hindi film actresses of the 1990s in the pictures, wearing a sleeveless blouse and shorts in one. In another, she is seen wearing a white jacket with a dated look, appearing very confident, although she also reflects small-town sensibilities. Another full-body picture has Priyanka wearing a silk blouse, black miniskirt, black stockings and open-heeled, wooden clog shoes with high heels. There is a glow—a lot of light—on her face and her hair.

There is every attempt in those pictures to make Priyanka look older, but her innocent face reveals the child, the teenager who was looking at an uncertain world, far bigger than she could ever imagine. Even though she had lived in the US for a few years by then, the pictures cannot hide the small-town Uttar Pradesh girl in her.

'She was rather shy at first,' Suri says from his store in Bareilly. This was before digital cameras arrived and so Suri couldn't instantly show the pictures to Priyanka. But as the shoot progressed, Priyanka seemed to get more and more confident. Besides taking the pictures, the photographer also applied make-up on Priyanka's face. 'She had a mark on her face,' he recalls. A few days later, Suri gave Priyanka and her father the 'portfolio'.

The next thing Priyanka recalls is that she was sitting at home eating her meal and watching Raj Kapoor's *Mera Naam*

*Joker* on television and she received a call from *Femina*. She had been shortlisted for the Miss India contest. She had to be in Delhi for an interview in five days. They asked her to bring heels, but to not wear any make-up.

So she walked up to her mother and said, '*Mujhe Femina Miss India se call ayaa. Dekho main kitnee badee tope hoon. Femina ko pata hai main Bareilly main hoon. Woh mera naam bhi jante hain aur mujhe* interview *ke liye bulaya hai. Lekin aap to apnee beti ko* appreciate *hee nahin karte*[33] (I got a call from *Femina* Miss India. Look what a hotshot I am. *Femina* knows I am in Bareilly. They even know my name and have invited me for an interview. But you just don't have any appreciation for your daughter). Of course she had no idea then that her mother had sent the pictures.

Like any parent, her father was apprehensive. How would his teenage daughter travel by herself to Delhi? 'My mom said she would come with me,' Priyanka said, adding, 'She gave up her practice, to stay with me until I was almost 23-24.'[34]

Bollywood mothers have been known to accompany their young daughters to film shoots. But for Priyanka's mother to put her medical practice on hold for her daughter's career was remarkable, especially in the context of the Indian film industry. Years later, commenting on the #MeToo campaign and whether there were men like Harvey Weinstein working in Bollywood, Dr Madhu Chopra admitted that Priyanka may have lost some projects because she always insisted on accompanying her daughter in meetings with new producers.[35]

'Her parents always formed a very solid support system around her,' Priyanka's Miss India co-contestant Dia Mirza says, 'I really think, throughout her early film career, it was just the presence of her parents that gave Priyanka the confidence. Her mother is unbelievable, such a determined lady. She has so much

fortitude and strength and she was constantly giving Priyanka
that. That even gave her the confidence and strength to go out
and do anything she wanted.'

✓

India has been sending contestants to the Miss World and Miss
Universe pageants for several decades. The first Miss India title
was won by a Jewish Hindi film actress Esther Victoria Abraham
aka Pramila in 1947. Five years later, Indrani Rahman (later a
renowned Bharatanatyam dancer) and Nutan (who went on to
become a big Hindi movie star) won the titles in two separate
Miss India pageants. And in 1966, Reita Faria became not just
the first Indian, but also the first Asian, to become Miss World.

Stardom in films often follow the winners of beauty
pageants—as was the case with Nutan (although she had already
acted in a couple of films before 1952) and Leela Naidu who won
the Miss India title in 1954 (her first break came with the 1960
film *Anuradha*, directed by Hrishikesh Mukherjee). Zeenat Aman
won the Miss Asia Pacific in 1970 and a year later she appeared
in the supporting (some may say leading) role in Dev Anand's
*Hare Rama Hare Krishna* (1971). But some of these beauty pageant
winners already had film connections. Nutan's parents—Shobhna
and Kumarsen Samarth were part of the film industry before she
won her title and Zeenat's father Amanullah Khan co-wrote the
scripts of *Mughal-e-Azam* and *Pakeezah*.

Things had begun to change dramatically in the 1990s, when
the winners in the beauty pageants were more democratized
and many of the young women applying for the contests began
coming from middle-class families. In 1994, Sushmita Sen won
the Miss India title and went on to be crowned Miss Universe.
Aishwarya Rai, who was declared the runner-up to Sushmita's
Miss India title, won the Miss World crown. And a couple of

years later, both the beauty queens landed offers in Hindi films.

Sushmita and Aishwarya's big wins started a trend that lasted until the year 2000—young girls from middle-class backgrounds, hailing from smaller towns in India, started winning global beauty titles. Despite the fact that they talked about global peace and caring for the poor, these young women had another goal on their mind—a chance to act in films. The winners included Diana Hayden (1997), Yukta Mookhey (1999) and Priyanka Chopra (2000)—all of them had won Miss World—Lara Dutta (2000, Miss Universe), and Dia Mirza (2000, Miss Asia Pacific International). Both Lara and Priyanka came from families in the armed forces, as did Sushmita and Aishwarya.

The army background was not a coincidence. 'The girls were better equipped than the girls next door,' says Sathya Saran, who was the editor of *Femina* in the 1990s through 2005. Saran was closely involved in the Miss India selection process. 'The army background means wider exposure to different cultures and languages, and more interactions. It promotes an outgoing nature and great confidence.'

Writing for *Verve* magazine, journalist Sitanshi Talati-Parish says, 'Priyanka Chopra's strong-willed endurance could be attributed to (her) upbringing.' She adds, 'The lifestyle, bordering on nomadic...is bound to have repercussions...the ability to make friends anywhere, to pick up and move on and remain disconnected from the trappings of setting roots, and treating it like an "adventure".'[36]

And she echoed Saran's comment. 'There is also a tolerance towards and the ability to deal with people, while fostering an innate sense of confidence and approachability.'

The fact that quite a few young women from India had won the beauty pageants obviously caught the eye of international press. While remarking about the phenomenon, Barry Bearak of

*The New York Times* noted, 'Indeed, the Miss World crown may as well be displayed atop the jewelled inlays of the Taj Mahal.'[37]

⌢

The Canadian-Indian director Nisha Pahuja's multiple award-winning documentary *The World Before Her* (2012) explored the lives of two sets of Indian women—one was a set of young girls and women from smaller towns and rural parts of India who joined the 'right-wing Hindu militia', Durga Vahini; and the other was about young girls mostly from medium-level Indian cities who aspired for the beauty queen titles and a future of fame and fortune.

'To be a Miss India and be considered the most beautiful girl in India, imagine the exposure. But who's going to give them that exposure?' asks Sabira Merchant in the film. Merchant was the diction expert and a key figure in shaping and moulding the Miss India contestants from the mid-1990s until the beginning of this century. She even trained Priyanka Chopra, Lara Dutta and Dia Mirza for the Miss India title and then for their global title competitions. She was hired by *The Times of India* and *Femina* team, headed by Pradeep Guha and Sathya Saran.

'They get ads, they get films, they get contracts,' Merchant adds. 'Just to have the television exposure (and) it's not just Indian exposure. They get contracts in Singapore, Hong Kong, Middle East, UK.'

In Nisha Pahuja's film, there were many contestants who, like Priyanka, came from small-town, middle-class families. Shweta, one of the contestants in the film, observed that all her competitors were part of the urban middle-class India. And Ankita observed the change that has been gradually happening in India in the last two decades or more. 'It's wonderful to see the nineteen contestants out here,' Ankita said. 'There are contestants from Indore, Bhopal, Chandigarh. They are small towns and it is wonderful to see that parents allow them to come here and walk the ramp. This shows that people are opening to things now.'

The decision to train and develop the contestants so that they could successfully compete in the global beauty pageants started in full earnest when Guha and Saran sat with Madhu Sapre who was the second runner-up in the Miss Universe contest in 1992. The idea was to find out what exactly happened at the world competition level.

'She was so close and yet missed it,' Guha tells me about Madhu Sapre. 'A lot of what I did after that was the result of my conversations with her. She was the first one to give me an insight into what happens at the global contest, what are they looking for.'

'We realized that swimsuit was a major round and our girls had never really worn a swimsuit in public in India, except if they were swimmers,' Saran says. 'So they would go there (to the world competition level) and their whole body language would show their nervousness in wearing a swimsuit. And the body had to be very well toned for the swimsuit contest. Height was also important. Because we have sent people like Juhi Chawla (Miss India, 1984) who was just about 5.4.'

In addition to hiring Sabira Merchant, Guha and Saran also brought two more members into the training team— Hemant Trivedi for grooming and Lubna Adams for training the contestants to walk the ramp. *The Times of India* and *Femina* were in the beauty contest business to build the brands. It was always an advertising-driven operation. So big advertisers like Keventers and Ponds would become the lead sponsors of the shows held each year in four centres in India. 'In the process, we hit gold,' says Saran. 'We managed to not only build the brand and get money into the brand but we managed to find girls who would become international winners.'

As more and more Indian women started winning the international pageants, some detractors maintained that it was all a business game being played by global cosmetics brands keen to enter the Indian market following the economic liberalization policies introduced in the early 1990s.

Others suggested that the contests were perhaps fixed. 'The Miss World competition was held in London, but it was an Indian network that sponsored the show worldwide,' Barry Bearak wrote in *The New York Times*, referring to the 30 November 2000 event where Priyanka Chopra was crowned Miss World. 'Indian designers did the costumes. An Indian was among the judges. Indians made up a large portion of the live audience.'[38]

Guha dismisses that talk, calling it 'rubbish'. 'It's a sad thing that people couldn't accept that we were winning because of our own efforts,' he says. 'There had to be some other reason why we were winning. People seem to lack confidence in ourselves.'

Saran agrees with Guha. 'If you watch the girls (who won the international competitions) on screen (including Priyanka and Lara Dutta), you would find they stood out in the way they answered, in the way they conducted themselves. It was more than just the training the girls received. It was about building their confidence.'

'It was telling them you can do it and we are with you,' she adds. 'Whatever you want we will give you. If you can't think fast, we will help you. If you think you are not confident because you don't stand tall, we will help you. We will teach you how to dress tall, stand tall, walk tall.'

Saran recalls tracking models and other potential contestants including Aishwarya Rai whom she chased for three years because a make-up man she knew said there was a potential Miss World hanging around. 'Every time she would say she would join the contest but then she would not show up, because her parents didn't want her to do it. So finally, she came the third year (1994).'

In the following years, there were others who came out of nowhere—unknown faces and names from small towns whose parents had submitted pictures and application forms. One such name was Priyanka Chopra who was 17 at that time and a resident of Bareilly.

⟋

'I remember her (Priyanka) because we didn't notice her in the beginning,' Saran recalls. 'I noticed her at the talent contest, because she sang beautifully. I told Pradeep she is going to win something.'

Guha says he was impressed with Priyanka from the beginning. 'But for some reason relative to the others, she didn't come up as the obvious choice. She grew through the contest. I think she needed a little more confidence. I think she wasn't quite sure initially whether this was the thing she wanted to do. She came in a bit tentatively. By the time the contest started she seemed a lot more collected and definitely more confident of herself.'

Part of the reason Priyanka felt unsure was because she was an outsider, as compared to some of the other contestants, including Lara Dutta who was already a professional model.

'Priyanka was completely new to everybody in Bombay,' Guha says. 'It takes time to try to create new relationships. So initially she felt a little out of place. But she kind of grew in confidence as the contest progressed.'

Another person who remembers Lara Dutta and Priyanka Chopra from the Miss India contest days is film-maker Karan Johar. Sometime in late 1999, Karan was invited by the organizers to give a motivational speech to the Miss India contestants. He clearly recalls seeing Lara and Priyanka in that room. 'I didn't meet or talk to Priyanka although I think she was sitting up front. But I did talk to Lara. She was sitting alone, quietly at the back row, and I thought, "Who is this attractive girl?"'

It was a usual occurrence. People would always notice Lara Dutta first. She had the refinement and body language of a successful model from Mumbai. Priyanka, the unsure contestant from a small town, would struggle to get noticed, even though she had spent a few years in the US.

'I remember Lara as being very self-possessed,' Saran says. 'She spoke very well. She had a very modulated voice. She was very polite, very well-mannered. If you look at the entire history of our contestants she stands out. You can't fault her on anything. She was quick and very well-read. Which made all the difference. I remember she dressed immaculately. She wasn't stunning in what she wore, but it was never wrong.'

One person who remembers Priyanka from the first day—and with a slightly different perspective—is Dia Mirza, who had come to Mumbai for the beauty pageant training from Hyderabad. The first day the contestants met was in the ballroom of Mumbai's Ambassador Hotel, where their stats were measured. And then the young women stood up, one at a time, to introduce themselves.

'I will never forget Priyanka with long, thick, lustrous black hair,' Dia recalls. 'She was wearing black pants, a white shirt and she had an American accent. But she spoke with such confidence. All of us were like bumbling fools really, so anxious.' *The Times of India* and *Femina* did not provide hospitality to the young contestants, so they had to find their own accommodation, clothes, make-up and travel details.

'We had all left home for a long period of time on our own, but I remember her mother was with her and she had this crazy confidence,' Dia adds about Priyanka Chopra. 'And that's actually my most vivid memory of Priyanka through the pageant. I remember breaking down multiple times, sobbing. There was a lot of pressure, we were so young, and the time, the amount of work we put in on a daily basis was tough. We were clocking 15 or 16 hours of work per day, with 7 a.m. workout sessions, and most of us had not worked out a day in our lives. It was the first time we were doing squats and lunges and jumping jacks. It was tough. But Priyanka was stoic, she was determined.'

Sabira Merchant has met hundreds of girls over the years while training them for the Miss India and then Miss World and Miss Universe pageants. But she remembers working with Priyanka Chopra and Lara Dutta very well. The sessions included speech and diction training where the contestants were taught to read loudly from books and magazines so they could feel confident about facing an audience and projecting their voices.

Priyanka had spent her teenage years in the US. And she had naturally acquired an American accent at the schools where she studied. 'It was an honest American accent which she had picked up naturally,' Merchant says while speaking to me about training the contestants. 'Nothing was put on. When you are that young, you are impressionable and you pick up the accent you are hearing all around you.'

But knocking out Priyanka's American accent became quite a challenge for Sabira Merchant. 'She had that kind of a nasal twang. I told her if she was going to represent India, she could not come across as a Yankee sounding person. You have to sound Indian in front of the crowd or at least you should get a global English accent and not American English.'

And Priyanka worked hard at it. At that time Merchant was teaching at Mumbai's SNDT University and she recalls Priyanka even following her there. 'And I would be like, "Now Priyanka we have done enough work. You can relax, you are okay." And she would say, "No, no, just one more question." She was so bent on improving herself. She was so keen that it was just unbelievable.'

But Merchant also found Priyanka a bit childish, not unusual for an excited teenager. 'She was always rushing into things,' Merchant says. In comparison, Lara Dutta was always very mature and had a natural, yet modulated voice. One reason could be that Lara was already 21 years old in the fall of 1999, while Priyanka was just 17. 'She (Lara) spoke very well. And she had the gift of the gab. Her vocabulary and choice of words was excellent. I worked very little with her, just to teach her not to do certain things.'

That year, the Miss India contest was held in Pune at the Poona Club. The date was 15 January 2000. The contestants faced a range of celebrity judges—actors Shah Rukh Khan, Juhi Chawla and Waheeda Rehman; cricketer Mohammed Azharuddin; media mogul and film producer Pritish Nandy; painter Anjolie Ela Menon, the then founder-chairman of Zee Media (and now Rajya Sabha MP) Subhash Chandra (Goel); fashion designer and perfume queen Carolina Herrera; and Marcus Swarovski, the great-great-grand nephew of the founder of the Austrian crystal company.

It was a day-long competition that started early in the morning, and included the swimsuit round. Finally, in the evening, the contestants faced the judges. Actors Rahul Khanna and Malaika Arora were the emcees. Each contestant picked the name of one judge to ask her a question. According to one news report, Juhi Chawla asked one contestant, 'If you were granted a sixth sense, what would you like it to be? The contestant was stumped, but then she responded, 'I would like to be a magician.'[39]

The same report said that Shah Rukh Khan asked a question of another contestant. The report failed to mention that the contestant was Priyanka Chopra. But then again, Priyanka was just a regular contestant at that time, not the star she is now.

There is a YouTube video of the classic moment—17-year-old Priyanka wearing a leather jacket (all contestants dressed alike for this round, and their clothes for the day of the pageant were provided by the organizers), with her hair open, facing Khan who was already a huge star then, having acted in films such as *Dilwale Dulhaniya Le Jayenge* (1995), *Kuch Kuch Hota Hai* (1998), *Dil Se* (1998), *Karan Arjun* (1995) and so many more hits.[40]

Shah Rukh started his long question by saying, 'I am as nervous as you are, I go meek in the presence of beauty.' And then, he posed the long question, 'Hypothetically, if you were to marry one of the following, who will it be? An Indian sportsman, like Azhar bhai—who would take you all around the world, make your country proud and make you swell with pride. Or an artistic businessman with a difficult name to pronounce like Swarovski, who would bedeck you with jewels and fine necklaces and you would never have to buy a chandelier for your house ever again. Or a Hindi film star like me, who has nothing better to do than to give you a complicated multiple-choice question about a hypothetical wedding like this.'

Then he added, 'And before you answer, let me tell you, whatever your answer is, none of it will prejudice my marks for you. I am sure Azhar Bhai and Swarovski won't mind.'

Priyanka kept a smile on her face, trying hard not to show any signs of nervousness. A girl from Bareilly was suddenly talking to Shah Rukh Khan in public. She held her breath, thought quickly and responded, 'If I was to choose one of these three very difficult choices, I think I would go to a great Indian sportsman.' People cheered, and Priyanka continued, 'Because when I come back home, or when he comes back home, I know I will be there to be his support to tell him I am proud of him, just as India is. To be able to tell him, "Hey look, you did your best and you are the best," and I will take immense pride in my husband who will be a man of strong character if he can bring so much pride to my country. Thank you very much.'

Clearly, Sabira Merchant's training combined with Guha and Saran's efforts to instil confidence in Priyanka had come handy. The audience clapped and even Malaika Arora remarked with a 'wow!'

After she became a Bollywood star, Priyanka said that during her teenage years, she was a *Dilwale Dulhaniya Le Jayenge* fan. And the irony is that years later there were rumours about Priyanka's relationship with Shah Rukh Khan. While there was never any clear evidence, the rumours did not die for a while. There was one report by Firstpost, where the website's photographer caught the two coming out of Shah Rukh's office in Khar at 3.15 a.m. on 18 January 2012.[41]

In November 2012, while talking to CNN IBN as he was promoting *Jab Tak Hai Jaan* (2012), Shah Rukh—with Katrina Kaif sitting by his side—said this about the rumoured relationship, 'To me what is most disturbing is that a lady who has worked with me has been questioned and somewhere down the line has not been shown the respect that I show her, or to all women.' And he added, 'She is one of the closest friends and she is very close to my heart, and will always be... She was a little girl who started her Miss World crowning with me. We have shared some of the nicest moments on screen and off it. It is extremely unfortunate for me, you know, a friendship gets a little spoilt.'[42]

In the fall of 2017, there were reports that upon Shah Rukh's suggestion, director Farhan Akhtar and producer Ritesh Sidhwani decided to replace Priyanka Chopra with Deepika Padukone in *Don 3*, a film that was supposed to be made in 2018. Later in the spring of 2018, reports indicated that Ritesh and Farhan were now looking for 'a new actress' to cast opposite Shah Rukh Khan.[43]

Priyanka had acted opposite Shah Rukh in *Don* (2006) and *Don 2* (2011). In a report about the casting development for *Don 3*, *India Today's* Ananya Bhattacharya wrote, 'For quite some time now, gossip mills have been abuzz with rumours about an extramarital affair between Shah Rukh Khan and Priyanka Chopra, back when the two were shooting for *Don 2*. Tabloids churned out story after story till Shah Rukh and Priyanka stopped being seen together in public, and the rumours fizzled out.'[44]

✧

Back in Pune at the 2000 Miss India pageant, Guha remembers a moment during that evening when someone in the jury had to be convinced about Priyanka's good chance as a contestant. 'Not everybody in the jury was initially in favour of her. One person mentioned she's too dark,' he recalls. 'I said, "Yaar come on—look at South American girls. They keep winning and some of them are pretty dark as are all the girls from Africa." So I said what are you talking about?

'I was always very certain about her and as I said this woman never made a mistake twice,' he adds. 'She kind of always improved on herself day on day, day on day. I knew that she would give in 200 per cent if she gets in.'

When the results were announced, there was a tie between the top contestants Priyanka Chopra and Lara Dutta. Guha and Saran had experienced a similar situation with Sushmita Sen and Aishwarya Rai in 1994. This time, they were better prepared and additional questions were posed to both Priyanka and Lara.

The final results were no surprise to anyone. The suave, elegant well-spoken Lara Dutta won the Miss India title. Priyanka Chopra, the girl from Bareilly, was the runner-up. Lara was crowned *Femina* Miss India Universe, while Priyanka became the *Femina* Miss India World. The second runner-up

Dia Mirza was given the *Femina* Miss India Asia Pacific title.

'We had stopped calling it the winner and runner-up,' Saran says. 'It was Miss Universe and Miss World. But the girl who spoke better and was given higher marks was sent for the Miss Universe contest. They want spokespersons, girls who can be emcees at shows and host TV and radio shows. The one who spoke better attended the Miss Universe.'

In 1994, the same game was played out when Sushmita Sen, the more articulate contestant, won the top crown and was sent to represent India at the Miss Universe contest while the first runner-up, Aishwarya Rai, went to the Miss World event. And the irony is that Rai, who was number two to Sen, became a bigger star after the two launched their film careers. The 2000 race was a repeat performance. While Lara Dutta came first in the Miss India contest, ahead of Priyanka Chopra, a few years after the two started their film careers, Priyanka became a bigger star.

Karan Johar believes that the distinction the Indian organizers made between the international contests was wrong. 'What people don't realize is that Miss Universe was never the bigger pageant,' Johar says. 'We also had it wrong. We were sending our Miss India number one to Miss Universe and number two to Miss World. But Miss World is a bigger pageant. So both Ash and Priyanka won Miss World—a more important title.'

Dia Mirza recalls the moment when the winners were announced in Pune. The top five contestants were huddled backstage waiting for the names to be called out. 'We were all holding hands,' Dia says. 'Priyanka just knew she would make it and Lara was the other one who had that confidence. The one who was really surprised that anything had even happened and who had won was me.'

'You even see on the cover of *Femina* with Shah Rukh Khan,' she adds. 'We were whizzed off to do the photo shoot with Shah

Rukh. Lara and Priyanka were looking straight at the camera with a lot of confidence and me standing there looking at Shah Rukh with this big smile saying, "I can't believe this is happening." It was like an out of body experience.'

The iconic cover for the February 2000 issue of *Femina* has Shah Rukh flanked with Dia on his right and Priyanka on his left. Lara stands on the left of the frame. The three women are wearing their crowns and identical saris—in different colours. Their *pallus* come in front, in the Gujarati style. They are all smiling. Shah Rukh is in a black suit and a black shirt and tie. He has that cool 'I-am-a-movie-star-I-don't-need-to-smile' look on his face.

Once the contest was over, Priyanka, Lara and Dia settled down in their routines to get further training for the international pageants. Lara had an apartment in Mumbai, but Priyanka and Dia shared a room together at the Taj Lands End, now as guests of *The Times of India* and *Femina*. Priyanka's mother gives all the credit to the training she received for her daughter's evolution into a beautiful young woman. 'After she became Miss India, she was groomed by the *The Times of India* and *Femina*,' Dr Madhu Chopra said in an interview.[45] 'That's when she began to change physically... She was always beautiful, but she became poised. She started putting it together.'

Priyanka turned 18 in July 2000 and her birthday was celebrated at Guha's residence in Mumbai. Dia celebrated her 18th birthday in December 1999, and Lara turned 22 in April 2000. The three women once again worked with Sabira Merchant, prepping for the big contest. Merchant had a series of two hundred questions she would ask. She also expected the young women to read the newspapers daily. One thing Merchant realized very soon was that Priyanka was very fond of Princess Diana and Mother Teresa.

'I told her clearly, "Please don't Princess Diana them, and don't Mother Teresa them,"' Merchant said. 'Because everyone would say, "Oh I love Princess Diana, she's my most favourite person." I told her, "Think of something original and clever to say." But she said she admired Mother Teresa the most. So I said, "Okay if you really want to say her name, then do so".'

On 30 November 2000, the Miss World contest was held at London's Millennium Dome. When Priyanka's chance came to answer her question, she was asked by the American television talk show host and former mayor of Cincinnati Jerry Springer to name a living person she admired the most. And her response was Mother Teresa, even though the Albanian nun had died three years earlier.

The next day's *The Guardian* reported that Priyanka who had said she wanted to be a clinical psychologist (in the later years she would change that answer to say that she wanted to be an aeronautics engineer or an astronaut) was the bookies' pre-pageant favourite.[46] 'I admire her (Mother Teresa) from the bottom of my heart for being so passionate and kind…giving up her life to put smiles on people's faces,' Priyanka told the judges with a big smile on her face. That was a sure sign of the Sabira Merchant training.

'I remember thinking, "Oh La La, girl you have made that mistake, which we wanted to avoid".' Merchant recalls. 'I spent so much time telling her not to say Mother Teresa's name and she did exactly that. She was young so you can't blame her. But I remember very well—because the video was played out to me—that she was breathing heavily, so fast that she was rushing with her breath. Obviously she was so nervous. When you are emotionally excited then you tend to rush into things and you keep taking little breaths in between.'

That night, Priyanka was crowned Miss World and awarded

70,000 pounds. She was crowned by previous year's winner Yukta Mookhey. Later, Priyanka would say that she mentioned Mother Teresa's name 'because she would be always alive for me.'

Priyanka's fans in Bareilly were elated. A banner was placed outside a hotel on the city's Station Road that read, 'Mimi (Priyanka's nickname at home), we are proud of you.' Another hotel decided to give her the world's longest greeting card on her return, in order to get the town listed in the Guinness Book of World Records, an obsession amongst many people in India.[47]

But some prominent voices in India were not kind to Priyanka's win, given her faux pas at the competition. She had even said India had a population of two billion people. Noted journalist and a member of Delhi's high society, Khushwant Singh ridiculed Priyanka Chopra, calling her a 'bimbo' and 'stupid'— 'We Indians send out some bimbo and she returns with the prize, and we act like we've conquered the world. This one is singularly stupid. She didn't even know whether Mother Teresa is alive or dead.'[48] An editorial in *Hindustan Times* also poked fun at the expense of the 18-year-old Priyanka, 'Perhaps Ms Chopra had taken the convent school line about the Holy Ghost a little too seriously.'[49]

'Priyanka won and came back and it didn't bother her one bit that she goofed up her answer,' Saran says. 'And she came back, like Ash did, still herself. Lot of people when they come back don't come back themselves. Priyanka was polite and friendly.'

Upon their return to India, the three beauty pageant winners that year—Priyanka, Lara and Dia—made a visit to Delhi to meet the then president of India, K.R. Narayanan. A short while later, there was a huge party at the Taj Mahal Hotel in Mumbai.

After that, Sathya Saran accompanied Priyanka for the homecoming party in Bareilly. But things were a little tense in Uttar Pradesh with its then Chief Minister, Rajnath Singh,

denouncing beauty contests as vulgar. 'There is no place for
such vulgarity in our society under my regime,' Singh had said,
a few days after Priyanka won the crown in London.[50] And he
was definitely not impressed that a girl from UP had received
the recognition.

But since Priyanka's father was in the army, the party was
held at the Army Officers' Club in Bareilly's cantonment area. At
a press conference, Priyanka gave a speech in Hindi. And then she
was heckled by a couple of people who said that she won even
though she gave the wrong answer. 'Did you pay money?' Saran
recalls some people asking Priyanka. 'She handled that well.'

Also present at the party was Rajiv Suri, the Bareilly-based
photographer who had taken Priyanka's pictures at his studio.
'That was the second time we met,' Suri says. Suri had been
instrumental in launching Priyanka's career, and although she
was not ungrateful, she had already moved into another world.
They would not meet after that. 'She was very professional but
we didn't talk after that,' he adds.

On the flight back to Mumbai, Priyanka came and sat next
to Saran and asked her opinion on what she should do next.
'I told her you have a year now as Miss World, so finish this,'
Saran recalls. 'I told her she was such a good singer, so she could
become a professional singer or even join politics. "We need
young people like you who are influencers," I said to her. And
she said, "Yes I have been thinking about that".' There was no
mention of a film career.

∿

In January 2001, a 37-year-old Indian woman living in Dubai
came up with a bombshell allegation. She claimed that she was
sexually abused by Priyanka's father, Dr Ashok Chopra, when she
was 12 years old. In a lengthy interview with *Savvy* magazine,

the woman—Shivani Saxena—alleged that the repeated incidents of abuse happened when Dr Chopra was posted in Ferozepur, UP, where he worked as a junior officer under her father, Dr Suresh Chandra Saxena. There were unsettling sordid details in the allegation.

'He started acting strangely,' Saxena was quoted by *Gulf News* as she narrated the first such incident that happened at her home when she was allegedly alone with Dr Chopra. 'When I tried to resist his advances he gagged me and sexually assaulted me. He even beat me up. It was very painful and quite traumatic. He left me totally shattered. While walking out of my room, he threatened to kill me if I told my parents or friends.'[51] Priyanka Chopra was still not the household name she is now. So the report in *Gulf News* identified her as Miss World—her only claim to fame at that time.

Saxena added that she was young at that time, hence afraid of Dr Chopra, and she tried to suppress the trauma, although she did share it with her husband at the time of her marriage. Then, as she watched Dr Chopra on televison around the time of the Miss World pageant, all her suppressed memories resurfaced. She had moved on with her life, she said, when she realized that her tormentor was Priyanka Chopra's father. 'He was seen smiling and in a second everything he had put me through flashed through my mind.' Saxena gave various statements to the press and at one point she indicated that her intentions were noble. 'It's more than just a personal crusade now,' she was quoted in a report in *The Telegraph* (published from Kolkata). 'I want to show other women that the stigma must lie with the assailant, not the victim, and for that, the truth must be told.'[52]

The Chopra family was shocked and denied the allegations. Priyanka was even asked about the allegation by the press present at her homecoming party in Bareilly. 'She handled it beautifully,'

Sathya Saran says. 'She was very fond of her father, very close to him.'

Saxena's lawyer filed a lawsuit again Dr Chopra, who, in retaliation, also went to court. At one stage, Saxena indicated that some compromise could have been worked out. Later, she told *Gulf News* that it was too late for a settlement. 'Now the news is out in the media, I cannot do anything,' Shivani said. Meanwhile, Dr Chopra told *Gulf News* that the allegations were 'bizarre and a total concoction.'[53] Some people claimed that it was Saxena and her husband's attempt to extort money from Dr Chopra.

In the pre-Internet days, the salacious gossip gained some traction in print publications. But Priyanka was not the star she is now, so obviously it was not that big a news. The lawsuits dragged on for years between courts in Uttar Pradesh—from Bareilly to Allahabad. Priyanka's father died in June 2013 after a long battle with cancer.

Then in 2017, there was a bizarre turn of events. The same Shivani Saxena and her husband, Rajiv, were back in news. Saxena was arrested by the Indian Enforcement Directorate (ED) in connection with the kickback distribution in the AgustaWestland VVIP helicopter scam. The arrest took place in Chennai where Saxena and the two companies she headed based in Dubai were accused and charges were filed under India's Prevention of Money Laundering Act (PMLA). Perhaps Saxena's karma had come back to haunt her.

⤴

Over the years, Priyanka Chopra's path crossed several times with those of Pradeep Guha, Sathya Saran and Sabira Merchant. Guha even visited her New York apartment during the *Quantico* shoot and posted a picture on Facebook.

'Her personality is very endearing,' Guha says. 'If she meets somebody, she makes that person feel very special and that's very important in a people's industry like the film business.' And Merchant adds, 'One thing that comes through about Priyanka throughout her career is the total confidence. She's a very, very confident, self-assured human being. And she's very hard-working.'

In 2010, Merchant was on a flight to Mumbai. Priyanka was on the same flight and she walked up to wish Merchant. 'She came over and said, "Oh ma'am, I am so happy to see you",' Merchant recalls. 'And I said, "Hi darling, everything okay?" She said, "Yes, yes, yes." And then she asked, "Why are you sitting here (in the economy class)?" So I said, "This is a silly question to ask. Why would I be sitting here? Because my ticket says so."

'So Priyanka stood up in the middle of the aisle and said in Hindi, "*Dekhiye sub log, yeh meri ma'am hain. Meri ma'am ne mujhe sub cheez sikhayin hai. Jaise main bolti hoon, jaise main chalti hoon, sub ma'am ne sikhaya hai. Ab ma'am yahan baithi hain aur main aage baithi hoon? Aise ho sakta hai* (Everybody, this is my ma'am. My ma'am has taught me everything. The way I talk, the way I walk, ma'am has taught me everything. Now ma'am is sitting here and I am sitting in front. How is this possible)? Then she asked, "*Main ma'am ko le jaa sakti hoon, mere saath? Aap sub log haan kijiye to main le jooangi captain sey pooch ke* (Can I take ma'am with me? If you all say yes, then I will take her after I have asked the captain)." So, they all stood up and clapped, "*Ma'am ko le jao, ma'am ko le jao* (You can take ma'am with you, you can take ma'am with you)."'

The captain came and asked Merchant to be a guest of the airline. 'And I was whisked inside the business-class section. She later said, "Ma'am I am very tired, I have been shooting for so long. Can I just rest on your shoulder?" So throughout the flight, she rested on my shoulder and slept.'

# 3

## POST MISS WORLD,
## EARLY FILMS

Courtesy: Shree Krishna International

*I*n February 2002, Karan Johar was on a flight to Kolkata from Mumbai. He was heading there to be a judge for Grasim Mr. India competition—the male version of the Miss India contest, now also a part of *The Times of India* group. In addition to Karan, the event had a range of other celebrity judges, including Sunil Gavaskar, Abhishek Bachchan, Raveena Tandon, Tarun Tahiliani and a-year-old Miss World, Priyanka Chopra.

In fact, Priyanka was on the same flight as Karan, seated right behind him. Here was Karan Johar, a Bollywood insider, son of a legendary producer and director of two hugely successful multistarrer Bollywood films—*Kuch Kuch Hota Hai* and *Kabhi Khushi Kabhie Gham...* (2001). And then there was Priyanka Chopra, the young 19-year-old from Bareilly who had suddenly become an international name. She definitely knew who Karan was, but looked uncomfortable in the setting. Her small-town upbringing must have made her realize that she was still not in Karan's league.

'I noticed her and thought it was strange,' says Karan. 'She was very quiet. Either she was shy and introverted or arrogant. Those are the two things you can think [of] because you are so accustomed to very well believing that people could be arrogant because of their standing in life, which is a stupid, premature judgement people make. More often people are awkward and more reticent.'

Good thing Karan was generous enough to give Priyanka the benefit of doubt. But at the same time, he was intrigued and curious.

'She was sitting [in] a row behind me and I kept staring at her,' he adds. 'In fact, every time I would get up and go and talk to someone she would be literally quiet, not reading a book, not eating, just quiet and staring down.'

Priyanka has travelled a huge distance since the day she took that flight, eventually crossing over the seven seas all the way to America like no other actor has done before. That crossing-over process would take a while but first there were duties to be performed. There were literacy campaigns for the Confederation of Indian Industry, support for the thalassemic children in Uttar Pradesh, adult education awareness programmes in Bareilly and volunteer work for the Polio Eradication Programme. And then, in the summer of 2002, Priyanka was invited to Libya to promote tourism and child welfare projects. Priyanka, however, seemed nervous about the tour.

'You hear so many bad things about Arab countries nowadays,' Priyanka told Rediff.com.[54]

It is not clear what 'bad things' she was referring to, but one has to forgive her since she was a 20-year-old when she made that statement. Those were the words of a naïve young woman, who had suddenly been thrust into the limelight and was supposed to have an opinion about everything. Fifteen years later, the star of *Quantico* and a UNICEF Goodwill Ambassador, Priyanka travelled to Jordan to meet Syrian refugee children and youth. She got a lot of credit for the maturity, warmth and compassion with which she handled her trip. Now she would never say that she has heard 'bad things about Arab countries'.

'But I am glad I did (go to Libya),' she said in an interview, adding, 'The Mediterranean is such a beautiful place—the quaint one-storeyed houses; the crystal clear ocean, though the Saharan climate was rather dry and sunny.'[55]

And she met the Libyan dictator Colonel Muammar Gaddafi. 'He was very cordial,' she said of the handsome Arab leader who was known to be equally charming and yet extremely brutal and power hungry. 'I was taken to see the remains of his former residence which was bombed by the Americans a few years ago.

The Colonel lost his daughter in that bombing, so that was a touching moment.'[56]

⌢

Priyanka began acting while she was also performing her duties as Miss World. Her acting journey started slowly and in rather unimpressive ways. Sathya Saran, one of Priyanka's guides during the beauty pageant days, had advised her to join politics or become a singer, but the newly crowned Miss World chose the obvious and, some might say, the safest route—acting in films. Acting can be an uncertain business but it can also be called the safest since it is a path well travelled by many young women, especially winners of beauty pageants.

Priyanka makes it sound like her entry in films, just like her victory in the Miss India and Miss World pageants, was all random luck and was unplanned. 'Honestly, films happened by fluke to me,' she told film journalist Rajeev Masand. 'I started getting film offers even before I won the Miss World title. Right after Miss India, I signed *Humraaz* (remake of *A Perfect Murder*, which itself was an adaptation of Alfred Hitchcock's *Dial M for Murder*), which was (supposed to be) my debut film.'[57]

In the same interview, Priyanka shed some light on why she thought winners of beauty pageants ended up acting in films. 'From what I have analyzed, the reason why everybody turns towards films is because once you go to a platform where you are popular and have tasted showbiz you perhaps want to retain it. You want to hold on it, and there is no other business in India that can give you the kind of popularity that a beauty pageant gives you... You perhaps only know the beauty pageant winners who come into show business...you don't know about the ones who become doctors, lawyers and take up many other professions after winning a beauty title,' she said.[58]

Priyanka did a three-month course—taking acting lessons from the Kishore Namit Kapoor Acting (Lab) Institute which also boasts of having trained a range of other actors, including Hrithik Roshan, Kareena Kapoor, Saif Ali Khan and Vivek Oberoi. The institute's website has the following slogans: 'We chisel Uncut Diamonds. We also Demystify Them.' 'Your Dream—Our Goal, Your Success—Our Dream.' In an interview with *Bombay Times* at the time of the release of *Krrish 3*, which starred three graduates from the institute, Kapoor was asked whether he thought Hrithik Roshan, Vivek Oberoi and Priyanka were destined to become stars. 'I've always maintained that talent can go only so far,' Kapoor responded.[59] 'After a point, you need to be passionate about your craft to achieve success in the industry. I remember their dedication in class. They weren't just students—they were disciples of the craft.'

Priyanka's first film on record was in Tamil language, something new actors often do to get acting experience by working in Tamil or Telugu movies. Aishwarya Rai's first break was also in a Tamil film—*Iruvar* (1997), a critically acclaimed take on the rivalry between M.G. Ramachandran and M. Karunanidhi. But *Iruvar* was directed by Mani Ratnam. Priyanka's first film *Thamizhan*, released in early January 2002—little over a year after she was crowned Miss World.

There was talk of several other films including K.C. Bokadia's *Ek Haseena Ek Deewana*, Kuku Kohli's *Asar: The Impact*, Satish Kaushik's *Hum Bhi Khush Tum Bhi Khush*, Guddu Dhanoa's *Gandhi* and Sanjay Gupta's *Musafir Hoon Yaaron* and *Aatma*. Eventually, none of these projects materialized. And there was the Abbas-Mustan film *Humraaz* (2002) where she was supposed to work opposite Akshaye Khanna and Bobby Deol. It was reported that Priyanka was in talks with Abbas-Mustan even before she had become Miss World. But the role eventually went to Amisha Patel.

'We had a mutual agreement with Priyanka that if she was crowned, she would first finish all her social work and promotional campaigns and then immediately begin working for *Humraaz*,' Abbas was quoted by Rediff.com.[60] 'We wanted to launch her. But she signed on some other films instead. So we offered it to Amisha... In retrospect, it is good that we did not have Priyanka Chopra. If you see the film, you will realize that Amisha has a very innocent look which is vital to her character. Priyanka would not have looked so innocent,' he added. The irony is that today Amisha Patel is nowhere in Bollywood. Her star did rise after the box office success of *Kaho Naa...Pyaar Hai* (2000) and *Gadar: Ek Prem Katha* (2001). But after a series of failures, she never bounced back. However, Priyanka has had a consistent track record with hits and some significant misses, and now she is even making waves in the US.

⸎

*Thamizhan*, directed by A. Majid, is best remembered for its lead actor Joseph Vijay Chandrasekhar. A review in *The Hindu* mostly talked about Vijay's character in *Thamizhan* and how it was different from his previous films. But *The Hindu* critic Malathi Rangarajan also mentioned that Priyanka had an inconsequential role in the film. 'Love has very little place in *Thamizhan* and so debutante Priyanka Chopra has precious little to do,' Rangarajan wrote.[61] 'But the world beauty could have done something about the weird wigs that she sports in some of the song sequences.'

My guess is there was little Priyanka could have done about her wigs, given she was so young and did not know much about the film industry. But in an interview in December 2001, the 19-year-old Priyanka Chopra seemed rather excited about her Tamil film acting experience. She mentioned how she took the project because of the reputation of the film's producer G.

Venkateswaran, and the lead actor Vijay who was very helpful
and sweet. 'The minute I knew that I was going to do a Tamil
film I started seeing Tamil films,' she said.[62] There was something
beautifully naïve and fresh about this young girl who had taken
up a role in a language she did not know at all. 'I also started
watching Tamil channels to know more about Tamil films,
particularly about Vijay. I also saw a few of his movies. I like
Tamil films. I am keeping my eyes open and trying to pick up the
Tamil accent. Tamil is beautiful but also very difficult. Learning
it will take a long time.'

*Thamizhan* was followed by a small role in Anil Sharma's *The
Hero: Love Story of a Spy* (2003) where Sunny Deol is presented
as an Indian super spy, a master of disguise and weaponry, who
breaks into songs, wins the hearts of two women (Preity Zinta
and Priyanka Chopra), and, even beats up a giant Canadian in
a nuclear lab.

Meanwhile in another scene, Priyanka, who plays Kabir Bedi's
daughter, gives a slight laugh in the middle of each sentence as
she says emotional dialogues to Deol such as: 'Wahid you know,
ever since I met you (small laughter), I just don't know what's
happening to me. *Har pal aisa lagta hai ki tum mere pass ho, mere
saath ho* (more laughter). *Kabhi hasne ko man karta hai, to kabhi
chumne ko* (laughter again). *Kabhi to aisa lagta hai ki tumhein dektee
rahoon.* (Another brief laugher) *Ekdum diwangee si chha gayee hai
mujh par* (Every moment it seems that you are close to me,
with me. Sometimes I feel like laughing, and sometimes I feel
like kissing. Sometimes I feel that I should just keep looking at
you. Total madness has taken possession of me).' Well, that was
the kind of roles Priyanka found herself doing in the beginning,
which were in strong contrast to the powerful characters she
played later, like Jhilmil in *Barfi!* or Kashibai in *Bajirao Mastani*
and many more.

Priyanka later confessed that acting with big stars like Deol was a daunting experience. 'My first film, my first day of shooting was with Sunny Deol and I was petrified of him. I was scared of him.'[63]

The film played in the US in a few markets. *The Variety* critic Derek Elley seemed smitten by Priyanka's beauty, referring to her as a 'stunning newcomer'. Later, in the review, Elley added, 'Mega-looker Chopra (Miss World 2000) making a solid screen debut as a modern urban miss.'[64] But referring to her small role, Rediff.com said, 'We will have to wait for *Andaaz* to figure out whether she can act.'[65]

For his new film *Andaaz* (2003), producer and director Suneel Darshan needed two actresses—both playing equal parts—to act opposite Akshay Kumar. The film was to be directed by Raj Kanwar, with Suneel on board as the producer. Suneel first considered the safe bet of going with the leading actresses of the time—Karishma Kapoor and Rani Mukerji. But he also wanted to do something unconventional. He had the recently crowned Miss Universe Lara Dutta in his mind.

Meanwhile, Priyanka Chopra's then secretary, Prakash Jaju, was persistent that Suneel should give the new Miss World a chance as well. 'I said okay, fine,' Suneel recalls. 'She walks into my office, I remember her to be of a darker shade. Our conventional heroines such as Kareena Kapoor were of fairer skin. She didn't have a conventional beauty, although she had still managed to win a beauty contest. So there had to be something about her.'

Suneel asked Priyanka to sit down and then he noticed her 'wonderful eyes and a fabulous voice.' He adds, 'I told Priyanka if you listen and you deliver in this movie you could become a Sridevi of sorts.' Priyanka also reminded Suneel of what he described as an actress 'from the bygone era.' That actress he says was Rekha. 'I have seen Rekha grow and evolve. She was also a dark-skinned girl, unconventional, compared to other girls of that time who were a lot prettier such as Hema Malini. But Rekha also succeeded with her husky, sexy voice, her beautiful eyes, and she had a body language.'

Suneel's brother, Dharmesh Darshan—director of the hit film *Raja Hindustani* (1996)—also recalls suggesting Priyanka's name. Dharmesh had seen Priyanka's song sequence from the Tamil film *Thamizhan* on television and he sensed a star quality in her. 'She wasn't a big name, but I liked her in that song. She had a certain energy,' Dharmesh says.

Suneel also liked the fact that Priyanka was accompanied by her mother on the first meeting and later during the shoot. 'At that point I realized here was an intelligent girl with an intelligent mother,' Suneel says. 'The father was a sweet man. It was a good family.'

Having Lara Dutta and Priyanka Chopra on board was a casting coup of sorts for Suneel Darshan. Lara got the higher billing, introduced on credits as Lara Dutta, Miss Universe 2000. Priyanka got the third card—introduced as Priyanka Chopra, Miss World 2000. Priyanka only appeared in the second half of the film and even though Suneel suggests that the two parts were equal, when watching the film, it is clear that Lara is the lead actress. A review on Rediff.com said this about the two actresses: 'Lara Dutta deserved a better debut to display her talents... Priyanka Chopra alone clicks with the audience, thanks to her skimpy outfits.'[66]

While Priyanka's acting skills were questionable early in her career, for a newcomer, she was quite confident in her scenes. But Priyanka's performance—awkward at times—was hampered by the ridiculous cringe-worthy dialogues she had to work with such as: '*Hum to ek katra hai mom ka, hamein khud main shamil kar lo, aag bana do,'* she says to Akshay Kumar. *'Apnee sanson ki garmee say hamare jism ko bhar do. Hamein rooh tak jala do. Is kadar barso aaj, hamaree barson ki payas bhujha do* (I am a little piece of wax, make me a part of you, turn me into fire. Come fill my body with the warmth of your breath. Come burn my soul. And rain so much on me that you can satisfy my thirst from a long time).'

After this dialogue, she and a confused-looking Akshay (that could also be his sexually turned on look) kiss, as we see thunder and lightning. And then, in her red silk dress, she dances to *Aayega maza ab barsat ka/Teri meri dilkash mulaquat ka* in Alka Yagnik's voice.

But perhaps the strangest scene in the film is the song 'Rabba Ishq Na Hovey', where Akshay is in a short red kurta, white pants and the two actresses are in leather outfits, showing a lot of skin.

It was probably that display of skin and sex appeal that got the two beauty queens the attention of the *Filmfare* magazine. The magazine's jury gave both Lara and Priyanka the best female debut awards at the annual ceremony held in 2004.

This is the world of Hindi films Priyanka Chopra stepped into at the beginning of her career—over-the-top and unreal dialogues in narratives where the female characters often showed a lot of skin and were mere sex symbols, desperate for the love and affection of their male counterparts.

A few years later, Priyanka would go on record to say that she would only work in films that would focus more on her acting abilities and less on her sex appeal. But in the early days, she lacked that bargaining power, as she was testing the waters of Bollywood and her films were yet to become box office successes.

Karan Johar saw *Andaaz* because Suneel Darshan had invited him for a screening. 'I remember thinking this girl (Priyanka) should improve her dancing at least—*thodi kamzoor thee* (she was a little weak)', Karan says. 'Then I heard that Veeru Krishnan—the choreographer of classic dance who had also done some roles in films, was teaching kathak to two of these girls—Katrina (Kaif) and Priyanka. Apparently, that made the biggest difference because the next time I saw Priyanka dance on the screen I thought, '*Arre isko kya ho gaya* (Wow, what has happened to her)?'

Dharmesh Darshan remembers getting a call from Priyanka's mother Dr Madhu Chopra. She was looking for a dance instructor for Priyanka. Veeru Krishnan had played a supporting role in Dharmesh's *Raja Hindustani* (1996). And so it was Dharmesh who recommended Priyanka, and also Lara Dutta and Katrina Kaif to Veeru Krishnan. 'All three of them would go to him at six in the morning,' he says. 'That was the only time he had.'

Priyanka would act again with the two Darshan brothers—in Suneel's *Barsaat: A Sublime Love Story* (2005)—with Bobby Deol and Bipasha Basu—and Dharmesh's *Aap Ki Khatir* (2006)—with Akshaye Khanna and Ameesha Patel. *Andaaz* was the launching pad for Priyanka and Lara. But as the years progressed, Priyanka's career took off in a much bigger way, even though there were enough bumps along the way. 'There are two kinds of actresses,' Suneel says. 'One who waits for the offers and the other who wants to go to seize them. Lara was more complacent. She wasn't aggressive. Priyanka Chopra was an absolute go-getter.'

*Andaaz* would be followed by four films in 2004—*Plan, Kismat, Asambhav* and *Mujhse Shaadi Karogi*—where Priyanka played the romantic interest of both Akshay Kumar and Salman Khan. A David Dhawan film, *Mujhse Shaadi Karogi* was like Priyanka's previous films, where she was essentially cast for her sexual persona.

In *Mujhse Shaadi Karogi*, Priyanka is introduced in a clichéd shot in white shorts and a top, emerging out of the water on a beach—again showing a lot of skin. She shakes her wet hair in slow-motion, as she walks out of the water. Next time in the film, we see her living in a house across Salman's balcony. She's wrapped in a pink towel. Just out of the shower, she wriggles and dances to 'Aaja Soniye'—as Bollywood actresses often do (Kajol did that in nearly half of the song 'Mere Khwabon Main Jo Aaye', wrapped in a towel in *Dilwale Dulhaniya Le Jayenge*). And when Priyanka opens her balcony's door, the towel drops and the camera quickly cuts to her feet. Seeing this, a startled Salman falls off the balcony. Fortunately, no bones are broken! But somewhere in that scene lies a peculiar David Dhawan brand of humour that continues to appeal to his fans.

But then, for a comedy film, Priyanka is really not funny in *Mujhse Shaadi Karogi*. She would take time to work on that skill, but in reality, Priyanka never managed comic roles well. In the later part of her career, she did handle daramatic and emotional roles rather well. Critics were pretty dismissive of Priyanka's performance in *Mujhse Shaadi Karogi*. 'Priyanka Chopra? ... She is average,' wrote the Rediff.com critic. 'She doesn't show any flair for comedy. She only lends glamour to *Mujhse Shaadi Karogi*.'[67] *The Hindu* critic barely mentioned her in one sentence, saying, 'Priyanka Chopra, who has been hyped a great deal, is nothing much to talk about.'[68]

And Jitesh Pillai of *The Times of India* had this to say about the film and Priyanka's performance: 'Only problem is that *Mujhse Shaadi Karogi* doesn't have a single original bone in its body... Priyanka Chopra's character could have been interesting but unfortunately she ends up as completely inert and wishy-washy.'[69] Pillai is currently the editor of *Filmfare* and Priyanka is a big star. Now it is doubtful that he and his publication would say anything unkind about the actress.

Priyanka would finally get a chance to display her acting

chops in a negative role created by the Abbas-Mustan team—in
*Aitraaz* (her fifth film to be released in 2004), which was inspired
by the 1994 Hollywood film *Disclosure* that had Michael Douglas
and Demi Moore.

In *Aitraaz*, Priyanka plays the role of a model Sonia who
believes that she needs to 'lend' herself and her body to
businesses who want to sell their products. In a confrontational
scene with Akshay Kumar, she says, '*Raj main ek model hoon.
Meri degree aur diploma meri khoobsoorti hai aur aage badne ke liye
mujhe us khoobsoorti ko aage karna padta hai. Bas* (Raj, I am a
model. My beauty is my degree and diploma, and to get ahead
in life I have to advance that beauty. That's it)! It's a part of
my profession... *Unhein apna product bechne ke liye meri body ki
khoobsoorti ki zaroorat hai, woh mujhe keemat dene ko taiyar hain*
(They need the beauty of my body to sell their product. And
they are ready to pay me the price I demand.) That's it. It's
strictly professional.'

But that dialogue written by Aadesh K. Arjun can also
apply to the early years of Priyanka's Bollywood career. During
those early years, Priyanka got projects where her sex appeal
and her glamorous appearance were the selling points for the
characters she played and it also helped her burgeoning star status
in Bollywood. This continued for a while until film-makers like
Vishal Bhardwaj, Zoya Akhtar, Madhur Bhandarkar and Sanjay
Leela Bhansali saw the real acting talent in Priyanka.

With *Aitraaz*, critics, who until now had been dismissive of
Priyanka Chopra, suddenly began to take notice of her. Anupama
Chopra wrote this in her brief review in *India Today*: 'Priyanka
Chopra, who until now was merely vacuous eye candy, chews up
the scenery playing a vixen in *Aitraaz*. She lusts, schemes, wrecks
and isn't afraid to look ugly. It's an impressive performance.'[70]
Syndicated critic Subhash K. Jha praised Priyanka, saying she was

now a bona fide star. 'A star is born! As the predatory social-climbing seductress who can go to any lengths to satiate her lust for life, Priyanka Chopra rocks the scene like never before.'[71]

*Aitraaz*, released four years after Priyanka was crowned Miss World, got her the ultimate recognition from the Bollywood film industry—a *Filmfare* award in the Best Actor in a Villainous Role category. She would later tell critic Rajeev Masand how difficult that role had been for her. 'I was 21 when I did *Aitraaz*. A film like that required so much maturity and for me, that's my best performance. I didn't know what I was doing. I was totally naïve... I was only listening to my directors then.'[72]

A year after the release of *Aitraaz*, Priyanka went on Karan Johar's popular TV show *Koffee With Karan*[73] (it was the first of her five appearances on the show) and made a surprising announcement that henceforth she was not going to show skin in films. 'It's a conscious decision,' she said when Karan asked what led her to make that decision. 'I don't think it is required, when you are performing as much. Even when I played the character in *Aitraaz* I didn't stoop to exposure—it was more the character I was playing, it was the way I spoke, the actions, the deliberate moves. I want to not be known for that. I want to be known for much more.'

To this, Karan asked if she was suggesting 'that the girls who show skin are not going to make it into the big league'. And Priyanka, who was only 22 years old at that time, replied, 'No I never said that. That's how I started... I did do *Andaaz* and I did wear a bikini. It's not something I can say I am ashamed of, but it's not something I want to do now. You want to be known more for your performance. I want to be known for the respect I will command than for people to say, oh she has a fabulous body. People have to look above that.'

Priyanka would more or less hold her ground on this issue

for the next four years, until she signed up to act in Karan Johar's production *Dostana*.

᠕

One of the drawbacks of actors becoming famous is that fans want to know details about their personal lives—what they eat, what they wear, where they party and, most importantly, who they are dating. Even Priyanka Chopra did not escape from this fate. While fans have admired her films, gossip magazines and other social media reports have often carried stories about her rumoured relationships with some of her co-stars. It started with Akshay Kumar.

*Aitraaz* was Priyanka Chopra's third film with Akshay Kumar. They would do one more film together—*Waqt: The Race Against Time* (2005). And then, they never acted again together. There were speculations that the two were in a relationship, while Kumar was married to former actress and now writer, Twinkle Khanna.[74]

Recently, Suneel Darshan said in an interview that Akshay and Priyanka were supposed to act in one more film—*Barsaat: A Sublime Love Story*, but then, Kumar pulled out because of pressure from his family. 'I guess it had a lot to do with the reports linking them to each other,' Darshan told *DNA* newspaper.[75]

The *DNA* story added, 'Akshay reportedly withdrew out of the projects starring the two together, after the speculative reports about their relationship began to affect his family life.' Later, it was Priyanka who made it official that the two were unlikely to work again.

In September 2004, there was a report in *The Times of India* about Akshay Kumar and Twinkle Khanna's big showdown in the lobby of a hotel in Goa. As a report in the newspaper mentioned, there were many witnesses to the big fight, but no one intervened.[76] That same report quoted a guest at the hotel: 'The fight happened in full public view and as both Akshay and Twinkle screamed at each other, one got the distinct impression that he had admitted to having an affair with Priyanka Chopra.'

But the true test for Priyanka came the following year when she made her first appearance on Karan Johar's *Koffee With Karan*. The show was in its first season and Priyanka was on episode 17 with Arjun Rampal, her co-star in *Asambhav* and *Yakeen* (2005). The show was broadcast on 26 March 2005—six months after *The Times of India* story on the Akshay Kumar-Twinkle Khanna fight in Goa. Karan Johar is known to ask somewhat awkward questions from his guests about their private lives, and many brush aside or joke about it. When he asked Priyanka the question about her rumoured relationship with Akshay, the 22-year-old actress seemed rather uncomfortable, but she was mature enough to smile as she looked at Karan and then at the camera, denying any truth in the story.

'I am just honestly really tired of it,' Priyanka said. 'There is enough that has been said, speculated, thought of, opinions of people and whatever. But it doesn't matter to me, because it doesn't matter to my family, as long as my parents are fine. They know what the truth is. My friends are fine. I don't have to prove anything to anybody.' She added that the rumours did upset her, showing her human side. 'Any kind of controversy [upsets you], not just an alleged affair. I seem to be crowned the controversy queen for some reason. I just so badly want to focus on my work. I was so happy that people were talking about my performances and my work.'

She did not talk about her decision not to work with Akshay Kumar in the future but did say she did not feel the need to speak to him so the two could clear the air. Karan gave Priyanka one more chance to say whatever she wanted to the media.

Looking straight at the camera, Priyanka said, 'Aren't you tired of it? I mean hello, it's been going on forever. Let's talk about something interesting and fresh.'

More than a decade later, in February 2017, Akshay, for the first time, addressed the issue during an interview. He was promoting his film *Jolly LLB 2* (2017) on the TV show *Aap Ki Adalat* where he was asked about his decision to not work with Priyanka in any film. 'Who tells you all these things?' Akshay responded to the question posed to him. And then went on to deflect the issue about the alleged romance between him and Priyanka.[77] 'This is not true. I have done around 4-5 films with Priyanka. I have worked with all actresses [of that time] except Rani Mukerji. It's not true that I haven't done any film with Priyanka.' And then he added he would 'work with Priyanka if any such film is offered'.

During her first appearance on *Koffee With Karan*, Priyanka had repeatedly said it was time for everyone to move on. So on the same show, Karan Johar took advantage of the opportunity and asked Priyanka about another man whose name seemed to be linked to her.

'Who is Harman Baweja?' Johar asked with a playful smile. Priyanka squirmed. She pushed back her hair. Although she continued to smile—perhaps a lesson she had learned during her Miss India and Miss World training—she seemed to be wishing she had not accepted Karan's invite to be on his show. 'Oh lord,' she said and then went on to explain who Harman Baweja was. 'He is Harry Baweja's son and I am doing their film called *Karam* (a 2005 film, directed by Sanjay Gupta and starring John Abraham; the film was a box office failure). And that's how I know Harman.' This was followed by a rather amusing set of questions from Karan, who seemed to know more than what Priyanka was ready to reveal.

Karan: Nothing happening there?

Priyanka: No he's a friend.

Karan: Oh, he's a friend.

Priyanka: I mean I know him.

Karan: (Giving a smile and sounding slightly sarcastic) You are just good friends?

Priyanka: Oh god, look at that smirk.

The issue died there. But Karan would raise it again the next time Priyanka appeared on his show.

Later, Karan told me that he had heard about Priyanka's friendship with Harman Baweja from Kareena Kapoor. At one point, Kareena and Priyanka were close and they would often go on double dates—Kareena with her then boyfriend Shahid Kapoor and Priyanka with Harman.

Priyanka did two films with Harman—*Love Story 2050* (a 2008 sci-fi film directed by Harry Baweja himself) and *What's Your Raashee?* (a 2009 film directed by Ashutosh Gowarikar where Priyanka played multiple roles). Both films were critical and box office disasters. But by the time Priyanka made her second appearance on Johar's TV show, broadcast on 18 February 2007,[78] she was somewhat opening up about her relationship with Harman Baweja. This time she was a guest on the show with Hrithik Roshan, after the two had delivered the hit *Krrish*. And Karan was back in his form, once again pushing Priyanka to talk about who she was dating this time.

After she hummed and hawed, Priyanka first said, 'I am kind of like in the middle', followed by, 'Well, like I said it is kind of getting there, yet not.'

So, Karan finally said it all in his next question, 'So rumoured, and I only talk about rumours and you can deny, you can confirm. It's entirely your call. Rumour is Harman Baweja who is the hero of one of [the] film you are doing called *Love Story 2050*. So will you come out in 2050, or will it be a little earlier than that?' Priyanka responded, 'Well, he's a really, really good friend. We hang out a lot. He's great company, but beyond that we don't know yet.' But Karan, like a nagging aunt, wanted to know more. 'Okay so that's the status right now?' he asked. 'You guys hang out a lot, you guys are friendly, and you don't know...' Priyanka finished the sentence for him, '...what the future holds.'

Reports indicate that Priyanka and Harman broke up after the failure of *Love Story 2050* and they acted together in *What's Your Raashee?* (2009) even though they were not dating at that time.

∿

Priyanka's early days in the film industry were mired with at least one more controversy. This one was related to her secretary/ manager Prakash Jaju who at some stage had a falling out with Priyanka, as well as her parents, and was fired from his job. Jaju who was actively involved in all aspects of Priyanka's professional, and sometimes personal, life felt he was suddenly out of the loop and he did not like that feeling. In 2008, Jaju was arrested by the police in Mau, Madhya Pradesh. The police were acting on a complaint filed by Priyanka's father, Dr Ashok Chopra, saying that he was threatening the family and making false allegations against Priyanka.[79]

Jaju had worked with Priyanka from her early days in Bollywood and he did get her a few plum assignments—*The Hero: Love Story of a Spy* and *Andaaz*. But he was also reported to be an obsessive and an intrusive man. And so, he was fired from his job. There were also some accusations of money being misused, while Jaju claimed he had not been paid his full salary.

The Prakash Jaju story did not die for a while. In the summer of 2014, Priyanka filed a lawsuit against another former boyfriend—model and actor Aseem Merchant (the two reportedly dated briefly when Priyanka was modelling before her film career started). Merchant had decided to produce a film called *67 Days*—referring to the number of days Jaju was jailed in 2008. Merchant maintained that the film was going to be Jaju's biopic. The complaint Priyanka's lawyer Anand Desai filed, stated: 'Our client is shocked to note that while all the news articles mention the proposed film as your (Jaju's) biopic, the promotions largely refer to our client and inclusion of aspects of her and her family life rather than references to you.'[80]

The complaint also charged that making the film would be 'violation of our client's rights, including right to privacy, defaming our client and lowering her reputation, seeking to subject her to hatred and ridicule.'

The film was eventually shelved.

Jaju has talked more about Priyanka, possibly making up stories, including a series of tweets in 2016 stating that the actress had once tried to commit suicide. This time even Priyanka's protective but otherwise media-shy and quiet mother came out to defend her daughter. A tweet from an account reportedly Dr Madhu Chopra's said, 'That lying bastard spent time in jail... His old mother and father fell at PC's feet begging forgiveness.'[81] The tweet has since been deleted.

During her first appearance on the *Koffee With Karan* show, Priyanka even suggested that Jaju may have been the person responsible for spreading stories about her relations with Akshay Kumar. 'I really do think a lot,' she said. 'Your every relationship, whether it is with your family or your friends or working relationship with your secretary, every relationship has a limit. And when you cross that limit is when it starts to get dangerous and it starts getting bad and unhealthy. And that's what happened with this relationship. He was my secretary and that's where he had to stay, but he started getting interested in other things.'

Controversies apart, Priyanka was already moving ahead with her one major goal in life—to become an actress of substance. And she was definitely getting there—slowly but surely. That process would start with films such as *Bluffmaster!* and *Krrish*.

# 4

# THE MAKING OF
# AN ACTRESS—I

*P*riyanka Chopra's acting skills took a while to evolve. She is one of those actors—like Saif Ali Khan, Kareena Kapoor, Abhishek Bachchan and even Aishwarya Rai— whose performances greatly improve when they work with top directors.

Priyanka is gorgeous and winning the Miss World title transformed her from a gawky teenager from Bareilly to a mature, intelligent adult, and an attractive woman. But for a good part of her career in Bollywood, she continued to be considered a sex symbol, instead of the fine actress she was slowly evolving into.

She has occasionally admitted to it, including that one time on *Koffee With Karan*, where she said, 'I think I have made my own way. I think I was a terrible actress when I started. I didn't even know the "act" in "actress". But I taught myself.'[82]

When Rohan Sippy set out to make his second film *Bluffmaster!*, he once again decided to work with his childhood friend Abhishek Bachchan who, at that stage, was riding on the success of a few hit films—*Dhoom* (2004), *Bunty Aur Babli* (2005). *Bluffmaster!* is the story of a con man who gets conned in a bigger game and it is clearly inspired by the Argentinean film *Nine Queens* (2000). There are similar scenes and the plot runs on a parallel track. Of course, Sippy, like other Bollywood film-makers, made essential changes and gave his film the Bollywood entertainment twists, from the songs to an attractive lead actress—Priyanka Chopra.

Reports suggested that there were casting issues with the film. Journalist Subhash K. Jha, who often has the inside pulse of Bollywood, wrote a report that Rohan had originally cast Aishwarya Rai for the role. But he then changed his mind and cast Priyanka. Jha quoted a rather upset Aishwarya as saying, 'How can that be? I've finalized everything, given Rohan the dates he wanted. Of course I don't have a written contract with them. But does one need to sign formal papers with friends?

In Amsterdam, Abhishek and I were talking about what fun it would be to shoot together again.' (Abhishek and Aishwarya had appeared as the leads in Rohan's first film *Kuch Naa Kaho* [2003]. The two would get married a year and a half after the release of *Bluffmaster!*). [83]

And she added, 'I ran into Rameshji (Sippy's father and producer/director Ramesh Sippy) a while back and we spoke about the project. How can Rohan do this? We're friends. We had so much fun doing *Kuch Naa Kaho*.'

When Jha asked Priyanka for a comment, she was diplomatic. 'I've no clue if anyone was approached before me. All I'm concerned with is what I've been offered. And *Bluffmaster!* seemed like a great deal of fun. Since some of the dates for Rakesh Roshan's *Krrish* got cancelled (because Hrithik Roshan had an accident), I decided to use them for *Bluffmaster!*' And she added, 'This interchange in roles happens all the time in this industry.'

At a Rediff.com chat, while promoting the film, Rohan was asked why he cast Priyanka in the film. 'I think the better question is why did she choose me!' he responded. 'I think she is talented, and she suited the part. What was also great about her is that she agreed to come onto the film even though it isn't a full-fledged "heroine's" role. She understood she was part of an ensemble cast, and really was a great team player!'[84]

'Instinctively, she is a fine actress,' Rohan told me in an interview I conducted at National Film Development Corporation's Film Bazaar in Goa in November 2017. 'That time we were also trying something different. It was lovely to have an actress who was on the same wavelength a part of the team. Even though time wise her part is not huge, but she is the bluffmaster.' He added that even though Priyanka's role was supporting Abhishek's character, she was comfortable and 'smart enough to understand that this is what her role required'.

The film was shot mostly in Mumbai and the days were often 14-hour-long. 'As luck would have it Abhishek's dates worked and we were able to shoot during the monsoon,' Rohan said. 'It's a little risky to work, but the payoff is great. And sometimes Priyanka would have to come at four in the morning because that was the window we had to shoot a particular scene.'

For most part, Priyanka looks stunning in *Bluffmaster!*, especially when she is dancing to the 'Say Na Say' song at her engagement party, wearing a white sari with silver work on the colourful border, and looking positively hot. The sari is tied low to show her waistline. Or in the 'Right Here Right Now' song that also features four sexy models and the rest of the cast and crew from the film, Priyanka is in a bikini top with extra straps hanging, pretending to be a singer with Abhishek dancing around her, the air from a fan inside the studio blowing her hair.

Rohan also recalls Priyanka joining the team's musical efforts for the 'Right Here Right Now' song, where she lends her voice, singing five words—'I am a good girl'.

But if Priyanka was hoping for a major recognition for her performance in the film, she was in for a disappointment. In the Rediff.com review, Priyanka got only five words in the mention. 'Priyanka Chopra is perfectly credible,' wrote Raja Sen.[85] And while Kaveree Bamzai of *India Today* liked the film, this is what she wrote in the last line of her review, 'The only loud things in the movie are the exclamation mark in the title and Chopra's pout.'[86] That would be the only mention of Priyanka in Bamzai's review.

One inside story during the making of *Bluffmaster!* caught on with the press and Priyanka's fans. During the making of the film, Abhishek Bachchan decided to give Priyanka the nickname Piggy Chops. That nickname stuck with her and for a while, Priyanka seemed fine with it. 'I find it cute to be called "Miss Piggy Chops",'

she told Rajeev Masand.[87] But then, to her surprise, that is how
she is introduced in the credits of *Taxi No. 9 2 11* (2006), where
she makes a guest appearance.

*Bluffmaster!* was referred to as a semi-hit by Box Office India.
But Priyanka's big hit—perhaps the biggest hit in her career so
far—would be released the next year. The film *Krrish* was producer
and director Rakesh Roshan's superhero sequel to his *E.T.: The
Extra-Terrestrial* inspired *Koi Mil Gaya* (2003). It was his attempt
to boost his son Hrithik Roshan's career. The result was a big
box office success—*Krrish* and the third part in the series, *Krrish
3* (2013) were huge hits. Critics were not satisfied with the films,
but Indian audiences bought the desi superhero—a masked man
with a cape, a do-gooder who saved kids trapped inside burning
circus tent and the film's leading lady from a gliding accident,
danced and sang songs with her and also fought bad guys. Kids
loved the idea of Hrithik Roshan being introduced as India's
answer to Batman and Superman. And so, kids and young girls,
smitten by Roshan's good looks and chiselled body, were the
biggest audience of the film.

*Krrish* received a range of negative reviews. *The New York
Times* generally treats Bollywood with kid gloves, but Laura Kern
said this in her review: '*Krrish* is overlong, schmaltzy, wholly
derivative and sprinkled with underwhelming song-and-dance
numbers. Coming from anywhere else, these elements might be
considered glaring flaws. In Bollywood they are not only expected,
but often, as in this film, they also appear as virtues.' [88]

In India, the Rediff.com critic saw one positive element in
the film, saying, 'While a lot of us might be scornful of *Krrish*,
it's heartening to see fantasy officially entering mainstream
Bollywood.'[89]

And critic Saibal Chatterjee trashed the film, saying it just
did not work. 'No narrative logic, no psychological realism and

loads of shallow romance complete with stale song and dance routines, but all in all three hours of undemanding, unalloyed fun. If that is the kind of cinema that is going to be the future of Bollywood, someone please give me a ticket to the moon. I am outta here!'[90]

Film journalist Subhash K. Jha earlier suggested that the role of Priya (Priyanka's character) in *Krrish* was first offered to Aishwarya Rai. 'Ash had more or less been finalized for *Krrish*. Even her dates and the fee had been negotiated. On the night before she was to leave for Bangkok with the unit, she was told she needn't go. Priyanka was doing the film.'[91] This change and that in *Bluffmaster!* must have created a great amount of friction between Aishwarya and Priyanka.

⌒

Priyanka was noticed in *Krrish*, but Rediff.com sensed she struggled with her role. 'Poor Priyanka gets an extremely tough role: A naïve girl who is initially taken in by a prank, scared but intrigued, and then smitten. Priya blows hot and cold as she then becomes worldly and (harmlessly) selfish, but is finally swept away by Krishna. In short, the actress has to convincingly be charmed, a much harder proposition than acting charming.'[92] The critic added that in the 1970s, Parveen Babi could have pulled off this role with great ease, but for Priyanka Chopra, it seemed like a tough job.

Seven years later, Rakesh Roshan was back with more of the Bollywood-friendly superhero adventure with *Krrish 3*. The film ended up scoring really high on the box office but it was a mess when it came to cheesy special effects, and derivative narrative with reference to several superhero films from Hollywood. And critics disliked it even more than *Krrish*. The Firstpost.com critic said, 'The film is two and a half painful hours of poorly presented, unexciting action scenes, awful computer graphics, unimaginative storytelling and Hollywood theft of the most blatant and shameless variety.'[93] Writing about Priyanka who once again plays Krrish's (Hrithik Roshan) wife, Priya, the Rediff.com reviewer said that her character is 'a shrill giggler with the most inane role possible.'[94]

The release of *Krrish 3* once again brought to surface a Bollywood rivalry that first surfaced since the release of Priyanka's 2008 film *Fashion*. Before *Krrish 3* opened, Priyanka said in many interviews that she was playing the lead role in the film and her co-star, Kangana Ranaut, only played a supporting character in the film. In a PTI story, Priyanka emphasized that she had never been insecure about sharing space in Hindi films. In *The Hero: Love Story of a Spy* and *Andaaz*, she appeared on screen only after the intermission. But she also insisted that she was definitely the lead actress in *Krrish 3*. 'I am the heroine of the film, I am playing Hrithik's wife and that is how it is,'[95] *India Today* quoted her in the PTI story.

But many critics mentioned that in the film, Kangana's villainous character had lot more shades than Priyanka's personality. The role was definitely more challenging than the one played by Priyanka. One story in *India Today* highlighted the differences between the two actresses' roles: 'There's not much for the leading lady to do in the film other than being rescued by the knight in shining err...black leather. Kangana, on the other hand, is more than a pretty face—she plays a mutant and that provides the actor in her with a huge canvas to play with... She makes her character look effortlessly sexy while maintaining her staccato expression throughout the film. Kangana simply goes for the kill with the role.'[96]

Priyanka and Kangana were first cast in the same film by Madhur Bhandarkar (National Film Award-winning director of

*Chandini Bar* [2001], *Page 3* [2005] and *Traffic Signal* [2007]) in *Fashion*. With a large ensemble cast, *Fashion* looked at the dark underbelly of India's burgeoning modelling and fashion industry, after the introduction of a liberalized economy. As India's middle and upper middle classes grew in numbers and their purchasing power expanded, they began to spend more and more money on consumer goods. The clothing industry and the high-end fashion industry also expanded with this increased demand. As fashion shows and beauty contests were broadcast on TV, they created a class of small-town girls who began to dream of glamour, becoming celebrities, high fashion and walking on the ramp. In fact, Priyanka played a small-town girl in the film, somewhat similar to the Bareilly girl she herself was. The only difference was that her character in *Fashion*—Meghna Mathur—had to fight with her parents to move to Mumbai. In real life, Priyanka Chopra's parents were happy to allow their daughter to enter the modelling, fashion and, ultimately, the film industry.

Clearly, Priyanka was the lead in the film, but Kangana had an interesting supporting role—of a model addicted to drugs and on a destructive path. Both actresses won National Film Awards for the film—in the best actress (Priyanka) and best supporting actress (Kangana) categories. But the press tried to make a big thing about their rivalry. Responding to these rivalry reports—even before the film was shot—Kangana told Subhash K. Jha, 'Barring Anurag Basu's *Life in a Metro*, most of my films have been solo-heroine films revolving around my character.[97] This is the first time I'm co-starring with another actress. I'm not insecure about it. Why should I be? Priyanka and I have distinct personalities and that's why Madhur has signed us to play the two very different characters.'

When Jha pointed out that whenever she was pitched against another actress such as Kareena Kapoor (*Aitraaz*) and Lara Dutta

(*Andaaz*) Priyanka had a way to give a stronger performance, Kangana seemed to take on the challenge. 'Good!' she said. 'It'd be healthy competition. We'll both do our best. A film shouldn't be like a kabaddi competition.'

Madhur remembers the press reports of the rivalry, but he also believes that too much was made out of nothing. 'There are some people who want to have their own space,' Madhur says. 'That doesn't mean they are moody. People did try to create the rift, but there was never a problem. They were very gracious to each other. Priyanka was very cool.' Madhur says that when he conceived the idea of making *Fashion*, he could only think of Priyanka Chopra to play the role of his protagonist.

Before she made *Fashion*, Priyanka had a string of flops— *Big Brother* (2007), *The Legend of Drona* (2008), *Chamku* (2008) and *Love Story 2050* (2008). Most of these films had not released when Madhur ran into Priyanka in the lobby of the Taj Hotel in Panjim, Goa. The two were there as guests and delegates of the International Film Festival of India. And Madhur's film *Corporate* (2006) was showing in the Indian Panorama section of the festival.

'I had only met her briefly at a few other functions,' Bhandarkar says. 'I said hello to her and that's when I said, "Priyanka I have something for you. I want to make a film on the fashion world." And the first thing she said, "Oh now you are going to target them?" I guess with *Chandini Bar*, *Page 3* and *Corporate*, people had started saying, "Madhur is always targeting some section of the society or the other".'

Two months later, they met again in Mumbai. The script was ready and Priyanka felt connected to Meghna's character. Madhur shot the film in a chronological order. 'I wanted the character to grow as we were shooting the film,' Bhandarkar says. 'Priyanka understood the graph I was tracking.'

Priyanka's love interest in the film was a relative newcomer,

Arjun Bajwa—a good-looking actor who had worked in a few Telugu films, but had not played a significant role in the Hindi cinema. Bhandarkar says that once he had cast Priyanka in the lead and, as it was a woman-centric story, he was sure that no big mainstream Bollywood actor would have accepted the role of Manav Bhasin. 'Actors have their own insecurities,' Madhur says. 'Most would not want to do a film if the actress was the protagonist. So I did not go down that road.'

Fashion became a defining film in Priyanka's career. Rajeev Masand wrote that the film follows Madhur's version of reality, but there are flashes of authenticity in the film. About Priyanka he wrote, 'Priyanka Chopra turns in a respectable performance, one that will inevitably go down as her best.'[98] Rediff.com's critic seemed somewhat surprised by Priyanka's performance in the film. 'Now either Ms. Chopra has learnt a few new tricks (as far as performance goes) since her last few outings or she really is Meghna Mathur (temperament wise) and was relieved to finally be able to play herself on screen. I suspect the truth lies somewhere in between.'[99]

Winning the National Film Award was just the cherry on the cake for Priyanka Chopra.

Despite a disappointing start in the year, Priyanka would end 2008 with another relatively important film, the one that had a lasting impression, at least for its popular songs and its comic timing. A few weeks after the release of Fashion, she was back on the screen with the Karan Johar production, Dostana, directed by Tarun Mansukhani. Once again, Priyanka plays a glamorous role, but this time with an edge, a certain coolness. And the fact that the film is set in Miami—and all outdoor scenes are shot in Florida—makes Dostana a fun watch and an important film—a big Bollywood production that started a conversation about homosexuality.

As was becoming common practice in Priyanka's career, the role of Neha Melwani, a fashion editor in *Dostana,* was first offered to Aishwarya Rai. She was supposed to act opposite her relatively new husband Abhishek Bachchan and Saif Ali Khan. But this time, Aishwarya pulled out of the project. One can only guess that the sexy look of Neha—in swimsuits and other tight-fitting dresses— was going to be a big challenge for Aishwarya who was now Amitabh and Jaya Bachchan's daughter-in-law. The first and the only time Aishwarya kissed on screen was in *Dhoom 2*. Also, there were reports that after she and Abhishek got engaged, Amitabh Bachchan had requested the *Dhoom 2* producer Yash Chopra to edit the kissing scene.[100] So, it is understandable that Aishwarya would be uncomfortable playing Neha's character in *Dostana*.

Aishwarya's loss was Priyanka's gain. The two did switch roles one more time on an earlier occasion. Priyanka was originally offered the lead in J.P. Dutta's *Umrao Jaan* (2006). But since she could not give the dates, the role went to Aishwarya. A remake of the 1981 masterpiece, the new *Umrao Jaan* was a critical and box officer disaster.

Karan Johar says that after Aishwarya's departure from *Dostana*, he and Tarun did not think of anyone for the lead role. 'I think she had just given *Bluffmaster!* and *Krrish,*' Karan says. 'She was in the zone where she was becoming hot. So we offered her *Dostana*.' Later, Saif Ali Khan also dropped out and was replaced by John Abraham.

There was the initial moment when Karan sent Tarun to meet Priyanka and the two did not find a connection. After Tarun narrated the script to Priyanka, he came back and met with Karan. 'I told him I wasn't sure if she was Neha. He asked what had happened and I said I don't know but she has not given me that vibe, if she is excited by the project.' Meanwhile, Priyanka also called Karan. She said, 'I love the script but I am concerned about the director.' Tarun says, 'She said, "He (Tarun) is such a serious person and I am wondering if he will be able to pull together a comedy."'

Karan had a hearty laugh. 'And he told us, "You both tried to act very officious while you both are completely mad people",' Tarun says. 'That's when we started hanging out, chatting and I realized that she was actually as mad as me. It was a great bonding and it changed everything after.'

But Priyanka had also made a public announcement that she would not expose her skin unless the script really demanded it. 'When it came down to the swimsuit shot, she (Priyanka) was a little hesitant because nobody had presented it in a way where the girl doesn't appear sleazy,' Tarun says. He sat her down, talked to her and even agreed to go shopping for the swimsuit with her. 'So she, me and (costume designer) Manish (Malhotra) went shopping in Miami. She was very excited (with a gold-coloured one-piece, backless swimsuit) and from that moment, she was on.' In any case, Tarun says that the film's outdoor shoot was in Miami 'where if you are not in a swimsuit then it is a problem'.

*Dostana* introduces Priyanka in a very Bollywood manner, keeping the mystery of her character while playing with her physical attributes. Bachchan and Abraham's characters arrive looking for an apartment (the interior scenes of the film were shot in a studio in Mumbai). The two pretend they are gay with the hopes to share a relatively cheap apartment. They are told by the real-estate agent their application would be approved, but Neha has to make the final decision. '*Yeh Neha kaun hai* (Who is this Neha)?' Bachchan asks. And we hear Priyanka's voice saying, '*Main Neha hoon* (I am Neha).' We see her hot pink lips and they part as she says 'Hi'. Then, we see her gorgeous eyes, green in colour, and her orange dress. There are many other shots until we see Priyanka's full face. The two dudes are thrilled.

'It is very important every time one wants a shot that projects glamour that one should not resort to sleaze,' Tarun says. 'You have to know how to shoot it, how she should pose, how she should stand. It is very easy for the camera to show the back and focus on the butt. We are mostly catering to a family audience, you don't want the audience to squirm and wonder why they are watching it.'

*Fashion* and *Dostana* were shot back-to-back and Priyanka's acting evolved during the two productions. But Tarun had to work with her to tone down the acting that she had picked up at the Kishore Namit Kapoor school and in her early Bollywood films.

'When she came to *Dostana* she came with a certain kind of acting quality that had become a norm for the Hindi film industry,' Tarun says. 'It was slightly over-the-top world. So when she gave me the first shot I remember going up to her and saying, "Don't do that. Just be yourself." When we were setting up the next shot, she walked up to me and asked, "Are you sure about it? Because it doesn't feel like acting." And my reaction was, "It is not meant to be acting. Be yourself." She started understanding what I was saying and her performance became more normal.'

There came a time during the shoot when Tarun and Priyanka really hit it off. And often Priyanka would have comments about a scene or a particular dialogue. 'Priyanka was the one who would come to me and point out if in a particular dialogue a word was used twice,' Tarun recalls. 'She would be like, "Why can't there be another word, because it is sounding like I am repeating myself." So she would keep me on my toes and that was by far the best thing I could have had as a director. I was constantly concerned that Priyanka will come to the set and ask me questions.'

*Dostana* did mixed business at the box office—or 'average' as sites that specialize on the box office of Bollywood films would say. The reviews were critical of the way the film portrayed the gay characters—that the film laughed at them and not with them. But the reviews always mentioned Priyanka's sexualized character Neha. As Raja Sen wrote in Rediff.com, 'Speaking of sexual dynamics, there's a considerable amount on display here in terms of Priyanka Chopra's dresses. Not that we're complaining one bit. The actress looks screen-scorchingly hot, and while there is a skimpiness overkill, we're too busy staring to make an issue out of it. She looks refreshingly at ease after a series of overdone roles, and her on-screen enjoyment is natural and fun. And did I mention those legs? Lord.'[101] And Rajeev Masand referred to Priyanka's Neha as a 'hottie-with-a-heart-of-gold.' He added, 'She looks smashing in this film, better than she's ever looked before.'[102]

One lasting legacy of *Dostana* is the hit song, 'Desi Girl', which has sort of become an anthem for South Asian women living in the diaspora—the US, UK, or elsewhere. 'Priyanka and I laugh about it,' Karan Johar says. 'She tells me, "Dude I get asked to dance to Desi Girl every time I go anywhere." It's the line *Dekhi Lakh Lakh Pardesi Girl*/Ain't Nobody Like My Desi Girl'. It applies to anyone who is a desi girl. It's not India-centric, or Pakistani or Bangladeshi. That branding also worked for Priyanka in America.'

ᔈ

When Priyanka Chopra was shooting in Miami, she had a visitor from Mumbai. Film-maker Vishal Bhardwaj flew all the way to Miami to narrate the script of the film he was planning—*Kaminey* (released a year after *Dostana*).

Vishal remembered seeing Priyanka in a film where he was impressed with her acting potential. He also sensed that she was an 'intelligent person'. And so he approached her for the role of Sweety.

'I wanted a slightly Marathi appearing actress, with a dusky look for the character in *Kaminey*,' Vishal says. He first approached Priyanka before she left for the *Dostana* shoot. He narrated the structure of the story since he was still working on the script, hoping that Priyanka would commit to the dates. 'I wanted to capture Bombay's rains and wanted to shoot during the monsoon season.'

'When she heard the narration from me, she first said no to the project,' Vishal adds. 'She said there was no role for the heroine in the film, since it was the story of twin brothers. But I told her, "Maybe you are not able to see it right now, or perhaps I cannot make you see. But once the script is ready your role will be a lot clearer." So I told her, "Don't say yes just now, but please also don't say no".'

And he promised to see her in Miami when the script would be ready. 'And she started laughing, saying, "Where will you show up in Miami?"' But he actually did fly to Miami and that is when she realized there was so much in the script. 'The character of Sweety was of a feisty, strong woman. I had told her that my female characters are always very strong. I added that this will be a challenge for you to play a Marathi girl. Then she accepted it.'

Priyanka worked extremely hard to get the Maharashtrian character right—learning the language from a coach who was assigned to her, and speaking with the film's crew in Marathi. 'I told her if you speak wrong, they will correct you,' Vishal says. 'When we started prepping I told her that on the set 90 per cent of the crew will be Marathi speaking, and I didn't want to dub her voice. I also didn't want a situation where after every shot some of the crew members would go in a corner and laugh at her.'

She even watched a few Marathi films to get the cultural nuances of Maharashtrians. Her mother would later tell me that it was for the first time she had seen non-Hindi language films. However, Priyanka earlier said she had watched a few Tamil films to prepare for her first film *Thamizhan*.

But more than anything else, Vishal was drawn to Priyanka's intelligence and her ability to adapt to the way the *Kaminey* team worked. 'What makes her special is that she is very spontaneous,' he says. 'I have the habit of changing the things on the set. Some actors come very prepared and if you change anything, they get thrown off. She would follow me a lot and there was a sense of respect. But she would also argue a lot—that comes with intelligence, where you think you can convince the other person.'

Priyanka looks quite convincing as a Maharashtrian, whether she dances as an excited bride in the song 'Raat Ke Dhai Baje', dressed in a green sari and a short red blouse, displaying her slim waist, or in the opening song 'Fatak', where she appears in the midst of AIDS activists, wearing large condom masks. She speaks in Marathi, '*Tu kuthai Guddu* (Where are you Guddu)?' And critics noticed her turn as a Marathi-speaking character.

Shubhra Gupta of *The Indian Express* wrote this about the film's lead actors (Priyanka Chopra and Shahid Kapoor): 'Savour a super-sexed up Shahid (his grungy, muscled, long-haired look is a killer), an equally sexy Priyanka (she does such a good job of playing a strong-willed Marathi "mulgi" that you overlook her immaculate French manicure, almost).'[103] Rediff.com's critic said, 'Priyanka Chopra's delightfully high-strung Sweety pulls off hysterical Marathi with impressive fluency.'[104]

Priyanka met with an accident during the shooting of a night scene where Sweety and Guddu (Shahid) are trying to escape on a scooter. To add to the dramatic look of the film, cinematographer Tassaduq Hussain had wet the road. Bhardwaj suggested that a double could drive the scooter, but Priyanka insisted that she would do it. And as she drove the scooter, it skidded.

'She was hurt,' Vishal says. 'I was sitting looking at the monitor and suddenly it seemed as if she was coming to the monitor. People started running and her face could have been injured. But fortunately Shahid's hand covered her face. She was very embarrassed. We thought we will pack up since it was already late—about 2-3 a.m. But she said, "No, I won't be able to sleep. You have to do a shot with me. Otherwise I won't be able to sleep. I feel let down and depressed." So we had to do a shot. That is Priyanka Chopra's dedication.'

It was because of Priyanka's dedication that Vishal also offered her the lead role for one of his most challenging films, *7 Khoon Maaf* (2011). The role of Susanna Anna-Marie Johannes—a woman who murders her six husbands—was very tough, definitely one of the toughest roles Priyanka had done. In addition to playing opposite several different actors—Naseeruddin Shah, Irrfan Khan, John Abraham and Annu Kapoor among others, Priyanka had to also age in the film, from a teenager to a mature woman in her 60s . 'She was very apprehensive, very nervous to do that,' Vishal says. 'There was a concern whether she will be able to pull it off or not.' So there was a lot of prep work and then at some point, Vishal asked her to be spontaneous in her performance.

'Priyanka actually became a part of the direction unit,' Vishal adds. 'She knew everything that was happening, what we were doing with the other actors. She used to come to our office and spend time with us. I have worked with many other actors. Movie stars usually live in their own world. Once the shift is over and they are done for the day, they have another life. Priyanka is very different. When she is in a film, she is your best buddy, your best assistant, she is like a spot boy. So she's available to you 24 hours. That is her job and she makes it her own, sometimes more than me. I would have to sometimes tell her that I was the director, it was my film and I knew my job. And then she would go, "Oh, sorry, sorry".'

One part of 7 Khoon Maaf—the segment where Susanna marries the poet Wasiullah Khan (Irrfan Khan)—was shot in Srinagar and the political conditions were tense in the city. Early one morning, there was a 15-minute shoot inside a mosque located in downtown Srinagar. It was a dangerous area and for security reasons and out of respect to the mosque, the police could not even take the guns inside. The crew was able to shoot the scene with Priyanka and Irrfan, and the police superintendent-in-charge was impressed. So Bhardwaj tried his luck and asked to take a quick shot at Lal Chowk. The superintendent agreed but the problem was that there was no place for Priyanka to change costumes.

'I said to Priyanka that the SSP has agreed but people will soon show up and we won't be able to take the shot,' Bhardwaj recalls. 'So Priyanka suggested that we should have people stand with sheets around a van and she could change her costume inside. She changed her clothes and within three minutes she was out. No mainstream actress would do something like this so quickly.'

On another day, the crew was shooting inside a house in Srinagar. The word spread that Priyanka Chopra was inside and nearly four hundred people gathered outside. A Central Reserve Police personnel came and told the crew to pack up immediately since the situation could go out of hand. But the shoot was supposed to go on until 8 p.m.

'Priyanka took my hand, led me through some narrow path and staircase (against the advice of the police officer) and waved from a balcony, requesting the crowd to let us complete our work,' Vishal says. 'You should have seen the crowd. They were jumping and cheering. We finished the shooting that day. The next day also they allowed us to shoot at that location. So this is Priyanka. She very is courageous.'

But Priyanka's biggest challenge was the day she shot the sex scene with Irrfan—playing a charming poet with a dark side. He is physically abusive while engaging in sex. 'Irrfan comes from theatre, he could transform into a monster, but Priyanka has no theatre background,' Vishal says. 'She was very afraid of how she would react to the physical abuse. I told her first drop all your inhibitions. Think like a master. Don't think otherwise. I was once told that, *"Seekho to shagird ki tarah, karo to ustad ki tarah. Karne ke time apne aap ko ustad mano* (Learn like a student, but when you perform, be a master. While acting and doing something, consider yourself a master)." I told her that she should consider herself an ustad like Meryl Streep in Irrfan's presence. That gave her the confidence. And she matched Irrfan in the scene.'

Vishal Bhardwaj says that Priyanka's evolution as an actor is remarkable, 'Hard work, and never being too happy with her work. She is always stretching to do better. If I suggested that she could change slightly, she would start to feel low, that she should have herself thought of it for her character. These things make you work. Then next time you go on the set, you know you have to keep working and not become too complacent.'

And then there is Priyanka's love for food. *'Khane ki bahut shaukeen hai woh* (She loves to eat),' Vishal says. *'Bhagwan ne usko kya* metabolism *diya hai* (God has given her an amazing metabolism). Usually, actresses will bring their boiled food for lunch. Priyanka will bring samosas, kachodis to the set. And the fat never makes its way to her body.'

During the climax shoot of *Kaminey*, the crew was standing right next to a bakery. 'When we got to the set in the morning, she smelled freshly baked bread and she went straight to the bakery. She's such a foodie.'

Vishal also reminisces about his friendship with Priyanka. 'I developed a great rapport with her,' he says. 'I have never had such a great rapport with any actor, as I had with Priyanka. I have done three films with Pankaj (Kapoor) Ji, so I guess the second actor is Pankaj Ji. But still it was never the way I connected with Priyanka. I have never had this much fun working with any other actor. She is still my only friend in the industry. She is so good and she is a very intelligent actor.'

ᔕ

It was during the *Kaminey* shoot that Priyanka reportedly became close to Shahid Kapoor. Shahid's much public relationship with Kareena Kapoor ended while the two were still making Imtiaz Ali's *Jab We Met* (2007).[105] That would also be Shahid's most successful film to date.

Perhaps the root of their relationship was the kissing scene in *Kaminey*. At least that was what Karan Johar suggested in his *Koffee With Karan* segment on 19 December 2010 with Shahid and Priyanka as his guests.[106] According to Priyanka, she did not want to kiss Shahid for the scene. The kiss was not written in the script. 'It was a surprise for the both of us,' Shahid said on the show. 'But Vishal Sir believed that it was something important, because he said there has to be a sequence in the film where you have to see these two people making love. Otherwise it looks very boring and outdated.' And to that, Priyanka added, 'The basis of Sweety and Guddu's characters was that they were going to have a baby.' And she also said, 'I have to say Shahid was quite gentlemanly about the thing and said, "It's entirely up to Priyanka if she wants to do it and if she is comfortable".' To that Shahid added, 'Because if it is not something discussed before then it's the actors' prerogative if it's something new.'

But Karan was simply interested in knowing if that was the beginning of the relationship. And he was persistent.

Karan: So did the chemistry steam after that?

Priyanka: I think we always had chemistry once we met...

Shahid: Once we started talking. We hadn't spoken until then.

Priyanka: I think we have had and we still do.

Karan: And that will continue?

Priyanka: Of course.

In the same episode, Karan kept digging for more and asking if the two actors were dating. At one point, Shahid said the only reason he wanted to be on the show was to clarify if he and Priyanka were dating and then, he turned to her and asked, 'Are we seeing each other?' And Priyanka responded, 'No, we are not.'

The fun and the banter continued between the host and his two guests. Karan asked at a point, 'What's the big deal?' So Shahid turned to Priyanka and said, 'I can't take the decision without you being involved. It is about the two of us.' Priyanka finally responded, 'I will answer this question. I don't like answering questions about my personal life, I never have and I never will. Until I come to the point where I feel that this is something I want to talk about.'

But before Karan moved on to his next set of questions he made the final declaration. 'I am not buying that,' he said. 'I am just announcing that you were dating. Whether you are dating or not right now, I don't know, because clearly with the chemistry that is clearly evident, it definitely shows there is something happening.' And he ended the show by saying, 'I had a great time. I may not have gotten any confirmations, but as I said we all have figured it out. We like it when love is in the air.'

The show ended with Karan's rapid-fire round. One question

put to Shahid Kapoor was: 'If you woke up one morning and turned into Priyanka Chopra, what would you do?' Shahid almost revealed their relationship by giving a hilarious answer, 'I would wonder what I am doing in Shahid Kapoor's bedroom and walk to the next wing, because that's where I stay.' (At that time, Shahid and Priyanka lived in the same building in Mumbai—Raj Classic on Yari Road, though their apartments were in different wings of the complex). Priyanka gave a shocked look, and her mouth opened with laughter as well.

Next month on Monday, 24 January 2011, there was an income tax raid at Priyanka Chopra's apartment. (There was also a simultaneous raid at Katrina Kaif's apartment.) As the practice goes, the income tax officers gathered in their office at 6 a.m. and were then led by senior officials to Yari Road. It was only fifteen minutes before the raid was conducted that the officers and the accompanying police were told which apartment and whose apartment they had to enter. At 7.30 a.m., when the officers rang the bell to Priyanka Chopra's apartment, the door was opened by a 'sleepy Kapoor, who was wearing nothing but shorts.'

The incident was reported in several newspapers and on Bollywood websites. It appeared to be a confirmation of the rumour that Priyanka and Shahid were dating. Later, there seemed to be an attempt to cover up, or at least give some explanation to what Shahid was doing in Priyanka's apartment. A few days later, Priyanka gave one such explanation when she said this to *DNA* newspaper: 'Yes, Shahid was there at my apartment when it (the income tax raid) happened. He lives just three minutes away from my home and it was but natural for me to give him a call when all that was happening. My mother was also supposed to be there but she couldn't make it. So I gave him a call and he rushed to my apartment just as he was (reportedly in shorts).'[107]

The three words in parenthesis—'reportedly in shorts'—were added by the newspaper.

Priyanka and Shahid's relationship eventually ended. After some well-publicized affairs, Shahid married a Delhi girl—Mira Rajput—in July 2015. On the *Koffee With Karan* episode broadcast on 5 January 2014, Karan talked about an earlier time when he and Priyanka were at a party and they saw Shahid there. 'When you are in the same fraternity, yes, you bump into each other,' she added.[108]

Priyanka's personal life has remained a subject of speculation among fans and gossip magazines. In a recent interview with *Filmfare*, Priyanka revealed an important aspect of her life. When asked about her relationship status, she gave a surprising answer that until last year she had been in a long-term relationship.

'I've been single after a really really long time,' she told Filmfare on 6 February 2018. 'I was in a very committed relationship. But since almost a year, I've been single. I've met a bunch of people. I've gone out with people. I let someone woo me but no... My mind hasn't exploded, not yet!'

Since the interview and even before she spoke about it, there had been speculations about who she was in a relationship with. Names of her male peers in the Indian film industry had been mentioned in conversations, but Priyanka refused to give any hints. For such a public figure whose life is closely watched in India and in the US, she definitely kept it under the radar.

But rumoured or actual relationships never stopped Priyanka Chopra from focusing on her work. And in the next few years, she did one project after another that showcased the actor in her. She seemed to be in a hurry with the projects. Perhaps she could see that her destiny would take her to the US.

# 5

# THE MAKING OF
# AN ACTRESS—II

*P*riyanka Chopra often tells talk show hosts and other journalists in America that she has acted in over fifty films. That sounds correct, if one counts Priyanka's page on imdb.com, which even includes all her guest appearances. But for Hollywood that sounds like a big number.

'I don't think De Niro has done fifty films,' Stephen Colbert said when Priyanka appeared on his talk show in early February 2017. 'Yeah, he probably hasn't,' Priyanka said, playing with her hair, trying to look shy, a bit modest. But it was the modesty of a true star. 'I do a lot of work.'[109] In reality, Robert De Niro has acted in nearly 90 films.[110] But he started his career in the mid-1960s, way before Priyanka was born.

However, even with the fifty films, Priyanka has only done a handful that can count as good cinema—where the roles challenged her and made her shine beyond the sex symbol image that she was typecast into for a while after she joined the film industry.

And in this mix of her good work, one must include *Don* and *Don 2*—both directed by Farhan Akhtar, who wanted to give a contemporary feel to the original *Don* (1978), directed by Chandra Barot, with Amitabh Bachchan in the lead, and written by Javed Akhtar and Salim Khan. Farhan cast Shah Rukh Khan to play the Don in his version. And he picked Priyanka Chopra to take on the role of Roma, originally played by Zeenat Aman. By 2006, Priyanka was on the edge of becoming a big star, having acted in *Krrish*, *Bluffmaster!* and the earlier films with Akshay Kumar, including *Aitraaz*.

Farhan made interesting casting choices, giving a more established actress Kareena Kapoor—she had already appeared in a range of films—including *Kabhi Khushi Kabhie Gham...* (2001), *Chameli* (2003), *Yuva* (2004) and *Omkara* (released earlier in 2006)—to reprise Helen's role of Kamini. The Kamini character dies in the beginning of _Don_. Roma definitely has a substantial role in the film.

In an interview with sifymovies.com just before the release of the new _Don_, Priyanka, seemed modest. 'When I was offered _Don_, I did not watch (the original) again because I did not want to do it like Zeenat Aman,' Priyanka said.[111] 'If I tried being like her, I would not have been able to do justice to Roma as Zeenat Aman had done a superb job. Comparisons are inevitable but Zeenat will always be the original Roma. I am just trying to recreate the character in a little different manner.'

Anyone who has seen the two _Dons_ will agree that Priyanka was by all means a far better Roma. There was a Bollywood tone in Priyanka's dialogue delivery, but it was definitely closer to reality. Zeenat, in her entire career, spoke Hindi with a strong accent. She always gave the sense that Hindi was a foreign language for her, and it was a struggle for her to speak it. Her acting abilities, too, were always questionable.

Even Karan Johar said this to me when comparing Priyanka to Zeenat. 'She was Zeenat Aman who became the actor,' Karan said alluding to the fact the both Zeenat and Priyanka started their careers as beauty pageant winners. 'She was kind of sexy, glamorous, but she went on to emerge as an artist.' Of course there was still time for Priyanka to emerge as a true artist, but she was already way ahead of Zeenat as an actress. The irony is that in the summer of 2017, Zeenat talked to the press about the possibility of a biopic based on her life. And she said she wanted Priyanka to play her character. 'I think she is very good and lovely,' Zeenat said,[112] 'Priyanka would be the ideal actress to play my part.'

Priyanka has some terrific moments in _Don_, including the first time she is introduced to us. In Farhan's updated film, Priyanka's Roma is shown performing martial arts with her slender, yet tight arms. It is almost as if she is performing a slow meditative tai-chi-inspired dance in a black tank top and black pants. Everything is sleek, modern, hip in the new *Don*.

For one critic, Priyanka's Roma was the biggest surprise of the film. 'Stepping into Zeenat Aman's shoes is a tough task, but she doesn't really waste time pretending to be the stunner's successor,' this critic wrote, being a bit too kind to Zeenat Aman.[113] 'Chopra handles her role with efficiency, looking every bit the competent woman of action—and a ravishing babe who fills out a skintight white jumpsuit deliciously. Roma is a hard part to play, but Priyanka has a no-nonsense air about her throughout the film. This is an actress willing to push herself, and has definite potential for screen magic. Not to mention a great smile.'

People will continue to debate whether Amitabh Bachchan's *Don* was better than that of Shah Rukh Khan's. But Priyanka made it clear in the movie that she was the new Roma and the audience had to forget comparing her with Zeenat.

*Don* was declared a hit by the film industry, and so five years later, Farhan planned a sequel. This time, freed from the constraints of the original 1978 film, Farhan focused on characters created by the duo Salim-Javed. But he took them beyond the tight structure of the Chandra Barot film. *Don 2* (just like the *Don* of 2006) essentially rests on the charm and screen presence of Shah Rukh Khan. But Priyanka's Roma is given a lot of material to work with.

This time, Priyanka has more action scenes and, again, we see her in her tank tops, or simply pants and shirt (she is an Interpol officer), looking attractive and menacing. And Shah Rukh's Don has an endearing line for her, '*Roma, Roma meri junglee billi, kab tak mera peecha kartee rahogee* (Roma, Roma, my wild cat, how long will you chase me)?' *The Telegraph's* Priyanka Roy had this to say about Priyanka's Roma, 'Priyanka Chopra kicks ass with some well-shot action sequences and shares crackling chemistry with Shah Rukh.' But she felt Priyanka failed 'to infuse Roma with the spunk of the first film.'[114]

*Don 2* has all the good intentions of being a smart thriller although it lacks edge-of-the-seat moments. But with its car chases and slick action scenes—many shot on the streets of Berlin—the film was a hit. There is now talk about Farhan Akhtar planning a *Don 3*. But it seems Priyanka Chopra will not be a part of that team.

One little fact worth noting about *Don 2* is that Lara Dutta plays the supporting role of Ayesha in the film. Priyanka and Lara had started their careers at the same time with the Miss India contest in 2000. Eleven years later, Priyanka had come far ahead through sheer hard work, and sure, some luck as well.

The next year, Priyanka Chopra acted in Anurag Basu's *Barfi!* (2012), definitely her best performance to date—and it was an extremely challenging role. In *Barfi!*, Priyanka plays Jhilmil Chatterjee, an autistic girl in love with her childhood friend Barfi (Ranbir Kapoor in his most charming and finest performance as a deaf-mute character).

But when Anurag first met Priyanka—based on the recommendation of his wife and co-scriptwriter Tani Basu—he was rather unsure if she was the right actress to play Jhilmil. 'She was looking so glamorous when I went there to narrate the story,' Anurag says. 'So in my head I couldn't imagine her playing Jhilmil.' Then, at one point, Anurag stopped and told her he wasn't sure if she was the right choice. 'She was baffled. She had never come across a director who would say to her, "Sorry I can't cast you." And her response was, "I am also not very sure about it."' It was then that Anurag suggested a couple of days of workshop with her to determine if she was indeed the right actress for Jhilmil.

It was an unconventional workshop. 'First day, it was about breaking the ice,' Anurag recalls. 'She was calling me Sir and giving me a lot of respect. I really wanted her to become my friend and not to have that director-actor relationship. So I asked her to hold my collar and abuse me in Hindi, to say all the bad curse words. She did that and shouted on top of her voice. It was only after we broke the ice that she could trust me.'

Priyanka spent time observing autistic children, their body language, and while she prepared a lot for the role, she was always concerned and nervous. Perhaps it was a good thing. Being vulnerable can bring out the best in an actor.

Jhilmil, as imagined by Anurag Basu, was supposed to have curly hair. And so Priyanka wore a curly-haired wig to play the character. On the first day of the shoot, Anurag found Priyanka crying in her make-up van. 'Somebody had told her that she looked like Sachin Tendulkar (with the wig),' Anurag says. 'Because she was taking a long time I went in to look and she was crying. She said, "I am so scared, I am not sure, Sir, how will I do it?"' And he adds, 'That is what makes her so special. She was not overconfident. Instead she was scared, she is always unsure whether she would be able to do it or not.'

For a female lead, Priyanka is first introduced nearly 27 minutes into the film. Then we see her lips as she blows air to fly a paper plane. And only two minutes later, after a few quick glimpses of her profile, we see her face as she bends down to look for her fish in a glass jar under the bed. Following this, there is a beautiful shot of Priyanka with her curly hair, looking from the back window of the car, her face partially hidden with light and the reflection of leaves as she stares at Ranbir. Priyanka gives a lovely, quiet, tender and a very restrained performance—a rare act for a Bollywood actor.

*Barfi!* was India's official entry for the foreign language Oscar, although it failed to win a nomination. Back home in India, many film observers accused the director of plagiarizing scenes from films ranging from works of Charlie Chaplin and Buster Keaton, to *Singin' in the Rain* (1952) and *The Notebook* (2004). But the film had a lot of charm, a lovely whimsical quality and it also had heartbreaking romantic tones. Most critics praised Priyanka for her performance. Anupama Chopra, writing for *Hindustan Times,* said, 'The surprise is Priyanka... She abandons the props of glamour and costumes and puts in a sincere effort to make you forget that you're watching Priyanka Chopra.'[115]

And Priyanka's co-star Ranbir Kapoor had this to say about her becoming the Jhilmil character, 'Priyanka is an autistic girl but she is like a puppy, who you would fall in love with. A beautiful puppy... A cute puppy.'[116]

But 2012 was a strong year for Hindi films. Sujoy Ghosh's *Kahaani* with its many twists turned out to be a surprise hit and Vidya Balan was much praised for her performance of a pregnant woman searching for her husband's killer. And so, Bollywood observers were not surprised when Balan ended up winning most of the awards in the best actress category, including the prestigious National Film Award.

Priyanka was clearly disappointed. On 5 January 2014, she appeared on the *Koffee With Karan* show. This is when Karan raised the issue about her *Barfi!* performance. 'Your performance last year (the show was recorded in 2013) truly won you all the laurels and all the praise that came globally for *Barfi!*—truly a stunning portrayal,' he said. And then he asked the delicate question. 'What happens, does it pinch you when sometimes you don't get the award you deserve? I remember...at the *Filmfare* award and I was on stage. I announced the nominations and I knew there was a prayer in your heart to win it. But you didn't. I looked back at you and I saw there was a sinking feeling in your demeanour. What does it really feel like?'[117]

Priyanka was honest and open about her feelings. 'This film for me was very special. And I knew I wasn't getting it (the *Filmfare* award) like before. But I sat through. My dad told me actually. He was ill, he was in the hospital at that time, and I told him I am going for *Filmfare*. He said, "Good luck, your performance was amazing."'

When Priyanka got to the show, she heard that she was not going to be the winner. 'I remember calling him (her father) and saying, "I am not winning it, so why should I stay?" And he said, "Because you are a good sportsman. Stay and clap for someone else, it's fine." So I decided I would do that. And yes it hurt me—that year specifically.'

'Did you think you were better than Vidya?' Karan asked her. 'I think my performance was a lot more nuanced and different,' Priyanka responded. 'For me it was completely differently done. But the film *Kahaani*, Vidya supported it completely on her shoulders. And it was a film entirely about her. So I understand. It is always a jury-to-jury decision. But I feel *Barfi!* for me was very, very special. I worked damn hard. It was really difficult.'

And Anurag adds, 'I was very disappointed. I won a few best director and best film awards but she didn't win and most of the time I felt Priyanka was a sure-shot winner. Vidya is a very good friend since my college time, but I think it was much more difficult for Priyanka to get into the Jhilmil character than for Vidya to play the *Kahaani* role.'

✓

The disappointment of not winning any major awards for *Barfi!* did not stop Priyanka Chopra from pushing ahead. From *Barfi!* to the next four years (2013–16), as she was beginning to look towards America, she also worked on a handful of films that became solid jewels in her Bollywood crown. These include *Goliyon Ki Rasleela Ram-Leela* (guest appearance) (2013), *Dil Dhadkne Do*, *Bajirao Mastani* (2015) and *Jai Gangaajal* (2016).

First in the mix was a guest appearance for an item dance number in Sanjay Leela Bhansali's *Goliyon Ki Rasleela Ram-Leela*. Starring Deepika Padukone and Ranveer Singh, this film about bloody clan wars in Gujarat was an adaptation of *Romeo and Juliet*. As with all of Bhansali's films, *Ram-Leela* was packed with excesses, but there was also spectacular beauty in it. And Priyanka's 'Ram Chahe Leela' dance, choreographed by Vishnu Deva where she entertains Ranveer's Ram, is one of the most sensual and sexy songs that has been shot for a recent Bollywood film.

Set in a palatial hall, decorated with thousands of candles (perhaps a nod to the Sheesh Mahal from *Mughal-e-Azam*), the song features several male guests sitting at the back—all with red turbans—and Ranveer Singh sitting on a couch, a marigold garland around his neck, drinking whisky straight from the bottle (the only clichéd part of the scene). Then we have Priyanka, her seductive smile, lifting her eyebrows, dressed in white—a choli and a dhoti—and her set of background dancers in similar outfits, but in blue. Bhoomi Trivedi, who was an *Indian Idol* contestant, sang the song, with lyrics by Siddharth-Garima and music composed by Bhansali himself.

As item numbers go, this one is a sure winner. A *DNA* report said that after a series of vulgar and tasteless item numbers that Priyanka had performed in the recent years in her not-so-great films—'Babli Badmash' *(Shootout at Wadla*, 2013), and 'Pinky' and 'Mumbai Ke Hero' (both from *Zanjeer*, 2013), she 'has redeemed herself with her latest number in Sanjay Leela Bhansali's *Ram-Leela*.'[118]

'I saw you in the song in *Ram-Leela*,' Karan Johar said to Priyanka on the 5 January 2014 episode of *Koffee With Karan*. 'It was like a moving sex machine song, I thought. I want to know where all this sex appeal comes from?'[119] Priyanka first tried to act innocent, responding to Karan's question. 'It's just the way it is,' she said. 'I've never known anything otherwise.' But then Karan seemed taken aback and asked, 'Other than being sexy?' So Priyanka did what all actors do—she gave credit to her director. 'I don't know, it's not like I try and do it. The *Ram-Leela* song was entirely Sanjay (Bhansali) Sir's conception. That was his idea.'

The other film in Priyanka's filmography worth noting is a Kolkata-based criminal drama *Gunday* (2014), with Ranveer Singh and Arjun Kapoor in the lead, playing two refugees from Bangladesh who become gangsters. As it often happened in her career, Priyanka again got the third billing. Critics trashed *Gunday* and the film could easily be forgotten, except for a couple of things. The film has high energy and a captivating song between Ranveer and Arjun—'Tune Maari Entriyaan'—with such a large cast of characters and background dancers that it seems like half of Kolkata is performing in the song. And second, Priyanka's look in the film—hair braided on one side of her shoulder and draped in a series of stunning Bengali saris, selected by the film's costume designer Subarna Ray Chaudhuri, who had previously worked on films like *Parineeta* (2005), *Lootera* (2013) and *Bajrangi Bhaijaan* (2015).

Although Chaudhuri now lives in Mumbai, she grew up in Kolkata. In dressing up Priyanka for *Gunday*, she drew on her memory of seeing women at the Durga Puja pandals in Kolkata. 'I remember seeing beautiful girls in their 20s and even married women who would wear nice sexy sleeveless blouses, matching them with Bengali saris,' says Subarna. So she decided to do away with the traditional look of Bengali women wearing half-sleeve blouses and saris with red borders.

Her experiment worked. In the film, Priyanka wears handloom

embroidered blouses including *kantha*. They are matched with handloom saris—including Dhaka muslin saris Subarna got from a supplier in Bangladesh. The Dhaka saris, she explains, are starched and look big on women.

'I would get these saris, take out the starch, then have them treated with lots of fabric softener,' she says. 'And then the saris become as soft and fluid as *malmal*. Priyanka has a beautiful body, so she does not have to have a puffy look. You should be able to see her contours.' Some of the blouses Subarna picked were backless. 'If you remember Moon Moon Sen, how she wore her blouses. She looks so sexy,' Subarna says. 'Many women in the 80s would wear those sexy blouses.'

Priyanka wore more than ten of the twenty saris Subarna showed her. She also asked her to pick up another thirty that she bought for herself. And in addition to that, Subarna bought Assamese bamboo hair clips that looked lovely on Priyanka's hair. Sometimes she only wore gold hair clips and flowers in her hair.

Priyanka's Nandini, who is later revealed to us as a police agent, looks like a gorgeous modern Bengali woman of the 1980s, including the scene where she is a cabaret dancer. But most critics were so busy tearing apart the film they did not see any sense in praising Priyanka's look. Calling the film 'utter garbage', critic Raja Sen had this to say about Priyanka in his review: 'Somewhere in this mess is Priyanka Chopra, looking like a bobblehead and making about as much sense. Her commitment to the part is in the way she sashays, and while she delivers most dialogues better than the boys, she's given a maddeningly inconsistent character.'[120]

But at least one critic, David Chute—an American who is a keen observer of Bollywood films—saw a lot more in Priyanka's take on Nandini. Writing in *Variety*, Chute said, 'Chopra brings so much conviction to the role of the femme fatale that she sweeps away all our recent memories of upstarts Katrina Kaif and Deepika Padukone, who have the natural endowments but miss the all-important bold attitude—the what-are-you-going-to-do-about-it swagger that stirs men to rise to the challenge.'[121]

ᔕ

While Priyanka Chopra was working on *Gunday*, she was also in negotiations to act in *Mary Kom* (2014)—Omung Kumar's biopic on the life of the Manipuri boxer Mangte Chungneijang Mary Kom, who has won a medal in each one of the six world championships. This was going to be Omung's first film who had until then been an art and production designer for films such as *Black* (2005) and *Saawariya* (2007)—both directed by Sanjay Leela Bhansali, who would step in to produce *Mary Kom*.

'We approached only Priyanka because I wanted her, and because she fits the bill completely,' Omung says. 'She's one dedicated actress who would give everything for the role. And this film and this role were so complicated. It wasn't just acting. She had to be the character. She had to become a boxer, which no other actress could have done.' It helped that Omung had worked on a couple of films with Priyanka. He was the art director for *Waqt: The Race Against Time* and *Love Story 2050*.

And Omung wanted a big star, since he was not an established name himself. He was sure he could not sell the film based solely on Mary Kom's name. *'Arre kisko pata thee yeh story? Poore India ko maloom nahin Mary Kom kaun thee* (Who knew this story? In India hardly anyone knew who Mary Kom was). People don't know anything beyond cricket.'

But a major controversy broke out when it was announced that Priyanka Chopra, a Punjabi woman, would play a Manipuri character. And it did not help that the film-maker and his production team hired a Hollywood make-up artist to give Priyanka heavier eyelids so she could develop more Asian features.

'That idea was dropped,' Omung says. 'The prosthetics were not working because it was a boxing film. The prosthetics would come off every time after the fight scene. We did a trial run but then avoided that completely.'

But Omung and his production team's plan—even though it had been abandoned—sounded like an awful idea. This is what I wrote in a 28 April 2013 column in *Mumbai Mirror* about the plan: 'I cannot emphasize how bad all of this sounds and I am surprised that people from Manipur and other neighbouring states have not taken offence to this plan. To me the idea smacks of strong racist tones, almost at par with the time when Hollywood would apply black paint on the faces of white actors—going back to Al Jolson in *The Jazz Singer* (1927) and Peter Sellers in *The Party* (1968).'[122]

The point of contention was not the debate around Omung deciding to add prosthetics to Priyanka's eyes, even though it was decided against. It was more about the fact that this option was even considered. And the unfortunate thing is that many in the film industry easily accept the argument that only a big star can draw audiences to a film like this. Surely, a well-made film with a strong script could have worked with a lesser-known actress. There were many qualified actresses from the Northeast who could have played the role that went to Priyanka.

Omung withstood the controversy. And he waited for the moment for the controversy to die. 'To prove them (the naysayers) wrong we said when the first poster will come out, you will all be surprised and believe her character,' Omung says. 'I did nothing except to put some freckles on her face, little make-up under her eyes. And she looked the part with the fringe on her forehead. People started believing that she was Mary Kom herself.' He hired two Manipuri dialect coaches as well. Even though the film was in Hindi, the tonality was such that it had to feel like

Manipuri, and yet they had to make sure that the large audiences in the Hindi-speaking belt of India could understand it. On top of that, Omung surrounded himself with actual boxers—even cast them in the film.

The film's shoot was broken into two halves. After weeks of training for Priyanka, Omung shot the climax scenes and every boxing match in 20 days. Post that, Priyanka went back to the *Gunday* shoot in Kolkata and also did her item number for *Ram-Leela*.

But then, just when Priyanka was about to come back for the *Mary Kom* shoot, her father Dr Ashok Chopra passed away. 'That was a major setback,' Omung says. 'It happened before the main shooting and she had to stop exercising. But in one week, she came back and she said, "Life has to go on and my father wanted me to do this."'

Omung recalls a moment of fun in the shooting. After he first narrated the script to Priyanka, she went and ate a huge burger. 'I recorded it,' Omung says with a laugh. 'I can't show it to anyone, but I knew after that narration she would not have another burger. Because once she signed up for the film she was going to starve, go on a diet and build up muscle.'

*Mary Kom* won a National Film Award in the Best Popular Film Providing Wholesome Entertainment category. But the film did not excite the critics. In her Firstpost review, critic Deepanja Pal said, 'Omung Kumar's *Mary Kom* is a bland film that quickly becomes boring because there's no tension in the story.'[123] Livemint's Sanjukta Sharma praised Priyanka even when she found the film to be flawed. 'Priyanka Chopra throws herself into the part, supplying energy and heart,' Sharma wrote. 'Her physical preparedness for the role is remarkable. Beyond the impossible callisthenics in the local gym or in the mountains of Manali (Omung abandoned the idea of shooting the film in Manipur because of security concerns and instead shot it in Manali), she manages to tap into the woman and the fighter despite the extremely superficial writing and sloppy editing.'[124]

The film was a moderate success at the box office, or a 'semi-hit'—to use a Bollywood term. Perhaps Mary Kom's story needed a smaller film with less of Bollywood trappings and more of authentic touches—an actress from the Northeast for sure, as well as a tighter script.

∿

Bollywood actors tend to jump from one project to another with ease. But in Priyanka's case there was a sense of urgency, as by 2012, she was already travelling back and forth between India and the US. So it was no surprise that while she was working on *Mary Kom*, she had already found her next Bollywood project— Zoya Akhtar's third film *Dil Dhadakne Do* (DDD), a movie about a rich dysfunctional family on a cruise with their closest friends.

Priyanka was not Zoya's first choice to play Ayesha Mehra, the bright, successful married daughter of Kamal and Neelam Mehra (Anil Kapoor and Shefali Shah), who also has a secret that she is afraid to share. She finds no connection with her arrogant, sexist husband (Rahul Bose), and would much rather not be in the marriage. In what would have been a casting coup, Zoya first considered real-life cousins, Ranbir Kapoor and Kareena Kapoor, to play the Mehra siblings. But Ranbir was tied up with another project and could not give dates for a year.

So, Zoya looked at her second options—she selected Ranveer Singh to play Kabir Mehra and Priyanka Chopra to play his sister Ayesha. 'I wanted an actress who would look like a part of the same family,' Zoya says. 'Priyanka is an amazing actor. I always wanted to work with her. She hadn't done a part like this.' Zoya adds, 'Priyanka is supremely impressive, she's incredibly bright and hard-working. She's empathetic as a person, she genuinely has compassion for characters. So even if you give her a flawed character, she will find humanity in it. That's who she is.' Priyanka is known to have strong work ethics. It was not enough that she was doing an extremely challenging job playing the role of a boxer in *Mary Kom*. She would wrap up the *Mary Kom* shoot after a gruelling 12-hour schedule and then, she would head to Zoya's apartment at 10.30 at night, with the script and her notebook. 'We would go through scenes and make notes. She doesn't take anything for granted,' Zoya says.

Zoya also describes Priyanka as a generous actress and a team player who worked very well with an ensemble cast. And she was not affected at all by the decision that Anil Kapoor and Shefali Shah got higher billing in the film's credits.

Zoya recalls the day when the film's poster was going to be shot—with the six main actors sunbathing on the deck chairs of the cruise ship. 'She called me and asked, "Are you coming?" saying that she was a little worried that they would want Ranveer and her in the middle. "And that's not your film," she said to me. I thought that was very cool of her. She is very secure. And she has a macro vision. She wasn't just thinking about her character.' Eventually, the poster was shot with Anushka Sharma, Ranveer, Shefali, Anil, Priyanka and Farhan Akhtar lying on the chairs. Shefali and Anil were in the centre.

There were many moments in the making of the film that have stayed with Zoya, such as the day when Priyanka was running a 103-degree temperature and she showed up for the one-take song '*Gallan Goodiyaan*'. Or the fact that Priyanka did not know how to play tennis or racquetball. And Zoya is not a sportsperson either. So she asked Rahul Bose to choreograph three or four moves for Priyanka. 'Every day in the middle of the day she would go for training with him.'

Perhaps one of the most difficult scenes to shoot for Priyanka and Rahul was when they are in bed and his character wants to have sex with her, but she is not interested. 'Sex scenes are always awkward to shoot when you have the entire crew hovering around,' Rahul says.

'I was extremely wary about that scene,' he adds. 'There's scrutiny and there's truth that you have to discover in that scene. You have to gradually ask the other person how comfortable it is going to be. You have to pretend that this person has been your girlfriend or your wife for many years. So if you are kissing, surely you have kissed her many times before that. You should know where the other person's mouth and nose is. But another actor can say, "No, no I can't kiss you before the scene." So it's that kind of non-acting, weariness that you exercise. But she was absolutely prepared. We are going to do it and we will. It wasn't like, "Don't touch me here," none of that stuff.'

DDD gave Priyanka many moments to shine as an actress— the quiet looks she gives when taunted by her mother-in-law (Zarina Wahab) or her husband. It is a beautifully nuanced performance for a mainstream Hindi film and her role is also very well-written. It is perhaps for the first time in a recent Bollywood film that a big star plays an unhappy married woman. And then she finally dares to ask for a divorce. 'I tried very hard Manav,' she says to her husband. 'But I can't pretend anymore. I don't love you.' It is also a first when in the midst of an argument and tension, she grabs her former boyfriend Sunny (Farhan Akhtar) and kisses him.

In an interview with ABP News's Yasser Usman, just before the release of the film, Priyanka spoke about being nervous when acting opposite her director from *Don* and *Don 2*. '*Jab Zoya ne mujhe pehlee baar bataya ke yeh Sunny ka kirdar play kar rahe hain, main to thodee see* awkward *ho gayee.* Director *jo hote hain na, woh* boss *hote hain* film *ke* set *par...* As a director *jab maine Farhan se baat karnee hotee thee, main pehle Shah Rukh ko boltee thee.* Directors *thode se* intimidating *hote hain* (When Zoya told me he is going to play Sunny's role, I became slightly awkward. Directors are bosses on the film set. As a director, if I had to talk to Farhan, I would first go talk to Shah Rukh. Directors can be slightly intimidating).

A few months after the release of *Dil Dhadakne Do*, Farhan was quoted in the press saying that he thought highly of Priyanka. In response to a reporter who was seeking a reaction from Farhan on the news that Priyanka was going to star in the Hollywood film *Baywatch* (2017), Farhan said, 'Wonderful, congratulations to her. I have had the highest regard for her talent. More and more power to her...' [125]

Overall, there seemed to be a lot of goodwill amongst the cast and crew of DDD. Like the characters from the film, for a few weeks they were stuck on a cruise ship in the middle of the Mediterranean Sea. 'One day, we were hanging out on the deck in the evening, and somebody said, "Man, I don't have any network and I can't get in touch,"' Zoya recalls. 'And Priyanka said, "Guys please look at this. We are sailing, the sun is setting over Africa. We are really lucky." And that's the thing about her. She's really happy to be doing what she does. She doesn't take anything for granted.'

And Rahul Bose remembers Priyanka fondly for her bag of savoury snacks that she had brought on the ship. 'We would always dip into her snack basket in the evening.'

◡

Priyanka acted with Ranveer in three back-to-back films—*Gunday, Dil Dhadakne Do* and then Sanjay Leela Bhansali's *Bajirao Mastani*—where they played husband and wife. It was a rare chance for the two actors to portray three different kinds of relationships—lovers in *Gunday*, brother-sister in *Dil Dhadakne Do* and then a married couple in *Bajirao Mastani*. Plus, Priyanka also performed the item number in *Ram-Leela*.

'I think that we are extremely fortunate that we have had the opportunity,' Priyanka told *The National* at the time of promoting DDD. 'I think this is a testament to the film-makers who worked with us, who have put their faith in us and trusted us to be able to pull off all the different characters. But if you ask me, honestly, I think Ranveer is really more like a brother to me. We even look alike... So we can very convincingly be brother and sister.'

Still, it can be a challenge for two actors to change their emotions and feelings towards each other, film after film. 'It throws you off. It's a little bit out of whack,' Ranveer said in the same *The National* interview.[126] 'I think this one (DDD) will be the most convincing, because, as we always say...' Priyanka cut him and added, '*Humari feelings aisi hi hain ek doosre ki taraf* (This is what our feelings for each other are like).'

✧

When Sanjay Leela Bhansali first offered Priyanka Chopra the 'supporting' role of Kashibai in *Bajirao Mastani*, she was somewhat reluctant to say yes. Perhaps she wanted to work with different directors, and she had only recently made a guest appearance in Bhansali's *Ram-Leela*. She had even discouraged her co-stars Ranveer Singh and Deepika Padukone to make a second film with the same director and that too, so soon after the first one.

'She (Priyanka) did not want to do the film... She had said she wants to go,' Ranveer said at the trailer launch event for *Bajirao Mastani*. 'She said you all are mad... You are doing a second film (with Bhansali). But she is a fast learner...and got things quickly.' [127]

But later, Priyanka clarified why she accepted the role, and perhaps once the film was ready to be released, her perspective changed. 'People talk about Bajirao-Mastani's love story,' she said, adding, 'For me the biggest reason for playing Kashi was to play a character history has never spoken about. I've never played such a soft and vulnerable character.' And she revealed how Kashibai's character was quite the opposite of who she is. 'It's very hard for me to play a girl who can't protect herself because I'm a modern girl of today, I can beat up people, but that's the challenge for me to convince you to watch and your heart hurts for her. She is a wonderful sweet character.'[128]

Despite her getting third billing, it is fascinating to watch Priyanka play the Maharashtrian wife—her third take as a Marathi character after *Kaminey* and *Agneepath* (2012)—a proud woman, the spouse of Bajirao Peshwa. But in the movie, she has to set aside her pride as her husband falls in love with another woman—and that too, a Muslim. Often, just using her eyes, her facial expressions, and little gestures, Priyanka is able to bring so much love and empathy for Kashibai.

It is a rare moment in Bollywood cinema where despite the grandeur, excesses, huge battle scenes, spectacular sets and lavishly shot songs, all of which Bhansali is known for, his script gives the breathing space for his three main actors to act. And as a director, he is able to bring out the best in Priyanka Chopra. It is when you watch her perform in films like *Barfi!* and *Bajirao Mastani* you realize that this woman has truly become an artist, one of the best actresses of Hindi cinema.

On Priyanka playing a supporting role, director Rohan Sippy says it is a sign of her confidence in her abilities. In 2005, Rohan had directed Priyanka in *Bluffmaster!* 'When you come out of the movie (*Bajirao Mastani*) you connect to her very strongly. That's her security as an actress. This is how she thinks—"Whichever way you are going, if I do my job well I can stand out." That's a great attribute to have.'

Priyanka shot *Bajirao Mastani* when she was also working on the first season of her ABC television show *Quantico* in Canada and the US, at times flying over the weekends. While it is certain she only travels by first class, all this intercontinental travelling must have taken its toll. It became the job of Uday Shirali, who was hired on Priyanka's recommendation, to give her the look of Kashibai and to remove the stress of all the work and travels from her face.

In an interview, Uday talked of giving Priyanka the no-make-up look. 'She was undergoing a lot of physical and mental strain,' he said.[129] 'And it showed on her face. I had to take special care to make sure that her eyes didn't look red and puffy or there were no bags under her eyes. I could not use any make-up because it would look odd for a queen in a period drama. The eyes were naked except the long eyelashes and a bit of eye shadow here and there. Also, though kajal was available during the sixteenth century, only Mughals wore it. And there was no sindoor in her parting since Maharashtrian women did not wear it.'

As is expected from a Sanjay Leela Bhansali film, a lot of effort went into creating the look of each actor. With Priyanka, the details included a traditional Maharashtrian hair bun called *khopa* and a crescent moon bindi with a small dot. She wore *Peshwai Paithani* saris and a pearl *nath* in her nose.

Critics across the board praised Priyanka's performance. Rachel Saltz of *The New York Times* was not drawn to the film's central plot—the romance of Bajirao and Mastani. But she added, 'You may find yourself rooting for Ms. Chopra's pushed-aside Kashibai. She has beauty to spare, a good song and something the rest of the movie lacks—warmth and a touch of humour.'[130] And the critic for *The Guardian* wrote, 'Chopra never allows Kashi to become an afterthought: Those eyes register a wife's hurt every bit as vividly as they have happiness elsewhere.' [131]

Indian critics too were equally impressed with Priyanka's performance. Anupama Chopra wrote in the *Hindustan Times*: 'Priyanka Chopra might have the fewest scenes of the three, but she creates maximum impact.'[132] And the Rediff.com's critic wrote, 'Priyanka Chopra, who, while not in the title, owns *Bajirao Mastani*. Her role is that of the moral right, but Bhansali goes out of his way to imbue her character with selflessness and dignity. Chopra's terrific in the part, her intelligently expressive eyes speaking volumes and her no-nonsense Marathi rhythm bang-on.'[133]

*Bajirao Mastani* was declared a hit. Priyanka Chopra was ready to depart from Bollywood (although she has always maintained that she has not quit the Indian film industry) with a bang. But she still had one last film to work on—Prakash Jha's *Jai Gangaajal*, a sequel of sorts to his hit 2003 film *Gangaajal*.

⁓

Manav Kaul remembers the first day Priyanka Chopra turned up on the set of *Jai Gangaajal* in Bhopal. It was a scene in a crowed marketplace. Priyanka, playing the town's new superintendent of police, Abha Mathur, was wearing a black *pathani* salwar kameez along with Ray-Ban sunglasses—and she looked positively hot.

'I had just been introduced to her briefly,' Manav recalls. 'She was standing and someone said, "Your scene is ready". My jaw dropped when I saw her. She asked, "Are you ready?" And I told her, "I will take some time. You are looking stunning. I have to stop looking at you." I was suddenly the small town *ka ladka* (boy) and this seemed like my *pehli* (first) break.'

I then asked him how Priyanka reacted when he called her

stunning. 'She was very sweet and she knows she is stunning. But then after a point when you start shooting, you actually forget that you are shooting with Priyanka Chopra. She was so normal, like a regular *Bareilly ki ladki* (girl from Bareilly).'

Manav plays Babloo Pandey, a villain in the film. But her real confrontation in the film is with the deputy superintendent B.N. Singh (played by director Prakash Jha in his first major on-screen role), a corrupt man entrenched with the local mafia who has a change of heart when Priyanka's Abha Mathur becomes his boss.

'I told Priyanka that I was the one playing B.N. Singh and not even once she expressed surprise,' Prakash says. 'She is so sure about her own abilities, so confident. I noticed that on the set, even with the minor character actors, she would make sure they get the scene and perform the best because she knew if the other guys did well, then her work would shine.'

Prakash Jha has directed a number of films, so that part was second nature to him. But playing a major role was a new experience. 'Sometimes a funny thing would happen,' he says. At the end of a shot with Priyanka and me, I would turn to her and ask if I had done okay. And she would laugh and say, "Hello, you are the one who is supposed to tell me that I did okay. I am not looking at your performance."'

Priyanka had a very short time period to work on *Jai Gangaajal*—in between *Bajirao Mastani* and *Quantico*. 'She got the *Quantico* training of acting like a cop with us,' Prakash says, laughing. She arrived in Bhopal one day before the shoot and then spent nearly 12 hours with Prakash discussing her character.

For one scene, Priyanka's Mathur had to get into a fight with Manav's Pandey. The fight scene was fully choreographed. There were two moments when Priyanka was supposed to hit

Manav. 'She was supposed to punch me, and I said you can hit me,' Manav says. 'But when she hit I suddenly realized that she had just done *Mary Kom*. It was a real hard hit.'

The second hit was supposed to be a kick on Manav's chest, but by mistake, Priyanka's foot kicked him on his throat and she was wearing shoes. Manav says, 'I had just done a fighting scene with Farhan (Akhtar) in *Wazir* (2016). And I am a brown belt in karate so I understand fight.' But it did hurt him. In fact, he lost his voice for a couple of days.

Immediately after she realized she had made a mistake, Priyanka tapped Manav and asked, 'I hope I didn't hurt you,'—he recalls. 'I said, "I am okay." But she started crying. She thought she had hit me really hard. It wasn't bad and I wasn't complaining at all. We had to stop the shoot for half hour. She kept saying, "It's not done, I can't do this."'

'She is so sensitive—I didn't know that about her,' Prakash adds, 'She wouldn't stop crying. So I had to scream at her, asking her to stop.'

Despite her hard work (running from project-to-project and flying across continents to meet her obligations in India and the US), critics were not impressed with Priyanka's performance in *Jai Gangaajal*. Shubhra Gupta of *The Indian Express* felt Priyanka did not fit into the role of a policewoman in the Hindi-speaking belt milieu. 'As the take-charge-policewoman-in-a-tough-posting, Priyanka Chopra comes off as dressed-for-the-part and stilted,' Gupta wrote.[134] 'You can see she's trying hard, especially in some of the "action" sequences in which she has to kick and punch and thrash, but she's far too smooth for this part.'

And Namrata Joshi of *The Hindu* was equally disappointed, despite Priyanka's action scenes. 'As a woman cop all that she (Priyanka) is required to do is run, chase, fight, do hand-to-hand combat, thrash goons with sticks, fire shots, don *pathani* suits and police uniform, and wear cakey make-up,'[135] Joshi wrote. 'In other words, try to be like a man and have junior cops thank her for making a man out of them.' Then she concluded, 'Ironically, Priyanka looks off-colour, disinterested and uninvolved with the goings-on through most of the film.'

# 6

# GIVING IT BACK:
# PRODUCING FILMS

Courtesy: Excel Entertainment

*I*n mid-2014, there were reports that Priyanka Chopra was toying with the idea of producing films. She had conversations with her friend and director, Madhur Bhandarkar—the only film-maker who got a National Film Award-worthy performance out of Priyanka (for *Fashion*)—to act in a film called *Madamji*.

Reports indicated that Priyanka would produce and perhaps even distribute the film under her production house, Purple Pebble Pictures. Other co-producers listed in the reports were Bhandarkar Entertainment and Ram Mirchandani's Rampage Motion Pictures.[136]

'I'm in love with everything to do with movies...the process, the creativity, the magic,' Priyanka told *The Times of India*.[137] 'This is an extension of that. I'm looking forward to the learning, the madness and the creative satisfaction of bringing a film alive.'

She later added, 'As a director, he (Madhur Bhandarkar) has a clear vision of what he wants and his choice of stories is intriguing and exciting. When he narrated this story to me, I knew it would be a great first project for me in production.'

'It was a very contemporary subject on the politics of that time—of an item girl turning into a politician,' Madhur tells me. But the project never took off, since Priyanka was busy with back-to-back films, *Mary Kom* and DDD. 'I didn't approach any other actress,' Madhur adds. 'Then *Quantico* started and I lost interest. We had basically developed the script with Priyanka Chopra in our mind.'

I ask Madhur about the similarity between the *Madamji* script and a Mallika Sherawat film *Dirty Politics* (2015), which dealt with a bar dancer called Anokhi Devi and her rise in politics. *Dirty Politics* did get made, but it was a critical and box office failure. Could that be the reason *Madamji* was shelved?

'No, nothing like that,' he says. 'That was also a woman-centric film based on the story of Bhanwari Devi from Rajasthan. We had nothing in common with that project.'

Later, Priyanka also acknowledged that *Madamji* was stalled because of her own scheduling issues. 'I have been spread so thin, it has been a little slower on the production front,' she told *DNA*.[138]

Eventually, the first film that Purple Pebble Pictures produced was in the Bhojpuri language—director Santosh Mishra's *Bam Bam Bol Raha Hai Kashi*. The film, starring Bhojpuri actors Amrapali Dubey and Dinesh Lal Yadav 'Nirahua', opened in theatres in June 2016.

In a September 2017 interview at the Toronto International Film Festival (TIFF), Priyanka's mother and producing partner, Dr Madhu Chopra, spoke to me about Purple Pebble's strategy. I asked her the reason behind picking a Bhojpuri-language film as the first film to produce.

'We wanted to start small,' Dr Chopra said, while acknowledging that the first year is always 'scary'. Then she added, 'There was less risk. You know, like we say in Hindi—*Ungli geeli karna*. We just wanted to wet our finger to test the waters.'

The other important factor was that Dr Chopra is from Jharkhand (carved out of Bihar in November 2000). 'That's my background,' she said about Bhojpuri language. 'That's my father's place. And it (Bhojpuri cinema) was an established industry.' Then she added, 'But Priyanka later said the mandate of our production house has to be newcomers, new stories and from other regions as well.'

ℓ

There is a do-gooder part of Priyanka's personality. Many other Bollywood actors are producing films with the intent of making good films and/or to make money. But Priyanka is doing it differently. In early January 2017, before the release of *Sarvann* (2017)—her Punjabi home production—Priyanka spoke to Dipps Bhamrah's popular BBC Asian Network radio show. And she said that she wanted to give back to the society and to the people who wanted to come in the entertainment industry.

'I do want to be able to use who I am... I came into the movie business to Mumbai with nothing at all, except my parents and my drive. I am extremely self-made. It's been a very hard, arduous journey, which has been quite solitary for me... because my choices have been different and not conventional. But that is the way I wanted my path to be, completely my own, unprecedented. And that is my plan with the production company as well. I want to be able to give support...the might of whoever I may be right now and the platform I have been given, to various regional films, Hindi films, English films. I want to be able to do television. And just be able to put out good stories...and have amazing artists—actors, directors, new talents get opportunities to be in the film industry when being an outsider is not easy.'[139]

Still, after years of doing films like *Mujhse Shaadi Karogi*, *Bluffmaster!* and *Dostana*, what prompted Priyanka to suddenly support regional films is a bit unclear, especially considering her mother said that as a child and teenager she never saw a non-Hindi language Indian film. Even during the years Priyanka worked in Bollywood, she showed no inclination to watch regional films. Two exceptions were when she watched a few Tamil films before she shot her first feature *Thamizhan* and then Marathi language films while she prepared to play a Maharashtrian woman's role in Vishal Bhardwaj's *Kaminey*.

'She might have read (the translated version of) a Marathi story I think,' Dr Chopra told Rediff.com in an interview. 'Or she probably watched a Marathi movie on a flight. She said they made wonderful stories, so let's start with regional and we will try and make as many regional films as possible.'[140]

During the TIFF interview, Dr Chopra talked further about Priyanka's motivation to go regional, saying, 'Priyanka, while she thinks straight, she also thinks a little differently. She said Bollywood has exploited every region in India. We take stories from different regions. In fact, in a couple of Salman Khan's films, the language was completely Bhojpuri. And you have stories out of Rajasthan, out of Maharashtra. But they all turn into big blockbusters in Bollywood. What have we given back? So that was her thinking. We will take their stories, use their talent and cast from their regions.'

In three years or so, Purple Pebble has made a few regional language films, including the Marathi-language, three National Film Award-winner *Ventilator* (2016). Directed by Rajesh Mapuskar, *Ventilator* is definitely the strongest film in the mix. There is the Punjabi film—Karaan Guliani's *Sarvann*—and a Nepali-language film from Sikkim, by first-time director Paakhi Tyrewala, *Pahuna: The Little Visitors* (2017). It landed Priyanka in a messy controversy when she promoted it at TIFF in September 2017.

For a new company, Purple Pebble went through some quick changes in the officers heading the top operations. The company's first Chief Executive Officer, Ishaan Dutta, was replaced by Sandeep Bhargava, who is more of a Bollywood insider and has given a corporate sense to some of the Hindi film industry's newer production houses—Viacom's Studio 18, B4U Relativity Media and Sanjay Dutt Productions. In the summer of 2016, Purple Pebble appointed Petrina D'Rozario, the founder of Women in Film and Television Association, as the company's Chief Operating Officer. D'Rozario stayed with Purple Pebble for exactly a year.

In early 2016, when the company was just about to get on sure footing, it landed in trouble with the Film Studios Setting

& Allied Mazdoor Union, whose General Secretary, Gangeshwar Shrivastav, claimed non-payment to union members who had worked on a project for Priyanka's production house. The union said that the studio had signed a contract to pay ₹36 lakh for a project of which only ₹20 lakh had been paid. Reminders were sent to the production house and one union member was quoted in *Mid-Day* newspaper, saying, 'Since we are daily wage earners, we are anxiously awaiting our payment to be cleared.'[141]

Regardless of the hiccups, Dr Chopra says that the company has now established a routine where scripts are submitted and vetted, and then a shortlist of projects are sent to Priyanka for her final approval.

'Once we made up our mind that we were going to all the regions, we started getting scripts from every region and then we have a team of people who shortlist them,' she explains. Some scripts are written in the regional language, but have to be translated into English, which according to her, becomes a double task for the writers. 'It takes six to eight months to green-light a project.'

Priyanka is only sent the scripts that are translated in English. So in addition to reading scripts that come her way for acting jobs, and of course performing her regular duties—from acting in *Quantico* (while the show was on) to participating in charitable events, walking red carpets for galas and visiting troubled war-torn zones as the UNICEF Goodwill Ambassador—Priyanka also reads scripts that are shortlisted for Purple Pebble projects.

'But our scripts she can only read on Sundays,' Dr Chopra adds as she laughs.

∽

Rajesh Mapuskar had worked as an assistant director for *Lage Raho Munna Bhai* (2006) and *3 Idiots* (2009). He later directed

*Ferrari Ki Sawaari* (2012). All three projects were produced by
Vidhu Vinod Chopra's production house. But for his first Marathi-
language film, *Ventilator*, he approached Priyanka's production
house. 'They (Vinod Chopra Films) only produce Hindi films,
not in any other language,' Rajesh says. 'So I went independent
for *Ventilator*.'

When Rajesh started the search for a producer who would
take on a relatively small Marathi film with a moderate budget
of ₹3.5 crore, he was pleasantly surprised to learn from his
chartered accountant that Priyanka Chopra was looking for
regional projects. 'Having Priyanka Chopra associated with a
Marathi film is a great platform because the project will get
immediate attention,' Rajesh says.

A meeting was arranged where Rajesh narrated the synopsis
of the story to Ishaan Dutta and Dr Chopra. 'They instantly
liked it,' he says. Then, by end of 2015, Rajesh had his first face-
to-face meeting with Priyanka who was in Mumbai on a break
from the *Quantico* shoot.

'I remember my first meeting with Priyanka in her office in
Bombay,' he says. 'I was a little stressed since I had never met
her and she was such a big star.' This was the case even though
Rajesh had worked with Vidhu Vinod Chopra and must have
interacted with the likes of Aamir Khan and Sanjay Dutt on the
sets. 'I was concerned how she would take the film, emotions
of a Maharashtrian family.'

But when he started to narrate the story—Rajesh describes
that moment as 'magical'. 'She made me so comfortable and it was
like just her and me in the room, where she was laughing, crying,'
he adds. 'I was enjoying watching her emotions, the way she
was reacting to the story. That's when I realized this is working.'

On the issue of Priyanka sponsoring smaller films, he says, 'I
think it is very bold, sensible. She has all the power, money and

muscle to produce these films. But I think somewhere this has to do with the fact that she is coming from such a grass-roots level herself. She is not from the film fraternity and she understands the emotions of an artist, a technician, a director, a writer. In her mind she must have thought that by giving a platform to these artists she would help them. There is much more satisfaction in creating smaller films with good content and stories. These stories need to be told and without Priyanka's support it would have been very hard. The economics of Bollywood doesn't allow you to tell the stories that are unconventional.'

Priyanka was in the US while *Ventilator* was being shot. So Rajesh worked closely with Dr Madhu Chopra every day. 'Her mother had put a lot of faith in me,' he says. 'There was no interference on that level. Because they were new, they were learning also. With first-time producers there could be many conflicts and resistance because they are also experiencing things for the first time. Somewhere we connected as partners and we had complete freedom.' But Priyanka was in touch with the team. She would often see the footage that would be sent to her. And she gave suggestions for the trailer and helped during the edit process.

Priyanka even sang a Marathi song for the film. 'We had an emotional song *'Baba'* in the film and we thought if Priyanka sang it, knowing about her bonding with her father and she is a singer, it could work well,' Rajesh says. And then, he adds, 'We didn't want to commercialize her and her father's relationship.'

But Priyanka was in New York working on *Quantico*. So through a few contacts within the Indian community, the *Ventilator* team hired Samarth Nagarkar, a Hindustani classical vocalist based in New Jersey to be Priyanka's voice coach. Samarth knew that Priyanka was a singer but he realized he would have to work on her Marathi pronunciations, especially to get the embellishments in Indian classical music she was not familiar with.

Samarth first got on Skype and discussed the song with Rajesh Mapuskar and the film's two composers, Rohan Gokhale and Rohan Pradhan. And then he spent a few hours in a studio in Manhattan with Priyanka, working on her accent and pronunciations. 'She's a very committed and professional artist,' Samarth says. 'When she takes on something she completely dedicates herself to it.' And he adds, 'She is a master at what she does as an actress, so one of her strengths was to get the emotions right when she was singing.'

He was surprised that Priyanka did not take a single break during the recording. 'The rest of the crew took toilet breaks, but she just stood there behind the microphone, perfecting the song.'

Nearly two and half hours long and with a huge supporting cast, *Ventilator* is a sweet story about a patriarch of a family and large clan who oversees, the Ganesh Utsav celebration. When the patriarch lands in the hospital, the entire extended family shows up in the waiting room of the hospital in Mumbai. Despite all the humour, *Ventilator* is the story of a son reconnecting with his estranged father. Priyanka's song *'Baba'* was tailor-made for the film.

*Ventilator's* large cast included film-maker (and sometimes actor) Ashutosh Gowariker in the lead. Ashutosh had earlier directed Priyanka in *What's Your Raashee?*, but Rajesh says this casting had nothing to with the fact that the director and the actress knew each other. In fact, Ashutosh was on board much before Rajesh approached Purple Pebble Pictures.

'I had been in touch with him,' Rajesh says. 'He was busy with *Mohenjo Daro* (2016), but he was contemplating what to do next. He loved the story. I was also very sure to cast Ashutosh, because he has the stature that is required for the character Raja (a famous director and the nephew of the patriarch) in the film.'

The year 2016 was a strong one for Marathi films with Nagraj Manjule's *Sairat* making over ₹100 crores. *Ventilator* also performed rather well, earning nearly ₹25 crore even though it was released a few days before the Indian government introduced the demonetisation programme.[142] *Ventilator* was the surprise winner of three National Film Awards in 2017. Rajesh won the Golden Lotus Medal for his direction, and the film was also recognized for its editing and audiography.

The success of *Ventilator* gave Priyanka a further impetus to making regional language films. 'She did not venture into producing a Hindi film,' Rajesh says. 'She is still going on with the regional films.'

Late in September 2017, the Film Federation of India announced that director Amit Masurkar's *Newton* (2017) would be India's official entry for the foreign language race at the 90th Academy Awards. There were a total of twenty-six films in the running, including *Mukti Bhawan* (2016), *Dangal* (2016), *A Death in the Gunj* (2016) and *Ventilator*. While all other film-makers welcomed the selection of *Newton* as the final choice to represent India, there was an odd response from Purple Pebble Pictures.

Technically, Priyanka did not make an official statement, but Rajesh spoke to the press about the actress and producer's disappointment. 'I told her not to worry, assuring her that only the best film would make it,' Rajesh was quoted by the newspaper *DNA*.[143] 'We were a bit disappointed when we learnt about the verdict the next day.'

Rajesh said that he was certain that Priyanka would have pushed the film more had it been sent out as India's official entry. 'Priyanka must be even more disappointed because she was always ambitious about the film. Had it been selected, she would have ensured that it was the most-talked-about film in the run to the

Oscars, especially since she is already an established name there.'

⌣

In early 2016, film-maker Karaan Guliani visited the Purple Pebble Pictures office. He wanted to make a Hindi film with Priyanka Chopra in the lead. Although the Purple Pebble team liked Karaan's script, they explained to him that Priyanka was tied up with *Quantico* and perhaps would not be available for a year and a half. It was then that the conversation shifted to regional cinema, and Karaan narrated the story of a Punjabi film that he was toying with. A call was placed to Dr Madhu Chopra who liked the idea. When Priyanka visited India, she heard the narration. And this is how Karaan Guliani's Punjabi film *Sarvann* was born.

Speaking on Dipps Bhamrah's BBC radio show, Priyanka said, 'This is a film about retribution, finding religion, finding yourself.'[144] *Sarvann* is a story about a Punjabi gang leader in Canada who accidentally kills another Indian there and then avoids getting arrested by escaping back to his village in Punjab. An uneven narrative, the film somewhat warms up in the second half when the killer falls in love with a young woman in the village, but because of circumstances, he cannot express his love to her. Also, in the second half, the plot begins to resemble the Raj Khosla film *Bombai Ka Babu* (1960), with Dev Anand and Suchitra Sen.

*Sarvann* boasts of a major Punjabi star—singer and now actor Amrinder Gill. As a tribute to Priyanka's late father, Dr Ashok Chopra (he passed away in 2013 after a long struggle with cancer), the film includes a well-known Punjabi *shabad*—'Mitar Pyare Nu'. Written by Guru Gobind Singh, the *shabad* has been sung by every major singer, from Mohammed Rafi to Jagjit Singh and even Nusrat Fateh Ali Khan.

In a Twitter exchange in early January 2017, I asked Priyanka about the recording and this is what she wrote back: 'He (her father) had recorded the song and we meant to release it but then he fell ill... It really feels like he's next to me when I hear it.'

Critics were not very kind to *Sarvann*. *The Tribune* gave the film a one-star rating. '*Sarvann* fails to fulfil the promise of being a different and entertaining film,' *The Tribune*'s critic wrote. 'With only good songs and Amrinder Gill, how do you expect *Sarvann* to carry the weight of broken, weak and disjointed script and direction on its shoulders? This one star is just for Amrinder Gill for trying to carry this weight, still.'

∿

For their third production, the Chopra mother-and-daughter duo took the project to Sikkim. Directed by former actress Paakhi Tyrewala, *Pahuna: The Little Visitors*, narrated the story about a group of Nepalis (the film is in Nepali language), fleeing the political violence in their country and finding refuge in the Indian state of Sikkim. The film is told from the perspective of two little children who get separated from the rest of the group, including their mother, but manage to survive with their charm and quick thinking.

Paakhi says she wanted to be true to the story and the people and so the film was made in Nepali language, even though she does not speak it. 'Initially I thought the film would be in Hindi, but as I started writing the script, I realized I would not be true to the film if it is not in the language spoken there,' she says. 'The kids spoke Nepali from Nepal, since they have come from there. But the adults they encounter speak Nepali as it is spoken in Sikkim.' And she adds that the entire region from Darjeeling, Sikkim and Nepal speaks one language—Nepali. 'But *lehja unka badalta rehta hai* (Their style of speaking changes).'

'I was very apprehensive,' Dr Chopra says about making a film in Nepali language. 'But Priyanka read the script and she spoke to Paakhi. She said, "We are making it. But just see it stays within the budget."' And Paakhi adds, 'Priyanka said, "Don't make it look like a regional film. I love your content. Make sure it's a good film."' She further explains that Sikkim only has two movie theatres, and there was little hope to recover the investment by showing the film in the Northeastern state. But Priyanka did not want Paakhi to compromise on the production quality.

And then Dr Chopra recalled another advice her daughter gave to Paakhi. 'She said, "If you make a good film we will showcase in India. If you make a very good film, it will go abroad to festivals."'

*Pahuna* premiered at the Toronto International Film Festival where Priyanka, Dr Chopra and Paakhi showed up to promote the film. Introducing the film on the world premiere night, Priyanka touched upon why the film was important to her team. But her rambling speech ended up creating a lot of controversies.

'This movie is from the perspective of our two protagonists, our two kids which (sic) are from a small village in Northeast India in Sikkim, which is a Northeastern state which deals with a lot of violence and insurgency because of political unrest,' Priyanka said. 'And it is basically set in a world where these kids have to run away from Nepal with their families and are displaced from where they live and have to run as refugees into India. It talks about issues such as the refugee crisis, the displacement of children, when adults take decisions for them. As we are seeing it in the world right now with DACA. It's such a relevant topic.'

Priyanka made similar statements the next day in a few interviews. It was clear that she was dealing with too much information and was mixing up details. For one thing, there is no political unrest in Sikkim. And it seemed that she got confused between Sikkim and Nepal. Then there was the reference to DACA—an American immigration policy. But perhaps, Priyanka forgot that she was no longer in the US. Instead, she was speaking in Canada, where most people were not familiar with DACA. The next day, speaking to *ET Canada*, Priyanka made another factually incorrect statement. 'This is the first film ever that's come out of that region, because it's very troubled with insurgency and troubling situations,' she said.[145] In reality, there have been quite a few films made in Sikkim, including *Ralang Road* (2017), which played in the competition section of the Karlovy Vary International Film Festival in 2017. Then there is Vijay Anand's classic *Jewel Thief* (1967).

There were many angry reactions to Priyanka's statements and she was trolled on Twitter by many who seemed upset (and perhaps rightfully) by her factually incorrect statements.[146]

Priyanka gracefully accepted her folly, and apologized. In a statement she sent to Sikkim's tourism minister Ugen Gyatso, she said, 'My comment, made during an interview at the prestigious Toronto International Film Festival 2017, where *Pahuna* made its worldwide debut, was misconstrued. I was talking about the Sikkimese film industry and also the subject of the film, where I mentioned how Sikkim was grappling with the refugee situation caused by insurgencies. I had meant by the "neighbouring countries". I am fully aware that Sikkim is an incredible host nation to so many refugees and our film shows exactly that through the children's point of view.'[147] Even her apology has an error. She referred to Sikkim as a nation.

She added, 'I have always taken pride as being someone who is informed about the world but this time, some of the statements made were incorrect and while I should have been better informed about certain facts, I take full responsibility for what I said. I understand now that our film was not the first

Sikkimese film to be made, but our aim has always been to provide local talent, both actors and technicians, a global platform to shine... I understand the impact of the statements made and hope that the people and government of Sikkim find it in their hearts to forgive me.'[148]

Priyanka's apology was accepted, especially by Gyatso. NDTV.com quoted the minister as saying, 'I condemn Priyanka's statement. Being an international figure, it's a very disappointing comment on her behalf. It has definitely made us feel bad and sad but she has apologized to us through a mail, likewise, her mother Madhu Chopra also apologized over phone today in presence of Sikkim media persons.' [149]

∿

It seems that Priyanka Chopra's critics have moved on. But the thing that her critics did not realize was that she said the same thing about Sikkim a few times during her visit to Toronto. It was not a one-time error on her part when she spoke to *ET Canada*. Priyanka has been the UNICEF ambassador for a number of years, having travelled to conflict zones in Africa and the Middle East. She travels extensively around the world and with her television show *Quantico* she often gives the impression that she is somewhat of an expert on all things related to FBI and CIA.

She of course had, and continues to have, noble intentions of making films in regional Indian languages. And the jury is still out in terms of how successful she has been in that regard. But she clearly does not have the complete knowledge about all the regions of India. One can say that Priyanka is not alone. Many Indians are clueless when it comes to the Northeastern states.

But the world expects more from celebrities. Their opinions and voices matter. George Clooney or Angelina Jolie speak about Africa or other troubled regions of the world and their voices carry. The press covers their moves and their words. And so, they have to be cautious and knowledgeable about what they say. In that regard, Priyanka failed a major test. She is a celebrity— her words carry weight and are reported every day. But she has proven time and again that she is still a global celebrity in the making. She can meet the Pakistani activist Malala Yousafzai at the UN, and Syrian refugee children in Jordan, but she is not at Angelina Jolie's level yet. That comes from experience, a deeper understanding, a world view, having strong advisers and moving beyond just looking glamorous on the red carpet. It involves focusing on what really matters to the world, what to speak and how to speak. Priyanka's training is still incomplete in that regard.

In the recent years, Priyanka has landed in other controversies as well. She posted pictures of herself and her brother on Instagram, smiling and posing in front of the Holocaust Memorial in Berlin when she was visiting the city to promote her film *Baywatch*. One picture is of Priyanka with big round-framed dark glasses, her red luscious lips, and the words 'Holocaust Memorial #Berlin.' In the other photo, she poses with her brother with the message, '@siddharthchopra89 and I being tourists. There is such an eerie silence here.'

Tourists take selfies when they visit historic monuments in other countries, but there is an unwritten rule that one does not take selfies or pictures at sombre locations such as Ground Zero in Manhattan or the Holocaust Memorial in Berlin. But to Priyanka, taking a picture in front of Berlin's Brandenburg Gate or the Holocaust Museum—all of it meant the same, it seems. Somehow, a world view, a greater perspective of how to perceive and react to significant global events, was missing.

As expected, there was an outrage on Twitter. One tweet read: 'Priyanka Chopra took selfies at the Holocaust memorial… is this another attention seeking stunt??? Shouldn't have done that.'[150] Another read: 'Taking selfies at the Holocaust memorial was tasteless and frankly very ignorant and stupid.'[151]

In the age of social media when the wall between celebrities and the audience has been broken, criticisms such as these do affect even the rich and famous. The tweets led Priyanka to delete the two images.

In October 2016, Priyanka posed for the Indian edition of *Condé Nast Traveller*, which carried stories about why people travel. She stood in the balcony of a tall building, with the backdrop of Manhattan. She was wearing a white sleeveless tank top with four words in a box. Three of the words—'Refugee, Immigrant, Outsider' were struck out. The fourth word read 'Traveller'. Again there was Twitter backlash that Priyanka had been insensitive to the refugee crisis. 'Maybe your editors need taste editing. I get what you are trying to say. But you just trivialized a serious refugee issue,' said one tweet. While another read: 'Extremely insensitive in midst of biggest refugee crises. All other options listed are forced on people not chosen.'[152]

Priyanka had to apologize again. This is what she said to Barkha Dutt on NDTV: 'I'm really, really apologetic about the fact that so many sentiments were hurt. I was very affected and I felt really, really horrible and that was never the intention.'[153]

Obviously Priyanka did not intentionally make these blunders. Will these minor errors in judgement happen again? That is quite likely. But these are relatively minor hiccups and eventually should not impact her life and career goals.

# 7

# THE HOLLYWOOD CROSSOVER BEGINS

On Sunday, 27 September 2015, ABC broadcast the first episode of its much touted television drama—*Quantico*, an action thriller set around the FBI training facility in a town by that same name in the southern US state of Virginia. In India, the show was broadcast a week later.

The show's lead character Alex Parrish, an Indian American FBI trainee, is played by Priyanka Chopra—a big first for an Indian actor, who was mostly unknown in the US until then. But to understand Priyanka's journey—the crossing over and becoming part of the mainstream American popular culture—one must shift the focus slightly, to understand the brain behind the Bollywood star.

That brain, or the person who made Priyanka what she is now, is Anjula Acharya, an Indian American who grew up in Britain. In fact, Anjula speaks with a lovely British accent and often narrates her experiences of growing up in a Punjabi immigrant household in Buckinghamshire, UK, at a time when it was impossible to see South Asian characters on television or films.

Speaking in a HuffPost Live interview in 2014, Anjula said that the motivation and passion for introducing an Indian actor like Priyanka to the US came from 'being a child (in the UK) and going through a lot of racism, and never having role models who looked like me or acted like me (on television or films).' And in a 2015 interview with Livemint she said, 'The biggest thing I felt was the way we were perceived and presented on TV was so derogatory and grossly misrepresented.'[154]

In another interview, this time with *Forbes*, Anjula said, 'People did not really understand our family and I guess they just relied on what they saw on TV or heard about South Asians to inform their decision on who we were.'[155] She recalled one TV show—*Grange Hill*—where there was an Indian character—a young girl from a conservative family. If her father saw her even talking to a boy, he would force her to get a virginity test. 'I'd be bullied in school even harder the next day than I already was,' Anjula added.[156]

Anjula and her then husband, Ranj Bath, moved to US in 2000. Like his wife, Ranj was equally interested in popular culture. Few years later, the two, along with another partner, quit their corporate jobs and raised a substantial amount of money—$6 million—to launch a website, DesiHits.com, with the goal of bridging the gap between Western and Indian popular culture.

One of the major investors in the project was Jimmy Iovine, CEO of Interscope Records (in 2014, his company was bought over by Apple Inc.) who has also worked with artists such as Lana Del Rey and Eminem. Iovine was keen to see diversity emerge in American popular culture. He told *Variety* that he signed on the minute he met Anjula and heard her pitch. 'She told me what her idea was,' *Variety* quoted him as saying, 'I thought it was an incredibly creative platform and one that doesn't exist.'[157]

Danny Boyle's unexpected hit *Slumdog Millionaire* (2008) made stars out of its lead actors—Freida Pinto, Dev Patel, Anil Kapoor and Irrfan Khan. All the actors had success of varying degrees in Hollywood. But for sometime, the biggest name celebrated in Hollywood was A.R. Rahman. Rahman won two Oscars for *Slumdog Millionaire*, including one for the song 'Jai Ho' that, for a brief period of time, became a phenomenal hit in the US. The DesiHits.com team banked on the popularity of 'Jai Ho' and recorded a remix of the song with Rahman and The Pussycat Dolls. The song's video played at parties, in dance halls, gyms and at Bollywood dance classes across the US.

The remixed 'Jai Ho' was a one-hit wonder internationally for Rahman, following the success of *Slumdog Millionaire*. His career took off in spurts—he received two more Academy Award nominations, this time for Boyle's *127 Hours*. Eventually, however,

Rahman's career fizzled out in Hollywood. But the DesiHits.com team remained persistent.

They followed up with a few more remixes—bringing together Sonu Nigam's voice with that of Britney Spears, for the original song 'I Wanna Go'. Another remix combined the talents of Lady Gaga with Bollywood composers and brothers Salim and Sulaiman Merchant. And in November 2014, Anjula accompanied Lady Gaga on a tour of India. Among the guests at Gaga's show after the Formula 1 race in Greater Noida in Uttar Pradesh was the Bollywood star Shah Rukh Khan.

Then, one day, Iovine asked Anjula who she thought was going to be the next big idea out of India. 'I thought a lot and then said I want to do something for my people,' she says. 'We see Latin and African American pop stars, but there's never ever been one from India, who has broken the pop culture. Somebody who is huge and has the ability to expand into different markets.'

And suddenly she remembered having seen Priyanka Chopra in a video from Rohan Sippy's *Bluffmaster!* 'I was living in Silicon Valley doing tech venture capital work and I wasn't even in the entertainment-music business, but I saw Priyanka in the video and I remember thinking she has the swag, she's so cool.' She did not know if Priyanka could sing, but she suggested the Bollywood actress' name as a potential singer who could be introduced to the West.

After the Miss World pageant, Priyanka's acting career did take off, but the quality of the films she got improved only over a period of time. A reluctant singer, she also carried a secret desire to one day sing in Bollywood films. People who heard her sing thought she had the talent, but she was also afraid of attempting to become a singer, especially at a time when her acting career was slowly taking off.

Perhaps it went back to her childhood fear of being picked to sing often. 'I was always one of those students in the class who would be asked to go and sing in front of the class to entertain everyone whenever a teacher was not around,' she said in an interview.[158]

During the shoot of her first film, *Thamizhan*, her director G. Venkatesh and her co-star Joseph Vijay Chandrasekhar heard her hum and then coaxed her to sing a song for the film. She was young (the film opened in 2002 when Priyanka was only 20) and did not have the clout to say no. The song 'Ullathai Killathe' would be featured in the film. It is a playful, upbeat song. In the video, Priyanka has a tiara on and is wearing a blue dress—something Cinderella would have worn to the grand ball. She is accompanied by Vijay and a group of background dancers, wearing outfits of animated characters.

There were other offers for her to sing, but Priyanka always seemed shy. One major Bollywood music personality who heard Priyanka's voice and realized that she definitely had something in her was her friend and composer/singer Vishal Dadlani.

'Priyanka is someone who goes above and beyond, with sheer determination and hard work,' Vishal says. 'She can do anything she chooses to, and singing is just one among her facets. She has a natural gift, a smoky, husky tone of voice. We recorded her for a song—that eventually wasn't used, because she didn't feel ready—in *Bluffmaster!* in 2004 or 2005. It was a jam in the studio, with Shekhar (Vishal's partner Shekhar Ravjiani) and I composing/producing on the fly, and Priyanka dropping her vocals in, quite effortless, really. It was a song of love and loss, and the lyrics were mine. Between Rohan Sippy, Shekhar and I, we convinced her to do it over a few days of insisting that only she would sing that one.'

The song Priyanka recorded with Vishal-Shekhar still remains a closely guarded secret. 'That song is lying unreleased with us,'

Vishal adds. 'Now that she's a global megastar, maybe someday, if she wishes, we'll take it out.'

Flash forward to 2010 and in California, Anjula was trying to explore on her own whether Priyanka Chopra could be made into a global singer. She called her contacts in India only to discover that Salim and Sulaiman Merchant had also recorded a demo with Priyanka. And she got a copy of that recording and played it for Iovine and David Joseph, Chairman and CEO of Universal Music UK. The group decided to go to India to meet Priyanka. 'Priyanka is an idea,' Iovine later told *The Los Angeles Times*. 'You get it within 30 seconds.'[159]

But first, Anjula tried calling Priyanka. 'She was filming *7 Khoon Maaf* and I am not sure if she took my first call seriously,' she says. 'I had to stalk her for months because she would not take my call. I love to tease her about it now, but she really made it hard.' Later speaking to HuffPost Live, Priyanka laughed and responded to the stalking part by saying, 'In my defence, I was in a really intense movie at that time and actors get like that sometimes.'[160]

The truth is that if Anjula had not been persistent, there would have been no *Quantico*, none of this media hype, talk show appearances, magazine cover stories, red carpets, appearances at the United Nations, invites to powerhouse galas, no listings of Priyanka as a powerful, influential woman, the hottest next thing. She would still be in Bollywood doing her regular work. She would have perhaps reached the peak of her career like several actresses before her—Juhi Chawla, Rani Mukherjee, Madhuri Dixit, Preity Zinta, Karishma Kapoor—married now, with children, but desperately hoping for a big break to make a comeback in an industry that is not too kind to actresses who cross the mid-30 age cut-off point.

Once the contact was made, Anjula travelled to India to meet

Priyanka. She was accompanied by David Joseph and Andrew Kronfeld, Executive Vice President, Marketing, at Universal Music Group International (UMGI).

'She was still in two minds,' Anjula says about Priyanka. 'I remember saying to her all you have to do is to go to the studio and give one try. You don't have to make a commitment. She got into a studio and fell in love with it.' The group listened to Priyanka sing and they all talked. 'When we came out, David and I said at the same time, "She's the one!"' Anjula adds.

And then it was a question of building a strategy of introducing Priyanka Chopra to America. 'I spent time analysing pop culture in America and how stars are today,' says Anjula who, in addition to managing Priyanka's career, is also a partner in the venture capitalist firm Trinity Capital. Priyanka's other half of management is handled by Troy Carter who heads Atom Factory, a talent management and full-service film and television production company. Carter's clients include Lady Gaga and John Legend.

Anjula adds, 'I realized early on that I didn't want to make her a pop star, I just wanted to make her a star. And what form it came in didn't matter, because she is a multitalented individual. We decided not to box her because it is so hard to find stars who can do everything.'

And then a few years later, Anjula's strategy changed. 'The process for me changed from "I want to make her a star to I want to make her a face in America."'

In February 2012, Priyanka signed up with Creative Artists Agency (CAA)—one of Hollywood's leading talent agencies. She was represented by David Tagioff who was earlier a director at DesiHits.com. Three years later, a little after Priyanka's TV show *Quantico* was launched, she switched to William Morris Endeavor Entertainment (WME).

Some years ago, it would have been hard to imagine an Indian actor making it this far in the US market. In this new journey, there have been some major misses and the road was initially rather choppy for Priyanka Chopra, but there were also some hits, and then it seemed there was no looking back for her. Despite the news on 11 May 2018, that *Quantico* has been cancelled, she still has a solid chance to make a comeback in the West.

As Karan Johar says, 'She is our hugest crossover success story. I think with everyone else when they cross, it is over only.'

⟡

In the fall of 2014, I did an email interview with Priyanka Chopra. I asked her about singing and why that was important to her. 'I've always loved to sing, and I come from a very musical family,' she wrote back. 'It was actually my father's dream for me to do this, so it's also been quite an emotional journey, writing and creating all of the songs during his last few years. As you probably know already, I am a self-confessed "daddy's little girl" ;-) (She has a tattoo in her father's handwriting on her right wrist, proclaiming that). I'm a very creative person, and singing/songwriting is really another avenue for me to explore and express my creativity.'

Today, Priyanka has three singles released. Her first song— not released as a single—was 'In My City', with rapper will.i.am, founding member of pop group Black Eyed Peas. It was featured on the NFL (National Football League) Network's 'Thursday Night Kickoff'—the pregame show for the football game. The song premiered in September 2012.

At the time of its release, the song was referred to as a single and was supposed to be a part of an album that Priyanka was going to release the next year. The album was being produced by Grammy Award-winning producer-songwriter RedOne (a.k.a. Nadir Khayat), the Morocco-born artist behind the success of

Lady Gaga. He has also worked with Jennifer Lopez, Pitbull, Enrique Iglesias and Nicki Minaj.

In a November 2012 report, *The Los Angles Times* quoted a very enthusiastic RedOne as saying that he was certain the album, and every song, would be a hit. 'Priyanka fits perfectly,' *The Times* quoted RedOne as saying. He referred to her potential appeal. 'I thought, "Oh my God, this girl could be a huge global star." It's something fresh for the world to hear.'

Prior to singing songs in the US, Priyanka took voice lessons from the Mumbai-based coach Samantha Edwards. Much of Priyanka's training with Edwards happened in between her shooting of *Barfi!*. 'She started out a bit shy of it, but all the experience and training with her coach Samantha, has really got her places,' says singer and composer Vishal Dadlani. But Priyanka has always been grounded and the reality was clear to her. She was being well-guided by Anjula and the rest of the team working with her, but America was an uncharted territory and the shift to singing was still an experiment. She was officially not known as a singer—not in India and definitely not in the US.

And she spoke openly about it to *The Los Angeles Times*. 'I don't want to come into (America) saying I'm this big star. I'm a new artist and nobody knows me here and I'm not delusional about it... It scares the crap out of me... I know I have flaws.' But *The Times* reporter Gerrick D. Kennedy did notice that Priyanka's body language, her persona, the entourage that moved with her—all of it gave the appearance of a pop star. 'Her sultry smile, body-hugging dress and towering heels command attention.' What Kennedy failed to realize was that this was the result of her fame in Bollywood and being a celebrity in India, something Priyanka had been managing rather well since the age of 17 when she was crowned Miss India.

'In My City' was Priyanka's attempt to reconcile with all

the cities she had lived in, 'Being from an army background, I've grown up in many cities—Bareilly, Ladakh, Pune, Boston, New York, Chicago, Delhi,' she was quoted as saying by website DigitalSpy. 'In a strange way, the song is dedicated to every city which has influenced me.'[162]

The song got love from some Hollywood personalities. Joseph Gordon-Levitt said he was adding the song to his iPod playlist. 'I came across Priyanka's new track and found the song very upbeat and refreshing. She is beautiful and extremely talented,' Gordon-Levitt was quoted in a statement.[163] On 10 April 2012, Priyanka reacted to Joseph's statements which were carried in several Indian publications by thanking him on Twitter. And Ryan Seacrest announced the single's release on his *E!* show by saying that Bollywood was 'about to take over Hollywood'.[164]

Priyanka convinced the Interscope Records team, which was releasing the song, to introduce it in India before it opened on the NFL show. In the first week, about 1,30,000 copies of the song were sold and downloaded in India. No surprise here since Priyanka is a huge star in India, even though she was not known as a singer. But in the US, the sales were much slower—only 5,000 songs sold on iTunes in the first week with no radio play.[165] The signs were not too good for a new pop singer trying to break into the already crowded market in the US. But Priyanka was not ready to give up.

The main video of the song had a bubblegum pop quality to it—fun energy, with a sexy-looking Priyanka Chopra dancing around. Five and a half years later, in the spring of 2018, the video had 37 million hits on YouTube. That is an impressive number, although Dhanush's 'Kolaveri Di', introduced a year earlier, had 146 million hits by the spring of 2018.

'In My City' was a big break for Priyanka if she was seriously considering making it in the mainstream American market. It was the theme song for the Thursday night football show for two seasons. But Priyanka's team and NFL took a big gamble on the song. Until then, NFL's opening songs were performed by artists like Faith Hill, Pink, Hank Williams Jr. and Cee Lo Green. For the clip that played before the pregame show every Thursday in the fall of 2012, the video showed Priyanka dancing to the song, wearing sexier versions of team T-shirts, interspersed with football players in action and the regular talking heads of the show. The Bollywood star of *Aitraaz, Dostana* and *Bajirao Mastani* was suddenly appearing to be a part of a phenomenon as American as apple pie!

But with the release of the song, Priyanka encountered a lot of hateful backlash from some American football fans. An article on Yahoo.com about Priyanka received some of the worst kinds of comments.[166] The comments have since been deleted. According to Anjula, an editor at *Billboard* asked Yahoo to disable those comments. But here is a sample of what was carried on the site:

'Who the hell is she…her names sounds middle eastern.'

'Seriously…in all of America, they couldn't find one good-looking American singer to do this but instead choosing someone who probably doesn't even know what a "hut" is?'

'Next we'll have a string of cheerleaders named "PATEL"'

'She looks ayrab?!'

'I thought she was hot until i found she's an Indian… yuchhhhhhhhhhhhh'

The comments rooted from a lot of racism and ignorance, and there were some deeply offensive words that are best not repeated. 'My strategy was to take her to one of the biggest pop culture brands—NFL—and we were getting backlash,' Anjula recalls. 'They were so offensive. They said things like you should go back to your country and get gang-raped. Priyanka was beside herself. This was her first outing in America and this is what people were saying. And there wasn't a big uproar with people saying it was terrible and wrong. Generally not many people stood up. And it was a very hurtful time for her and for all of us.'

Publicly, Priyanka was calm and diplomatic about the criticism. In an interview with *The Wall Street Journal* television, she said, 'I've been in the limelight, in a public space, for very long. I understand dealing with brickbats and bouquets. And I've dealt with racism. I think the only way to go forward is to shut the detractors with your work. Instead of harping on the fact that, "Yes, I'm called a terrorist, because I happen to be brown and from South Asia," and on getting hate mail saying "You're not white, why should you be on NFL?" Despite that, I'd rather focus on the millions of other people who've been sending emails or tweets and saying it's amazing.'[167]

Anjula is all praises for Priyanka for continuing to look forward. 'She's a risk-taker in every part of her life,' she says about Priyanka. 'When you have a safety net, then you do not need to take risks. It takes sheer guts.'

But Priyanka was certain that the safety net would stay there for her. She never cut off her ties with Bollywood. She was definitely not planning to pack her bags and give up acting in Bollywood films to become a singer. That remained her bread and butter at that time.

In response to a question from *Spin* magazine whether she was aiming for a crossover into the US market, she said, 'I don't know if it's a crossover. I'm not leaving where I was, and I'm not here either. The Indian movie industry has made me who I am. I'm not saying "That's done, and I'm here."'[168] She referred to her move towards America and pop music as 'organic'.

The issue of the crossover and the repeated question about it bothered Priyanka. In an email interview with me, she seemed a bit irritated with the question regarding her strategy to crossover. But she also put a positive spin on the question, making herself appear as the first Indian star who was extending her scope of work beyond the Indian borders.

'To me it is the same career,' she wrote in the email. 'This is by no means a "crossover", I am beginning to hate that word! I am and always have been a global citizen who entertains a universal audience, and I really hope more talent from India takes a global view.' And then, she suggested that she would love a situation where her career would develop so that she could combine acting in films and singing songs. 'I always say...movies are my heart, and music is my soul. Stay tuned...'

∿

The year 2013 was a busy one for Priyanka as she slowly made attempts to gain foothold in the US. That summer, Priyanka released her second single 'Exotic'—the song and its accompanying sexy video featured Cuban American rapper Pitbull. Speaking to ABC's once highly rated news show *Nightline*, Priyanka described the song as pop music with a 'twist of some chicken tikka masala'.[169]

That was not the kind of answer many Indians, especially those in the diaspora, would like. While chicken tikka masala may be one of the most popular Indian dishes among Americans, it is not a dish in India. Food connoisseurs and leading Indian chefs consider it as clichéd Indian food. By equating her new song with that dish, Priyanka seemed to be entering that similar clichéd territory.

There were also some rumblings in India that Priyanka was pandering to the West and to its stereotypical image of Indian women. Gursimran Khamba, a stand-up comedian with the popular group, All India Bakchod, is not a fan of Priyanka's singing, and had this to say about 'Exotic': 'After replacing will.I.am with a man who refers to himself by a canine breed, ie Pitbull, Ms. Chopra has returned with a song with lyrics that are even more spectacular. My personal favorites are "Mumbai Cuba baby let's go"—making her the *first* person outside the CPI(M) to willingly want to go to Cuba. Also, "I'm feeling so exotic, I'm hotter than the tropics"—an earnest attempt if there ever was one at teaching her young fans geography.'[170]

The *Hindustan Times* wrote, 'Priyanka Chopra's Exotic is more odd than exotic. A video that conjures up images of a glittery Jennifer Lopez gone wrong to candy floss Britney style shots, Priyanka has tried it all. Moving from In my City will.i.am to Exotic Pitbull, Priyanka seems to go the Lopez way quite a bit. But PeeCee is no JLo.'[171]

And here was the irony. Priyanka had spent years trying to prove in Bollywood that she was more than just a sex symbol, a beauty pageant winner who looked hot in body-hugging western clothes. After winning the National Film Award in 2008 for *Fashion* and later acting in a film like *Barfi!*, which opened in 2012, she was back to being a sex symbol—albeit for a different market—a hot item girl in a pop song with a touch of rap music added, to increase her potential audience. This was how her marketing machine in America thought of selling her.

The criticism in India puzzled Priyanka. 'I don't know how that is so, considering I have Hindi lyrics in the song,' she told me in an interview in the fall of 2013, when I suggested that she may be pandering to the West. 'The song is very me. This is an English album. It's an international album with Hindi lyrics. So how does it mean that I am pandering to the West? I think that's wrong.' I suggested that maybe it was so because she was going with the Western perspective of India being an exotic land and Indian women being exotic as well. People in India want to move beyond the orientalist notion of the country as the land of snake charmers and tigers. To that, she responded, 'I like the fact that I am called exotic. I like the idea of that.'

Anjula adds that the song 'Exotic' had actually done well in the Indian market. 'There are always a small percentage of people who want to create drama,' she says. 'I just stopped taking them seriously. It's like the backlash Warris (Ahluwalia, New York-based Sikh designer and party-going-celebrity who had modelled for GAP ads in the US) got from the Sikh community that he was modelling with a turban on and he had women draping themselves over him. As if we don't do that in Bollywood? I think everyone should just chill out. To me Priyanka is exotic. You find that word offensive, I apologize. But majority of women would like to be called exotic.'

The song and the video did win Priyanka at least one fan in the West. The popular celebrity site PerezHilton.com had this to say about 'Exotic': 'The perfectly fine Pitbull and his curvy collaborator are so HAWT on the beach that you'll need to cool off with cold shower after it's all over!!!…The catchy track has a fitting title because, between the Cuban-American rapper and his gorgeous Indian goddess, they really are a deliciously exotic duo!!!'[172]

On 26 July 2013, the same day 'Exotic' hit the market, Priyanka showed up at Millions of Milkshakes—a store on West Hollywood, a city within the greater city of Los Angeles in California. With thousands of fans packing the town's famous Melrose Avenue, she made her own concoction of milkshake and named it—what else—Exotic. In branding a milkshake at Millions of Milkshakes, Priyanka was joining the ranks of other Hollywood celebrities—Miley Cyrus, Kim Kardashian, David Beckham, Katy Perry and Leonardo DiCaprio—to have a drink named after them.

Later in an interview, Priyanka told me that she was nervous since she hardly cooked. 'I kept thinking, "Oh God people will say I don't even know how to make a milkshake." I didn't want to embarrass myself.' The ingredients were her own choice, she said. 'I wanted to make it with almonds because that's my favourite. This was just an expansion of *badam* milk, added with caramel and bananas.'

The crowd outside the store mostly showed up because local radio and TV stations catering to Los Angeles' large South Asian population had announced that Priyanka was going to be there and would greet her fans. The numbers were so large that the Huffington Post compared Priyanka's popularity among South Asian immigrants to another Indian actress. 'Priyanka Chopra caused Aishwarya Rai-esque pandemonium on Thursday while she was visiting Los Angeles,' Huffington Post wrote.[173] Obviously the HuffPost writer was still stuck on Aishwarya Rai's brief and mostly unsuccessful attempt to make a mark in Hollywood. The writer also missed the point that Priyanka (the piece referred to her as a Bollywood vixen) was herself a big star in Bollywood and in the recent years, her stature had become higher than that of Rai.

Later, Anjula acknowledged that the crowd that came out to support Priyanka was predominantly desi. 'But we are seeing more and more non-desis,' she added.

A few weeks later, Priyanka was back in news. This time, she was promoting a Disney film *Planes*, in which she did a voice-over for a skunky Indian airplane Ishani, who participates in a world flying competition and is also the love interest of the film's main protagonist plane, Dusty Cropper (the voice of Dane Cook). This was perhaps the first time an actor from India was doing a voice-over for an American production—that too a Disney film.

Priyanka was apparently cast in the film because the director

Klay Hall had been a fan of hers since he watched *Dostana*. 'She's a triple treat—an actor, singer and dancer—and we noticed that when she came in to record her lines, she attracted the attention of a lot of people who'd stop by to watch her in action,' Hall was quoted in a press statement at the time of the film's release.[174] Hall has previously worked on hit TV shows such as *The Simpsons* and *King of the Hill*. 'Priyanka exudes heart, charm and warmth,' Hall added.

*Planes* also featured the voices of Terri Hatcher, John Cleese, Julia Louis-Dreyfus, Val Kilmer, Sinbad and Cedric the Entertainer. Clearly, Priyanka was in esteemed company. To her credit, Priyanka tried to bring a bit of Indian authenticity to the Ishani character. Ishani's accent has a natural Indian tone. 'I was very clear about that,' she told me at the time of the film's promotion. 'You know that stereotypical accent that most people see Indians speak with? I was clear that I didn't want that. That's really not how all of us speak. I wanted to keep it real. And (director) Klay (Hall) was fine about that. He actually liked that I had an Indian accent. He was glad it wasn't exaggerated and stereotypical. I tried to get a few Hindi words here and there and that made Ishani unique.'

Critics trashed *Planes* and most in the West failed to notice Priyanka Chopra's presence in the film. The film had a 25 per cent score on Rotten Tomatoes Tomatometer. *The New York Times'* Neil Genzlinger critic wrote: '*Planes* is for the most part content to imitate rather than innovate, presumably hoping to reap a respectable fraction of the box office numbers of *Cars* and *Cars 2*, which together made hundreds of millions of dollars.'[175] *Variety's* Justin Chang, taking the easy way out, did not miss using the word 'exotic' in describing Ishani: 'Ishani (Priyanka Chopra), a striking Indian beauty who becomes an exotic love interest for Dusty.'[176]

Earlier, during 2013, Priyanka and Anjula were sitting in a lounge room at the Heathrow Airport. Priyanka was skimming through *Elle* magazine when she suddenly saw an ad for Guess Jeans. 'She just slapped her hand on the Guess ad and said "Make me a Guess Girl."' Anjula laughs as she recalls. 'I looked at her and asked, "You are joking?" and she said, "No I [am] not." And I said to her, "Priy, you are not blond haired with blue eyes," and apart from Naomi Campbell, all other Guess girls (Claudia Schiffer, Anna Nicole Smith, Paris Hilton) have been blond. And she just shrugged her shoulders and said, "I will be the first."'

'When she gives me a job like this, I take it very seriously, and we made it happen through CAA,' Anjula adds.

In an interview with *The Hollywood Reporter*, Priyanka said that the process of her becoming the Guess Girl for the holiday season of 2013 was smooth. 'It happened within three seconds of meeting Paul (Marciano, CEO of Guess),' Priyanka told *The Hollywood Reporter.* 'He just said, "Oh my God, you're a Guess Girl, I have to shoot you. Get your management to call me."' The same story also quoted Amber Tarshis, SVP marketing for Guess North America, as saying the company did not necessarily approach Priyanka because of the music she has been creating. That is a somewhat unfortunate statement, considering Priyanka Chopra was such a big star in India. And it is strange for Tarshis to say that because her boss Marciano seemed to know a lot about Priyanka's life beyond just the few songs she had released in the US.

In an email interview with me, Paul Marciano says this about Priyanka Chopra, 'My first reaction when I met Priyanka face-to-face at Guess was almost speechless in the sense that she is so strikingly beautiful but so down to earth, so approachable and such a great attitude that the minute she walks in the room, you could feel her presence everywhere.'[177] He adds, 'The qualities I look for in Guess models are always the same that I feel very strongly for our brand which is to be feminine, confident, adventurous, open-minded of new career paths, and always of course fashion conscious. And Priyanka had exactly all that.'

Marciano adds that he knows there are many beautiful actresses, models and singers in India. 'But a lot of them stay in India, being so busy with their careers there, and do not really wish to pursue other continents as a personal choice.'

When talking to *The Telegraph*, Marciano compared Priyanka to the classic Hollywood beauties. 'She reminds me of the young Sophia Loren and the top actresses of the 1950s,' he said. [178]

California-based Indian American journalist Sheila Marikar says that Guess most probably chose Priyanka because they realized how big she was in the Indian market. 'They understood that she had a huge appeal in the Indian market and also in the Middle East,' Sheila says. 'And she has that look, you can think that she could be multiple ethnicities. She doesn't fit into just one category. Her ability to be a chameleon in that respect worked in her favour of what Guess wanted...'

Guess's India strategy started a few years earlier when the company opened its first store in Mumbai in 2005. India was the 68th country the clothing retail chain entered (they now have presence in nearly ninety countries). There was already a market ready for the Guess brand. 'India has been on our radar for some time now,' said Giulino Sartori, Vice President of international retail at the time of the opening of the Mumbai store.[179]

Around the time Paul Marciano signed up Priyanka Chopra to be the face of Guess, the company's fortunes were on decline. The four Marciano brothers had gone on their separate paths and there were lawsuits among them. More importantly, Guess's

market share in the retail clothing world was on a decline.[180]
Priyanka Chopra thought she had broken the glass ceiling
when she landed the modelling assignment with Guess. 'I am their
first brown model,' she told *WWD*, feeling rather proud of her
achievement.[181] It was definitely an achievement. And speaking
to *The Hollywood Reporter,* Priyanka said, 'With Guess being such
an iconic brand associated with such beautiful iconic women over
the years, it's amazing to be a part of that legacy.'[182] But the
truth lay somewhere in between. Marciano's company needed
Priyanka Chopra—her reach in India and beyond—perhaps a lot
more than she needed this modelling assignment.

Then there was the surprise. Guess hired the Canadian
singer Bryan Adams—also a well-known photographer—to do
the shoot. Priyanka told various publications how Adams was
famous in India and his concerts would always sell out. 'We
love him,' she said to *The Hollywood Reporter*, sounding like just
another fan of the rock star. 'We know all his songs and all the
lyrics.'[183] Later, talking to BollywoodJournalist.com, she referred
to the musician as a man with a 'certain *daal-chaawal* (humble)
quality. It was fun working with him and we listened to a lot of
Hindi songs while shooting for the campaign.'[184]

Priyanka looks stunning in the black and white images that
Adams shot in a Mediterranean-style villa. With her hair open,
at times loosely tied on the top, she is often shown in high
heels, printed summery dresses, and always with a wicked, fun
smile on her face. The advertisements appeared in a series of
magazines—*Harper's Bazaar, Paper, Nylon, Elle, Marie Claire, WWD
Collections, The Hollywood Reporter* and the *WSJ Magazine*. More
than the music and the voice-over in a Disney film, it was these
ads that set the stage for the launch of Priyanka Chopra's career
in the US.

Before the launch of the advertising campaign, *WWD*

magazine asked Priyanka if she felt ready to take on the Western market, and her response was exactly what a Western publication and the Guess team was looking for. She said she partly grew up in the US and referred to herself as an 'amalgamation' of the East and West.

'I'm not too American and I'm not too Indian, but I'm a global citizen, and that's what most people are today,' Priyanka added.[185] 'And I don't want to have to change who I am to try and fit in or cater to a certain audience.'

After the launch of the campaign, Priyanka was invited to open a Guess store in London. 'I told the Guess team there will be a big crowd,' Anjula Acharya says. 'But they didn't realize how big as all the radio stations were broadcasting to avoid Regent Street because a Bollywood star was there. There were thousands of people who showed up. Priyanka shut down the street in London.'

∾

Since 2014, Priyanka has released two more singles. In April of the same year, she took more risks and recorded a cover of Bonnie Raitt's 1991 hit song, 'I Can't Make You Love Me'. 'We were in a car when Jimmy (Iovine) suggested Priyanka should listen to a demo Ester Dean had recorded,' Anjula says. 'And Priyanka was totally thrilled. She was like, "I love this song and I love this version."' But later, Priyanka realized the challenge she was facing. The song has been sung by a number of solid singers, from Adele to George Michael.

'She was nervous,' Anjula adds. '"What if they don't like my vocals or my singing. What if my vocals don't hold?" she asked.'

But with an electronic dance beat—although the song still has its ballad tone—Priyanka's cover took off. The video featured Priyanka with the hunky American television actor

Milo Ventimiglia (*Heroes*, *Gilmore Girls* and now *This Is Us*). In between moments of heartbreak, pillow fights, and jumping on bed, Priyanka also applied henna on Ventimiglia's back, writing his name and throwing Holi colours at him. She spent time explaining Holi in an interview with *Elle* magazine. 'There's a festival in India called Holi, it's a festival of colours, and that's what we do. It's ridiculous. Everyone's drunk in the day, and everyone's throwing each other into colour, and swimming pools are like, pink or purple... And I wanted to have a part of India... my Indianness in the video, but not obviously.'[186]

But the song was a moderate success. As expected, it did very well in India. And in the early summer of 2014, the US edition of *People* magazine recommended it as the single of the week.

In August 2017, in the middle of a packed schedule of projects, travels and her obligations, Priyanka dropped another single, one more EDM (electronic dance music) song—'Young and Free'. Australian producer and DJ Will Sparks collaborated with Priyanka for the song.

*The Los Angeles Times* had said that Priyanka's album would be released by Desi Hits! Universal—a label owned by Anjula Acharya and Jimmy Iovine—in early 2013. That has still not happened. But it is clear that while her music career has not exploded as compared to some of the other projects she has undertaken in the US, she is not giving up.

'It all depends,' Anjula says about the release of the album. 'The word in the music industry is that you have to read the record. Nobody has albums out without two or three singles. Also this is a good problem. In India her music is an instant success. The day after the song is released, we are on top of the charts. But here when you are a new artist—and even when you are not a new artist—it takes so long to build up the momentum. I remember John Legend had a single out in September 2013, but it became a huge hit only in May 2014. It takes a while for people to hear it and for the song to percolate across the globe to get traction.'

# 8

# *QUANTICO* AND FAME IN THE US

THE FBI'S TOP RECRUIT IS NOW THEIR MOST WANTED

QUANTICO

SUNDAYS 10 CTV

FBI

ABCON
utdoor

Church Of
St George
The Martyr
→

Photo: Aseem Chhabra

*H*ow does an actor, a celebrity in one part of the world, become famous in another country—a large nation like the US—where most people tend to be inward looking, and are not much focused on popular culture in the rest of the world? I pose this question to Anjula Acharya. She had told me that her goal was to make Priyanka Chopra 'a face in America'. But by 2014, despite some of her music singles and the big splashy Guess jeans campaign, Priyanka was still not a household name in America.

'There are two ways to become a household name—through a scandal or hard work,' Anjula says, in response to my question. And she should know, since she has watched American popular culture rather closely. 'If she had an affair with Ashton Kutcher (for example) then she would be famous tomorrow. I think in Priyanka's case it is hard work. Our strategy is to build her one brick at a time in America's heart.'

Those words would come true a few years later. Priyanka had started spending a lot of time in the US in 2013–14, in between also finishing her Bollywood commitments. *Gunday* and *Mary Kom* released in 2014. *Bajirajo Mastani* and DDD opened in 2015 and her last Bollywood film *Jai Gangaajal* in early 2016.

California-based journalist Sheila Marikar interviewed Priyanka for *The New York Times* in Los Angeles in January 2014. Her piece ran in *The Times* a month later. Sheila admits that she had not followed Priyanka's career in India. But she had a sense about the Bollywood actress. It was Priyanka's singles and especially her face as a Guess spokesperson that made Sheila pitch the story to *The Times*.[187]

'It occurred to me that this was the first time I had seen an Indian woman get this kind of exposure in the US,' Sheila says. 'But all I knew was that she was getting into the American market more as a model, a pretty face rather than as an actress.

Once when I met her I started talking about her ambitions and
the things she was trying to do in Hollywood. I realized that it
was much more than just being a model for an American brand.'

Priyanka and Sheila talked over lunch, sitting outside on the
sidewalk of the posh Beverley Wilshire Hotel, right where Rodeo
Drive meets Wilshire Boulevard in Beverly Hills, California. This is
the same hotel where nearly thirty years earlier a Los Angeles call
girl—Vivian Ward (Julia Roberts) fell in love with the businessman
Edward Lewis (Richard Gere) in *Pretty Woman*, a film everyone
loves. 'Los Angeles doesn't have as much foot traffic as other
cities, but this is a pretty prominent intersection,' Marikar says.
'There were tourists and tons of people walking around. She
and I sat outside, and not one person came up to her. No one
recognized her. She was wearing sunglasses, but she wasn't in
a disguise or something like that. She was out there herself.'

Things changed fast in less than a year when Priyanka's face
was plastered all across America for the ABC TV show *Quantico*.
'And that was probably one of the last times that happened for
her,' Sheila adds. 'Because now certainly if she is eating anywhere
in the US there are people who would come, take photos of her
and get her autograph. She is a very recognizable celebrity now.'

Anjula's prediction of winning American hearts one brick
at a time came true sooner than Priyanka had expected. But in
her mind she was already a star and it was just a matter of time
before America would get to know her.

She arrived for the photo shoot for *The Times* story with a
large entourage of twelve people. 'When we walk into a room,
it's like *Ocean's Twelve*,' Sheila quoted Priyanka as saying in the
article, referring to the entourage as 'Team P.C.'. Her publicist
had earlier asked Sheila if *The Times* would provide Priyanka
with a stylist. Perhaps, they thought *The Times* photo shoot
would be similar to that of the glossy magazines like *Vogue* or

*Vanity Fair*. So Sheila informed the publicist that *The Times* did not have the budget for a stylist. The talent could appear as they wanted during the shoot. Still, Priyanka brought a whole rack of clothing.

'She had the air of the star, of someone who is very famous, even though she wasn't that famous in America yet,' Sheila recalls. 'It is because of Bollywood and the level of stardom she had attained in India. She knew exactly what her hair should look like. She talked about how she knew when she saw good lighting. She's been in this business for so long that it is second nature to her. She doesn't need a photographer to tell this is the right way to stand. She just knows.'

∿

People can try and chart the course of their lives and careers, but there are always unexpected events which trigger things forward, perhaps even in the direction where one may not have thought of going. In Priyanka Chopra's life, that chance happening was in 2012 when at a dinner party, she and Anjula Acharya met with Kelli Lee, a casting executive at ABC—the Disney-owned American television network. The party was hosted by Ron Meyer, Vice Chairman of NBC Universal. 'It was like a 10-people dinner, and we ended up talking that night,' Priyanka told *USA Today* about the first meeting with Lee.[188]

Priyanka Chopra first took baby steps into American pop culture with her singles, but it is not clear if she was aiming for network television after that. However, she had a pat answer when she was asked why she had considered television to be her first acting vehicle in the US. 'I want to go wherever my work takes me. I want to be able to tell stories globally, entertain globally.'[189]

In Bollywood, stars host reality TV shows or appear on them as judges. Priyanka herself was the host of the TV reality show

*Fear Factor: Khatron Ke Khiladi*. She anchored the third season in 2010. But few switch to television once their careers have taken off in films. There have been some exceptions—Amitabh Bachchan (*Yudh*), Anil Kapoor and Shabana Azmi (*24, India*). In all the three cases, the stars acted in mini-series.

The same can be said for Hollywood. Rarely does a big Hollywood star give up films and join television on a regular basis. Tom Cruise's film career needs a desperate boost, but he is definitely not considering television as the next move. However, some Hollywood stars did make what appears to be a temporary shift to television in series and mostly outside network television. That lot includes Kevin Spacey and Robin Wright (*House of Cards* on Netflix), Matthew McConaughey, Woody Harrelson, Colin Ferrell and Vince Vaugn (*True Detective* on HBO) and the recent outing of Nicole Kidman and Reese Witherspoon (*Big Little Lies* on HBO).

But Priyanka had an empty slate to write on in the US. Her acting career in Hollywood—whether in television or films—was not going to be determined by her star status in Bollywood. She has been asked this question enough number of times—why start all over again, when you have it going so good? 'But there was a time when people (in India) didn't know me also, right?' she told msn.com.[190] 'And I had to introduce myself to people. It feels exactly like that.' When she was pushed, she added, 'I've worked for 13 years in one of the most prolific film industries in the world and then, to come to a completely new country, without familiarity… It was a little scary.'

Film critic Anupama Chopra states that the steps Priyanka took are rare for any industry. 'Here is an A-list actor, who had the courage and ambition to become a newcomer again in another industry.'[191]

Priyanka will never admit to what drove her to make the

move. But film-maker Karan Johar, in an interview, tells me what could possibly be the answer to this puzzle. 'Like everybody else in the business she is ambitious and has a desire to do great work,' Karan says, as he assesses Priyanka's career in India. 'But I always thought that there was a bit of Priyanka that felt she deserved much more and didn't get as much as she can.' Karan suggests that Priyanka had more or less peaked out in her career in Bollywood, but she wanted more—projects that would not only recognize her talent, but also challenge her.

Keli Lee—the ABC executive at that dinner party—had something in common with Anjula. Korea-born, Lee came to the US when she was two years old. 'As a young Korean girl growing up in the US, I learned about American culture through watching television programmes,' Keli told Forbes.com.[192] 'At the time, there was very little diversity on television and no one who looked like me or my family on television.' It is a standard statement that many foreign-born Americans make. The statement is so often repeated that it sounds like a cliché. But there is a lot of truth in it. This truth became the guiding force for Asians like Keli and Anjula. They started their journeys in different corners of the world, but their goals were similar.

Keli joined Disney/ABC, rose through the ranks, and then, in 2001, she launched a programme called *ABC Discovers: Talent Showcase*, an initiative to find people of colour and other races to be represented on television shows. Her team auditions thousands of potential actors of different ethnicities and along the way they have discovered the likes of Oscar-winner Lupita Nyong'o (*12 Years a Slave*), Golden Globe-winner Gina Rodriguez (*Jane the Virgin*), Jesse Williams (*Grey's Anatomy*), Randall Park (*Fresh off the Boat*), Chadwick Boseman (lead in Marvel's *Black Panther*), and Cornelius Smith Jr (*Scandal*). Keli is also the brain behind some of the biggest recent diversity-focused castings on television—

Sandra Oh (*Grey's Anatomy*), Sofia Vergara (*Modern Family*) and Kerry Washington (*Scandal*).

Keli remembers the dinner in 2012 and making that rare discovery. 'Even in Hollywood, it's not everyday that a global superstar like Priyanka walks into a room,' she told Forbes.com.[193] 'And even rarer to meet someone who has the total package of beauty, intelligence, talent, warmth, vulnerability, generosity and charitable spirit. I knew she belonged on ABC.'

Keli and Anjula remained in touch, while Priyanka was in India shooting her films. The conversation went on for some time and, finally, Keli flew to India with Anjula to talk further with Priyanka. Priyanka was shooting for *Gunday* at that time and Keli again charted out the possibilities for her, giving examples of Sandra Oh, Sofia Vergara and Kerry Washington. Priyanka made a few things clear to Keli. 'I didn't need to do anything unless it happened to be the right thing,' she was quoted in *Vanity Fair* as saying. 'So I told her, the only way I would do it is if you find me a show and a path which first will put me in the same position that I am in India.'[194]

In December 2014, Priyanka's team announced that she had signed a one-year TV development deal with ABC. Priyanka released an official statement emphasizing on how she had always been a fan of ABC's shows and the network's efforts of reflecting diversity through its characters, and how she felt honoured 'by the opportunity to share my talent with a game-changing network'.

Sheila Marikar would later remark that her February 2014 piece in *The New York Times* may have triggered the ABC deal. 'What Anjula told me was after my article came out, she used the article as a bargaining chip between ABC and FOX,' Sheila says. 'They were competing with a development deal with Priyanka and suddenly there is a *Times' Style* section piece about how she is the next big "it" girl in America. Anjula presented the article saying, "Hey *The New York Times* is saying this. Which one of you wants to sign a development deal with her?"'

The one-year deal meant that either ABC would develop a project for Priyanka or cast her in an existing project. Priyanka was handed twenty-five scripts for pilot shows to read. She picked four and said *Quantico* was her top choice. And later, she said it was also ABC's top choice.

*Quantico* was created by Joshua Safran whose previous works include the hit shows *Gossip Girl* (CW network) and *Smash* (NBC). In September 2014, trade publications announced that Safran had signed a deal with ABC for the show *Quantico*. The show was described as *Homeland* meets *Grey's Anatomy*. The show revolved around a group of diverse FBI recruits who go through twenty-one weeks of training to become special FBI agents at Quantico, the agency's academy in Virginia. The show was designed to engage the audience by giving them clues about a potential terrorist among the recruits. 'The show is structured to give those at home the fodder to play FBI agents themselves,' Joshua told *Entertainment Weekly*.[195] Joshua partly roped in his impressions about a family member who may have been a CIA agent. But at the time of the writing of the show, Alex Parrish—the role Priyanka Chopra plays—was supposed to be a Caucasian male character.

'Well of course,' says Eric Deggans, TV critic at National Public Radio (NPR), when I mention to him that there was a possibility that Alex Parrish would have been a white man. Eric talks to me from his office in Florida. His writings often focus on race and diversity in American media. 'Every good part starts with a white man,' he adds.

And then the day came when Priyanka went to audition for the role in the presence of Joshua Safran and producer Mark Gordon. This is the first time the star of *Fashion*, *Bluffmaster!* and *Dostana* was going to audition for a role. She showed up wearing a designer dress and carrying a fashionable handbag. Joshua was confused—not sure what character she was going to read. 'She walked in the room, and it was like the molecules shifted in that way that superstars have,' Joshua later recalled in an interview with *The New York Times*.[196] 'I was very confused because I didn't know who she was, but we all sat up straighter.'

'She walked in with all of this Priyanka-ness,' Joshua told *The Wrap*. 'I was like, "This person feels like a star—how come no one has found her?"'[197]

Later, when *The Times* reporter Kathryn Shattuck narrated Safran's reaction to Priyanka, she laughed. 'Ah, I love that, when it happens at hello,' she said. 'I make sure my walk is a good entrance. My heels and my hair.'[198]

But by now, Priyanka was keen to break it into Hollywood and she was ready to ignore this very America-centric view—this time reflected by Joshua Safran—that a big global star is not a star until America and Hollywood discovers him/her. In the globalized world, actors and other talents should certainly go wherever work takes them, but Hollywood's ignorance of entertainment industries outside the US shores—once again reflected in this belief that the *Quantico* team 'discovered' Priyanka Chopra—is astounding.

Months later, the *Quantico* team hired Sharbari Zohra Ahmed, a Connecticut-basesd Bangladeshi-American scriptwriter as the token South Asian to be a part of the show's Season 1 writing team. Sharbari co-wrote episode number 8 with another writer and then she wrote episode 13 all by her self. For Season 2, the show's producers hired another Indian-American writer Marisha Mukherjee. One day, in the writers' room, Sharbari was asked by her co-writers who Priyanka's equivalent was in Hollywood. 'I remember thinking Taylor Swift, just in terms of adulation,' she recalls. 'When you see Priyanka's Twitter or Instagram feed, the adulation that is poured on her by fans in India, and it is sometimes intimidating.' And then she also gave the name of Beyoncé. 'I said she is huge in India.' Some of her colleagues had heard of Shah Rukh Khan, but again, they had no perspective of his popularity. 'I was like you want a comparison, he is the combination of Tom Cruise and George Clooney and Harrison Ford when he was younger and Cary Grant. And they said wow! So that is something Hollywood has to wrap its head around. They are only starting to.'

Joshua's idea of Alex Parrish was a character hardened by tragedy. He never imagined Alex as a bombshell. But on meeting Priyanka, he realized that Alex could also have sense of humour and a heart. 'One of the things we talked about was, "Is she so glamorous that she can't play this regular person?"' Producer Mark Gordon told *The Times*.[199] 'What we quickly came to realize is that she's a huge star internationally, but she's actually quite regular.'

Then there was the question of Alex Parrish's ethnicity. In the show, as it was now broadcast, Alex is the child of an Indian mother and an American father who has spent time living in Mumbai, in India. 'When I got the part we had a whole debate we should change her name, make her more Indian, make her Anjali or something,' Priyanka told NPR's Eric Deggans a few months after the show was launched in September 2015.[200] 'I didn't want to change the character. I wanted to act like Alex.'

'Alex's Indianness was never the focal point of the show,' Sharbari Ahmed says. After Sharbari joined the writing team, the show's producers realized that she was also Muslim—something her name gives away immediately. The fact that Sharbari was Muslim became an added advantage. She could bring in subtle distinctions about the Muslim characters in the show.

'They said she's an FBI agent, she is an Indian American, but they didn't call constant attention to her Indianness,' Ahmed says. 'They put her in there and they didn't make a lot of hullabaloo about it. That was the wisest move when you don't understand what you are dealing with culturally. I did try and talk to the producers that she is so popular in India, the rest of South Asia, the Middle East, North Africa, Eastern Europe. I said there are a lot of us out there and we love our Bollywood movie stars and so it might not have been so terrible to reference her Indianness and the culture.'

There were minor references for those looking for Alex's Indianness. Right at the beginning of the show, in the pilot, as Alex is found in the rubbles of New York City's Grand Central Station, we notice the symbol Om on her bracelet. And in Episode 3, camera briefly pans around Alex's room and we can see a the small statue of dancing Shiva. But that was it.

'My American side is happy that she wasn't exoticized,' Sharbari says. 'But my desi, Bengali side feels like we had an opportunity here and I feel that we could have done more to push the diversity ball.'

It is important to note that while a network like ABC appeared to be progressive by constantly thinking of diversity, it was also shy to really push the envelope. It is cable TV and streaming services that actually bring shows that connect to the newer audiences. That happened with HBO's *The Night Of*, and the Netflix's *Master of None* (both shows won Emmys in 2017) and the Hasan Minhaj show *Homecoming King*. All those shows were streamed in 2016–17, the same time *Quantico* was running on ABC. While *Quantico* failed to bring in the ethnicity of its protagonist as a significant part of the plot line, those other shows along with the hit indie Hollywood film *The Big Sick*, from the summer of 2017, narrated honest stories about South Asians in America. The writers of these shows were not embarrassed about the South Asian experiences in America. The shows did not shy away from talking about those immigrant lives, in fact, they proudly displayed the differences of their protagonists. And they hit the right note not just with South Asians but also with the general audience as well.

As NPR's Eric Deggans says, 'If you create a show that is authentically about a culture, it will speak to people outside that culture too because they respond to the authenticity of it.' He adds, giving the example of HBO's hit show *The Sopranos* that authentically introduced the Italian-American culture of New Jersey. 'I watched that show because I don't know anybody like that. I really enjoyed learning about that culture.'

While Priyanka obviously looked South Asian, *Quantico*'s producers put her through extensive accent training. The American accent she tried to acquire was a matter of much debate, mocking and ridicule in India. It was almost like despite months of anticipation of seeing Priyanka Chopra—the first major Indian actor to appear on a network television show—many Indians were waiting for her to fail and they found her failure in her accent. People acquire accents for various reasons. In Priyanka's case, one reason was because she had lived in the US as a teenager, then, she also had to sing her singles sounding like an American. Now this major role on a television show required her to speak like an American. But sadly, her Indian critics were unforgiving.

Priyanka clarified that the accent training was hard for her, especially rolling her 'Rs' as Americans tend to do. And when the criticism in India hit her hard, she made a joke of it. Speaking in her mostly normal Indian accented English with a bit of Americanism thrown in, she made fun of the situation on *Late Night With Seth Meyers*, 'This is my fake accent, my Indian accent is a fake accent.'[201]

There was at least one journalist in India who defended Priyanka's decision to adopt an American accent while she acted in a television show in the US. This is what Buzzfeed India editor Rega Jha had to say in Priyanka's defence, 'The hate stems from a weird assumption that Chopra worked her ass off to make it to Hollywood, for India. For *us*. Now that she's there, how dare she reassimilate into the culture that shaped her adolescence? How dare she adapt for her work, rather than shout her Indianness from the rooftops at every opportunity? That luxury we happily granted to Hugh Laurie when he learned an American accent for *House MD* and to Renée Zellweger when she dropped her Texan drawl to become the very British Bridget Jones. Just imagine if all of England had protested Christian Bale's American accent in *The Dark Knight*, or if Australia disowned Heath Ledger for not making the Joker more Australian.'[202]

There were times when Priyanka felt the need to explain to the Western media why Alex Parrish had to have an American accent. But she explained it in a tireless and outdated manner. 'I didn't want to be this stereotype of what Indian people are usually seen as in global pop culture, you know?' Priyanka told *Vanity Fair*. 'We don't just have to be Apu from *The Simpsons*.'[203]

It is good that Priyanka took a stand on not wanting to sound like Apu Nahasapeemapetilon, but it also seems like she had missed the bus. Anti-Apu sentiments have been very prevalent amongst Indian American and other South Asian actors for a while now. Most Indian American actors on American television do not have to talk like Apu. There is even a new documentary, *The Problem With Apu* (2017), with several Indian American actors and comedians including Aziz Ansari, Kal Penn, Hasan Minhaj, Russell Peters (well, he is a Canadian American), Hari Kondabolu and Asif Mandavi discussing this issue. The documentary has been covered widely by the mainstream American press. And its success led to the Greek-American actor Hank Azaria—the voice of Apu on *The Simpsons*—to admit for the first time that he was 'perfectly willing and happy to step aside, or help transition it (the Apu character) into something new.'

⌒

In the late summer of 2015, I began to notice a phenomenon—first in the New York City subway stations, then on buses and at bus stands. There were large images of Priyanka Chopra across New York City—staring at us, an FBI badge against her pink full lips. The word 'QUANTICO' was typed in bold capital letters across Priyanka's face. Friends started mentioning seeing the same posters in Los Angeles, Florida, Chicago, Washington DC and elsewhere in the US. I saw a huge billboard in downtown Toronto. A friend even informed me that he saw the same ad behind a bus in Shanghai.

It was thrilling, yet hard to believe. Priyanka Chopra—the Desi Girl of *Dostana*—had her face all over New York City. And hardly anyone in New York City, other than desis like me, seemed to notice it first.

One of her fans, who goes by the Twitter handle @majinnuub and describes himself as an Indo-Caribbean, tweeted on 5 August 2015: 'Been seeing @priyankachopra on every bus on queens boulevard #Quantico !!' And Priyanka responded to the tweet as saying, 'I went to school at Robert F. Kennedy in flushing queens! What a full circle!'

One day, during the shooting of the show on the steps of the New York Public Library on Fifth Avenue, a crowd had gathered and people were taking pictures of Priyanka. *Entertainment Weekly*'s reporter Shirley Li, who was there to cover the shoot, heard this conversation between two women. 'Who is it?' Shirley heard the first woman ask, as she pushed to get a better look at the star. Her friend shouted back, 'It's Selena Gomez!' To which Shirley commented, 'Nope, not even close. It's Priyanka Chopra, one of India's most beloved celebrities (though still a relative unknown in the US) and the lead on ABC's new action thriller *Quantico*.'[204]

A relatively unknown actress in the US—then what happened? Why and how had ABC taken such a huge risk? Normally, in the marketing world, when you bank your whole advertising on someone's face, it has to be an established face. It is normally someone as big as Tom Hanks, Matt Damon or Julia Roberts. It has to be a face where within a millisecond the consumer knows who that is. One does not see a lot of that with someone who is not established in that particular country.

It was clear that ABC was using Priyanka's beauty as the only selling point for *Quantico*, apart from a hint that it was going to be a thriller related to FBI. Gitesh Pandya, editor of BoxOfficeGuru.com, a media consultant for Indian films, and a well-known observer of Indian popular culture in the US says, 'If you are somewhere in America and you don't know who Priyanka Chopra is, you could see the billboard which for most part is only her face and that alone is enough to get someone's attention. The consumer could then take the second step which is, "Let me watch the opening episode and find out more about it."'

Obviously, the network and show's producers hoped the advertising campaign would build an audience for the show. And the fact is that in the summer of 2015, Priyanka had a sizeable Twitter following of nearly 11 million (nearly three years later, by the spring of 2018 that number was up to 22 million). They were so confident in Priyanka's abilities to sell the show that in August 2015, they brought her to the Television Critics Association press tour, flanked by *Quantico*'s two producers Mark Gordon and Joshua Safran. It was becoming clear that Priyanka was going to be the face of what was believed to be an ensemble drama. And she charmed the television journalists by narrating the story about how Keli Lee came to meet her in Mumbai. But she added that she wanted to be seen as an actor first. 'I wanted to be cast for the respect of being an actor, not for the colour of my skin,' *The Hollywood Reporter* quoted Priyanka at the TCA event.[205] 'Going to school in America, I never saw anyone with my colour skin (on TV).'

Many Indian Americans felt a tremendous sense of pride in seeing large posters of Priyanka flashed all over. Sheila Marikar lives in Los Angeles and she had the typical reaction on seeing someone who looked liked her on billboards across the city. 'The degree to which ABC went behind her and the weight they put in for *Quantico*'s advertising and promotion, I can't remember that being done for an actor or actress who had been an unknown in America,' she says. 'For me, as an Indian-American woman, it was sort of gratifying to see someone of my own culture and heritage, to see them in this kind of light. It's surprising, but on the other hand, she's a beautiful woman. She has this multi-ethnic quality about her so it shouldn't at all be surprising in this day and age, given the demographics in America.'

*Quantico* opened to mostly positive reviews, earning a respectable 82 per cent fresh ranking on Rotten Tomatoes. In a tongue-in-cheek review, *The Hollywood Reporter*'s Tim Goodman wrote, 'You should definitely give *Quantico* a look if you're interested in a little mindless eye candy that has enough hooks of a larger mystery to possibly keep you entertained week to week.'[206] He added this about Priyanka, '*Quantico* is fronted by Bollywood superstar and former Miss World Priyanka Chopra, who will now attempt to conquer the last bastion of said world right here on American television.'

*The Wrap*'s Tim Grierson was less kind to *Quantico*. The

headline of his review gave away what he felt about the show—
*Priyanka Chopra Scores in Silly Spy Drama: ABC's series provides sexy
fun, but not smarts to match*. Finding faults with the plot Grierson
wrote, 'For a show about highly trained, incredibly intelligent
agents, *Quantico*'s pilot often succumbs to lame-brained plotting
and a less-than-convincing portrayal of its specialized milieu.'[207]
And on his blog, Grierson added his frustration with *Quantico*.
'I understand that one shouldn't take a show like *Quantico* too
seriously,' he wrote. 'Deeply soapy and filled with sexy, beautiful
people, this ABC drama is meant to be guilty-pleasure eye candy.
But does it have to be so dumb at the same time?' Nevertheless,
the show went on to the third season, although we would learn in
May 2018, that it would be its final season. And its publicity began
with just Priyanka on the new season's announcement poster.[208]

Priyanka was praised by *The New York Times'* critic James
Poniewozik who wrote, 'The strongest human asset in *Quantico* is
Ms. Chopra, a Bollywood superstar and former Miss World who
is immediately charismatic and commanding amid the otherwise
generic ensemble. If there's a problem with her casting, it's that
she may come across as too seasoned and assured to be persuasive
as a shaky, neophyte recruit.'[209]

*The Times'* James Poniewozik had a point there. A quick look
at the cast from *Quantico* indicates that most of Priyanka's co-
actors had played in indie films or other television shows. But
none of the women in the group had been crowned Miss World.
And nobody in that cast was as famous as Priyanka, given her
Bollywood status. Obviously, Priyanka was a much more seasoned
actress in comparison. Sharbari Ahmed also says that despite the
appearances, *Quantico* was never supposed to be an ensemble
show. 'She was going to be the leader,' Ahmed says. 'It was about
Alex Parrish and everybody around.'

There is a thinking that perhaps by pushing Priyanka's

persona, ABC was trying to also reach out to a larger audience—South Asians—especially affluent ones and other immigrants from the Middle East and other countries where Bollywood films tend to be popular. The thinking does make sense because network television ratings are on a constant decline. They are losing out to cable, streaming services like Netflix and other forms of entertainments now available to Americans.

'My hunch is when *Quantico* aired, people who enjoyed her work in Bollywood watched the show, since they see there is hardly any Indian culture on American television,' Eric Deggans of NPR says. 'But when they see that she is pretty standard action heroine character and a lot of those viewers you want to watch the show kind of fall off because it is not really speaking to them.'

*Quantico*'s ratings declined in the second season. There were speculations that the show would not return in the third season. Priyanka made quite a few trips to Mumbai in the spring and summer of 2017 with the hope of signing up one or more Bollywood films. She was reportedly close to working with Sanjay Leela Bhansali on his next production *Gustakhiyan*, a biopic on Sahir Ludhianvi. One report said that Priyanka decided not to take the *Gustakhiyan* project when she learned that Abhishek Bachchan was definitely Bhansali's choice to play Ludhianvi. A *Deccan Herald* report quoted a source as saying, 'For years Abhishek refused to work with her (Priyanka) after she replaced Aishwarya Rai in his friend Rohan Sippy's *Bluffmaster!* Now Priyanka felt uncomfortable working with Abhishek.'[210]

Eventually, nothing materialized from those trips Priyanka took to Mumbai. And then it was announced that *Quantico* was back for Season 3, although it would have only thirteen episodes, as opposed to the normal twenty-two episodes in Season 1 and 2.

'*Quantico* was a hit initially because a lot of people were curious about her, but I think the show they created for her

(Priyanka) was so average that it couldn't sustain the attention,'
Eric Deggans says. 'And it wasn't as game-changing a show as they
suggested it might be. I think the reason was that they created a
vehicle for her which was the kind of vehicle they would create
for a white star. I think that was a mistake.'

The decision of ABC to drag *Quantico* into Season 3 could
have any number of reasons, according to him. 'ABC wants to
be in the Priyanka Chopra business and they may want to keep
other people from being in the Priyanka Chopra business,' Eric
adds. 'It's hard to know what ABC is thinking. It's not like the
show was a failure. Network TV is at a point it can't just let go
of a show that draws an audience. But I do think ultimately it
wasn't that big a show as the people who put together the deal
were hoping it would be.'

Priyanka's popularity surged with *Quantico,* and in 2016, she
won the People's Choice Award for Best Actress in a New Series.
The award show ranks the lowest in terms of recognition for
artistic abilities, with votes gathered through online voting or
polls conducted by research companies. The same year, Dakota
Johnson won the award for the Favorite Dramatic Movie Actress
for her role in the critically panned *Fifty Shades of Grey* (2015). And
the best film of the year was *Furious 7* (2015), which according to
current estimates, is the sixth highest grossing film of all time.
None of these films would come close to winning a Golden
Globe or an Oscar.

On stage with John Stamos, Priyanka gave her first awards
acceptance speech in the US. 'I'd like to thank everyone who
voted for *Quantico*. My first year in America and to come to
another country and to actually get this kind of acceptance is I
guess what America is all about. So thank you all for accepting
me.' And among the people she thanked was her mother, and
her manager—Anjula Acharya.

The next year Priyanka was back at the People's Choice Awards where she won the recognition in the Favorite TV Drama Actress category. This time, she made the standard speech congratulating all the other actresses nominated in her category. 'All of these incredible actresses were the reason that I joined television,' she said, holding her glass trophy in one hand. 'They were the reason that I wanted to be the actor I am here today receiving this award. And being in the same category as them is just so overwhelming. Thank you to all of you who have accepted me and loved my show.'

After she thanked the show's creator and other producers, she shared a regular Priyanka moment with the audience. 'I am just a little psyched. Can I do a little wiggle?' she asked as she shook her hips and the audience cheered. 'Sorry, it's the concussion talking.'

The show was held on 18 January 2017. A week earlier, Priyanka was shooting an action scene for the show, wearing rubber boots, when she slipped on the wet floor and suffered a minor concussion. 'It was actually scary,' she told *USA Today*.[211] 'I've never got hurt before on-set while I do stunts, I always do them myself. This was just a one-off.'

While she was advised rest for a couple of weeks, Priyanka still showed up at the awards show. For a newcomer in the world of American popular culture, it was important for her to be seen and cheered by fans. And then of course, there was the surprise of winning the Favorite TV Drama Actress award.

Priyanka has always been known to stay connected with her fans. During the shoot of *Quantico*, she always made time for her fans—often South Asians, and more women than men.

'Bollywood fans are crazy,' Sharbari Ahmed says. 'Like Beyoncé has the BeyHive, they are the PriyankaHive. She would find as much time as she could to talk to these people, to give them a second. She rarely turns down autographs or says no to taking selfie. She genuinely loves them and doesn't go about huffing that it is so tiring to deal with fans. I found that to be endearing. She was not a diva and I thought she would be.' When *Entertainment Weekly*'s Shirley Li showed up at the shoot of *Quantico* on Manhattan's Fifth Avenue, she saw Priyanka mingling with scores of her fans. When one fan asked for a selfie, Shirley heard Priyanka saying, 'I'll come back, okay? If I do this with you guys, I'll get in trouble.'[212]

Then there were the small gestures of Priyanka that touched Sharbari. She tweeted to say that the Episode 13 in Season 1 *Quantico* was her favourite. And she tagged Sharbari, the writer of the episode on the tweet. On Diwali day in 2015, while Sharbari was sitting in a room in Brooklyn with her co-writers, a box of Indian mithai arrived. It was Priyanka's gift to the writers who had been spending long days and sometimes late into the evenings, creating the show about Alex Parrish.

'Everyone was like, "What's this? Is that really silver? Can you eat the silver?"' Sharbari says laughing. 'And I said, "Yes you can." It was great that she sent the Indian sweets without any explanation.'

# 9

# 'UNFINISHED':
# LIFE POST *QUANTICO*

*Quantico*, the show, may not have been a game changer. But it did change the game for Priyanka Chopra. Every week, millions of Americans sat up to watch the show. Now Priyanka is a very well-recognized celebrity, followed by paparazzi as she steps out on the streets of New York City with her dog Diana, whom she adopted a couple of years ago.

In November 2016, Priyanka visited the Buzzfeed office for an on-camera interview. The website brought four puppies for her to play with as she answered the questions. The frisky little dogs jumped around Priyanka's black leather pants and shoes. During the interview, she talked about how much she missed her cocker spaniel Brando in Mumbai, so when the interview ended, she decided to take one puppy home. And now the press and Priyanka's fans cannot have enough of Diana, the puppy, who even has an Instagram account—@diariesofdiana—with over 62,500 followers.

Since *Quantico* was on ABC, the network has made sure that the star had maximum visibility. 'When you get involved with a broadcast network like ABC they would put a lot of weight in terms of publicity and managerial help,' says journalist Sheila Marikar who worked for ABC News for seven years. 'I think once you sign a development deal with a network they want to make you a star, because they want their money's worth, and they want people to watch their shows, so people can exercise their muscle to make sure they see you and hear about your project.'

And so it was natural for Priyanka to appear on some of the more popular ABC properties—*Live With Kelly and Ryan*—where she made a few appearances, including on April 2017, when she co-hosted the show with Kelly Ripa; *The View* where also she has been a guest and a co-host; *Good Morning America*; and the late night show *Jimmy Kimmel Live*. She even did tequila shots on Ellen DeGeneres's daytime talk show on NBC. And she has been on other late-night shows including *The Late Show With Stephen Colbert* (CBS) where she charmed Colbert with the word 'dance' as she pronounced it in her British-Indian accent; *The Tonight Show Starring Jimmy Fallon* (NBC), where she played Holi with Fallon; and *Late Night With Seth Meyers* (NBC). She even appeared on another episode of Fallon's show where the two had a hot wings-eating face-off. There have been many other appearances and Priyanka continues to win over Americans with her self-deprecating sense of humour, and her adapting to all aspects of American popular culture and way of life.

One of the first comments many of the hosts would say to her is 'You smell very good'. It is amazing how the conversation about Priyanka's mysterious perfume is often brought up. On *Live With Kelly and Michael*, Priyanka joked, 'I just wake up like this.' When she appeared on *The Arsenio Hall Show* in October 2013 (around the time she appeared in the Guess ads), he asked, 'You smell good, what're you wearing?' And she responded, 'Well at the moment, the oil that OJ gave me. Thanks OJ (referring to one of Hall's crew member).'[213]

It happened again in early January 2017 on the *Jimmy Kimmel Live* show. Priyanka settled down on the guest chair and the first thing Kimmel said was 'You smell very good. You smell... you smell like you look. You smell just as good as you look, which is great.' Priyanka was overjoyed by the compliment. 'I love that,' she said. 'I don't know why it happens, but most of the interviews I have done in America open with that.'[214] Kimmel repeated himself, like a teenager who had a crush on the woman he was going to interview, 'Well maybe because you smell so good. Because I don't say that to everyone who comes out here.' 'I am so glad,' a beaming Priyanka added. 'I feel super special. I put in an effort.'

It is an interesting game that Priyanka seems to play on talk shows. She has the airs of an A-list star, something she has picked up from the years of being a celebrity in Bollywood. But she is also very relatable. She loves to become a part of a joke, like a friend one knows, a person you would love to hang out with at a party—not because she is Priyanka Chopra, but because she is like your best friend. And all the while her sex appeal and her star persona is also on display.

All this fame means that Priyanka Chopra is often the 'must invite' celebrity to galas—(her long trench coat-like Ralph Lauren dress at the Met Ball in 2017 was discussed, loved and ridiculed for a while)—awards events, including Oscars and Golden Globes. Only a few Indians have actually gone up on the stage to present awards at such major Hollywood gatherings. In 2008, the Hollywood Foreign Press Association invited Shah Rukh Khan and Freida Pinto to announce *Slumdog Millionaire* as one of contenders in the Best Motion Picture (Drama) category.

Priyanka presented the Golden Globe for Best Actor in TV (Drama) in 2017, because she herself was a major TV star in the US. Her co-presenter was actor Jeffery Dean Morgan. A year earlier, she was there for the 88th Academy Award, dressed in a sexy white dress designed by Zuhair Murad, who is from Lebanon. Priyanka appeared on stage with actor Liv Schrieber to present the Oscar for Best Film Editing. She also appeared at the 2016 Emmys, wearing a flowing red dress, and twirled around on the red carpet and even on stage. She co-presented the award for Directing in Limited Series or Movies with Tom Hiddleston, who had just broken off with Taylor Swift.

The gossip press in India and outside was full of reports about Tom and Priyanka flirting at the Governor's Ball that night. Famous people connecting with other celebrities is always fodder for gossip magazines. And there are always insiders who love to be quoted anonymously. It is hard to say whether anything ever

happened between Tom and Priyanka that night, but eonline.
com was sure about it. 'Tom had his arm around her and held
her close,' the website quoted an insider.[215] 'Afterwards, Tom and
Priyanka talked closely and were holding hands at one point for
a few moments. Priyanka fixed Tom's bow tie and then the two
kissed on both cheeks.'

Priyanka's fame also translated into appearing on magazine
covers. Living in New York, it actually seemed to me that every
month Priyanka was on at least one new magazine cover. Her face
was always seen on the news stands, in the subway stations and
above the ground. A quick search on the Internet shows several
magazines in the US with Priyanka on the cover in the last three
or four years, including *Elle, Maxim, InStyle, Cosmopolitan, Complex*
and *Harper's Bazaar* which listed Priyanka as the Hollywood's 'It
Girl' of 2016. It is a long list of women celebrities, starting with
Janet Leigh in 1960—the year she acted in Alfred Hitchcock's
*Psycho* (1960)—followed by Audrey Hepburn in 1961. The list
includes Elizabeth Taylor, Julie Andrews, Barbra Streisand, Tina
Turner, Diane Keaton, Meryl Streep, Julia Roberts, Gong Li,
Beyoncé, Jennifer Lawrence, and Lupita Nyong'o. And now it
has Priyanka Chopra's name in the mix. She is the only Indian
and the second Asian (besides Gong Li) in the list.

Sheila Marikar believes that Priyanka has entered the
mainstream entertainment business in the US when the time is
perfect for women. 'There is a whole resurgence of feminism in
the US, especially women of colour and diversity speaking out
about their experiences, how those are different from average
white experience. I think magazines and talk shows love her
because she has the diversity play, but she is also dialled into
Western culture and of course she is beautiful, so people are
going to tune in for that reason. She's taking advantage of that,
as she should.'

Priyanka has spoken a lot about diversity in the recent months. Although she has not charted her course in the US after *Quantico*, she clearly seems to be on a mission. And in any case, it is also clear that she really has nothing to lose. So, in an interview with *InStyle* magazine, she spoke about being denied a role in a Hollywood film because of the colour of her skin.

'It happened last year,' she told *InStyle*, 'I was out for a movie, and somebody (from the studio) called one of my agents and said, "She's the wrong—what word did they use?—physicality." So in my defence as an actor, I'm like, "Do I need to be skinnier? Do I need to get in shape? Do I need to have abs?" Like, what does "wrong physicality" mean? And then my agent broke it down for me. Like, "I think, Priy, they meant that they wanted someone who's not brown." It affected me.'[216] The memories of racism that she had faced as a student in the US came back to haunt her. But now, she has the platform and she would much rather address this issue and confront it head-on.

Priyanka scored the biggest jackpot of all with *Time* magazine, which named her among the 100 most influential people in 2016. Priyanka joined the prestigious company of a few other significant people of Indian origin, including Liberian-Indian physician and CEO of Last Mile Health, Raj Punjabi; environmentalist and activist, Sunita Narain; actor and comedian, Aziz Ansari; Google CEO, Sundar Pichai; Flipkart founders, Binny Bansal and Sachin Bansal; US Ambassador to the UN, Nikki Haley (she was the Governor of South Carolina at that time); economist and then Governor of the Reserve Bank of India, Raghuram Rajan; and tennis player, Sania Mirza.

That is an impressive company to be a part of. Priyanka's tribute was written by actor Dwayne Johnson (aka The Rock), her co-star in her first Hollywood film—*Baywatch*. *Baywatch* opened on 25 May 2017 and Priyanka played a villain in it, opposite

Johnson and Zac Efron. And this is what Dwayne Johnson said about the Indian actress, 'She has drive, ambition, self-respect, and she knows there's no substitute for hard work. We always quote the saying "Wear your success like a T-shirt, not like a tuxedo," and she really does—as big a star as she is, as global as she is, as beautiful as she is, there's this interesting quality of relatability.'[217]

Priyanka chose to act in a television show before she took on a film project. That could possibly be because ABC approached her first with the television project. But speaking at the Television Critics Association event in August 2015, she said that it was actor Kevin Spacey who encouraged her to do television. This was two years before Kevin Spacey had to step down from his hit Netflix show *House of Cards* after the embarrassing accusations of sexual harrassment.

'I was doing a master class with Kevin Spacey a couple of years ago,' she was quoted in a report in *The Hollywood Reporter*.[218] 'I asked him, "What (work) did you find most fascinating?" And he said television, when I thought he would say theatre.'

'I just don't know what Frank will do. It keeps you on your toes,' Priyanka recalled Spacey saying this about his *House of Cards* character. And she mentioned to him that she was similarly in the dark about what went on with her character Alex Parrish. 'They tell me nothing. Is that how TV works? That you don't know? It's frighteningly exciting as an actor.'

But if Priyanka was considering to have a longer and lasting acting career, television was possibly the right first avenue for her. Her focus on one television show and the fact that she is a big star meant that it would be more than acting. *Quantico* led to the building of the 'Priyanka brand' in America.

'Had she only done *Baywatch*, people would have noticed her during the promotion and then forgotten her,' says Gitesh

Pandya, editor of BoxOfficeGuru.com. 'Unless you have a groundbreaking film like *Slumdog Millionaire*. Otherwise, it's a very finite attention you get. It builds up rapidly, the movie opens and then it evaporates quickly. If it's a hit, it might be an extra month, but that's about it. With TV you have a season going on from September to May and you have got a lot of press activity and shooting in the summer. So it's a year-round project.'

Did Priyanka and her team think this through? Perhaps they did. *Baywatch* came and was gone. The film was panned by critics and audiences in the US did not rush to the film to catch the sexy tanned bodies running in slow motion on a beach in Miami. *Baywatch*—the TV show itself—was a bigger phenomenon outside the US. It had a huge following in India in the early days of cable television.

Priyanka tried her best to sell the movie, saying that such mindless entertainment was good for the world since we live in such tough times. 'I play a complete villain,' she told *Metro* in UK.[219] She did not mention that she had played the negative role a couple of times in Bollywood. 'It's so much fun to play a baddie in a comedy, because you can do the most ridiculous things and they work. It's such a fun, silly movie. I hope people will get a couple of laughs and enjoy themselves. The world needs a little bit of laughter right now.'

But all the promotion and travels around the world, including a surprise visit of Dwayne Johnson to India which created a media frenzy, did not shake up the film's box office performance—not in India and definitely not in the US. The film's US domestic gross was $58 million, while its budget itself was close to $69 million. Globally—in countries like China—*Baywatch* did decent business and finally ended up earning a total $178 million worldwide. But that was still not an impressive number. For a film that should have been review-proof, *Baywatch*'s domestic box office performance in the US was certainly impacted by the harshness of the critics.

'Thank heaven for Dwayne Johnson, whose foot-wide smile will not be switched off, and who saves the life of the movie,' wrote Anthony Lane of *The New Yorker*.[220] 'Whether it deserves to be saved is another matter.' *The Village Voice*'s Criag D. Lindsey called the film 'ill-conceived and out of whack.'[221]

*Baywatch*, the film, was quite flat and dull. It was never clear why the film's producers decided to revive an old television show when the images of sexy men and women running on a beach seemed quite dated. It was also not clear why Priyanka chose this rather weak film as her first Hollywood production. But this much is true—one of the only fun parts of the film was Priyanka's villainous character, Victoria. She was sexy, mean and funny at times. And she seemed to enjoy playing her character. Unfortunately, there was hardly any word of praise for her in the Western press. In fact, even though *Quantico* was a fairly successful show by then, Priyanka was often not featured in the *Baywatch* advertising campaign in the US.

But at least one critic in India—Raja Sen, writing for NDTV. com—suggested that perhaps Priyanka could be considering *Baywatch* as a visiting card. 'Playing an attractive drug-dealer, she cannily uses this film to deliver a barely-disguised showreel to studios in need of a baddie,' he wrote.[222] 'I'm not a Bond villain,' she even says, perhaps prophetically, in as many words, 'Yet.'

~

In July 2017, Priyanka Chopra attended Giorgio Armani's Privé Haute Couture Fashion Show in Paris. She posted a few pictures from that day on her Instagram account. In one photograph, Priyanka is standing in front of the Eiffel Tower in a white dress, where the back is longer than the front, showing her sleek legs in black boots. That picture got over 7,15,000 likes (she has 24.1

million Instagram followers). In other pictures, she is posing with Armani, and sitting with Isabelle Huppert and Sofia Loren. In a group picture, Priyanka is standing against the show's step and repeat banner, with Armani in the centre, flanked with Loren on his right and Naomi Watts on his left. Priyanka is standing in the middle of Loren and Kate Winslet. Huppert and Chinese actress Tang Wei (the lead in Ang Lee's *Lust, Caution*) are also in the picture.

Seeing Priyanka Chopra with Sofia Loren, it dawned on Shivan Govani, an observer of popular culture and a columnist for *The Toronto Star,* that the two seemed to have parallel careers. 'Like Loren, Chopra's career is built on an undeniable va-va-voom, and like Loren, she has undetected reserve of mettle.' Govani wrote in a large piece on Chopra just before the 2017 Toronto International Film Festival.[223] 'In the same manner that Loren was able to balance being an Italian star and a global one decades ago, Chopra is walking that very tightrope today.'

⌒

Hollywood has a magnetic draw that few can resist. It is definitely the most powerful film industry in the world with its reach and revenue (even though India makes a lot more films than the US). And so most artists around the world—whether they are successful in their home country or still struggling—dream of one day when they can work in Hollywood. In 1999, while promoting *East is East* in New York City, the late actor Om Puri told me that his one big regret was that he would never get roles given to Dustin Hoffman and Robert De Niro.[224] At least Om Puri managed to get small breaks in the West, including two Hollywood films directed by Mike Nichols—*Wolf* (1994) and *Charlie Wilson's War* (2007).

In 1967, Satyajit Ray visited Los Angeles, hoping to make his

Hollywood production *The Alien* with American studio funding, and he considered casting Marlon Brando or Peter Sellers or Steve McQueen in it. In March 1992, while accepting his honorary Oscar from his hospital bed in Kolkata, Ray said this about American films: 'I have learned everything I've learned about the craft of cinema from the making of American films. I've been watching American films very carefully over the years and I loved them for what they entertain, and then later loved them for what they taught.'[225]

During the peak of their careers, Indian actors, from I.S. Johar to Kabir Bedi and Shashi Kapoor, worked in American productions. Shashi had a long-standing relationship with the Merchant Ivory Productions, acting in six of their films. And like Om Puri, Shashi also acted in a few British productions.

Later, a number of Indian actresses attempted to swim in the Hollywood seas. Freida Pinto got a lot of attention after the success of *Slumdog Millionaire*. Soon after, she was cast in a large number of films, directed by A-list film-makers—Woody Allen's *You Will Meet a Tall Dark Stranger* (2010), Julian Schnabel's *Miral* (2010), Rupert Wyatt's *Rise of the Planet of the Apes* (2011), Tarsem Singh's *Immortals* (2011), and a few others. Most of the films, other than *Rise of the Planet of the Apes*, did not do well at the box office. And it was clear that Freida had nothing to do with success of the *Planet of the Apes* sequel. Freida's acting abilities were often questioned. She still works in Hollywood in films and television but she is not getting the plum roles she got immediately after the release of Danny Boyle's multiple Oscar-winning hit film. America's love-affair with Latika from *Slumdog Millionaire* is long over. Meanwhile, Freida's co-star in *Slumdog* and former boyfriend, Dev Patel, has become a relatively big star in Hollywood, with even an Oscar nomination—but then, he is a British actor.

Aishwarya Rai is the only big Bollywood star, in the same league as Priyanka Chopra, who made a concerted effort to work in Hollywood. Her public relations machinery and the agents pushing her made great inroads into American mainstream culture. Aishwarya was on the Oprah Winfrey show, where she taught the talk show host how to tie a sari. She appeared on the *Late Show With David Letterman* to promote her 2005 film with Gurinder Chadha—*Bride and Prejudice* (produced by Harvey Weinstein's Miramax). At the show, she charmed Letterman and even managed to get extra points with the audience, when he asked her if it was common for adult children to live with their parents in India. 'We don't have to make appointments to have dinner with our parents,' Ash replied. She got a lot of laughs for her quick retort. She also denied any plans to move to Hollywood. 'I will be happy to stay in my country,' she said. 'We are gypsies. I think as actors, or people belonging to the fraternity, we travel, wherever work takes you. I don't see at this point to have a permanent shift of residence.'[226]

But in her other TV appearances, Ash either rolled her eyes, giggled or got awkward talking about how she was not comfortable kissing in films. When Bob Simon of *60 Minutes* said that if she wanted a career in Hollywood films, at some point she would have to kiss men on the screen, Ash's response was, 'We'll cross the bridge when we reach it.'[227] That was a sure signal to Hollywood producers not to line up outside her house with scripts.

*Bride and Prejudice* did mediocre business at the box office. Aishwarya followed that up with *Mistress of Spices* (2005). A critical and box office disaster, the film was directed by Chadha's husband Paul Mayeda Berges. Both films did not help Aishwarya's career in Hollywood. She appeared in *The Last Legion* (2007) where she played an Indian martial arts expert opposite Colin Firth and Ben

Kingsley. Despite an A-list cast, that film also failed at the box office. Then, she had one major film—*The Pink Panther 2* (2009), a sequel to the hit *The Pink Panther* (2006), which itself was a remake of the original franchise films. But the second film did very poorly. 'At that time (the first) *The Pink Panther* with Steve Martin was a huge commercial success. During the development stage if an offer like that comes your way, you don't know how it will turn out, but it is a high-profile project. It could have been even bigger than part one. So I can understand someone like Ash taking such an offer,' commentator Gitesh Pandya says.

After *The Pink Panther 2*, Aishwarya's priorities in life changed. She got married to Abhishek Bachchan in 2007 and had a child in 2011. By that time, Aishwarya had put her career in India on hold. And Hollywood was history.

There is currently one Bollywood actor—Irrfan Khan—who continues to work in Hollywood, thanks to the exposure he got with *Slumdog Millionaire*. Previously, he also got a lot of critical acclaim in Mira Nair's *The Namesake* (2006). Irrfan has found the right way to straddle between projects in Hollywood and films in India.

Unlike Aishwarya, Priyanka did not arrive in the US with any baggage and hang-ups. She did hesitate to kiss in Indian films. But then she did so quite a few times in *Andaaz*, *Kaminey* and DDD. Anyone who wondered what Priyanka's position on kissing and sex scenes would be in the US just needed to watch the first five minutes of *Quantico*, Episode 1, Season 1, where her character Alex Parrish is having sex in a car with Ryan Booth (Jake McLaughlin).

Priyanka may have inspired one more South Asian actor to follow her path. It was reported that Pakistani actor Fawad Khan has been approached with a few Hollywood scripts. Fawad's career in Bollywood came to a halt after the 2016 political issues raised before the release of *Ae Dil Hai Mushkil* (2016) and, in any case, there is not much chance to grow in Pakistan. The Bollywood site Pinkvilla.com quoted a source as saying, 'Karan (Johar) told Fawad the cultural stereotypes of Asians playing cab drivers and terrorists had changed after Priyanka Chopra's Hollywood innings. That's when Fawad got interested.'[228]

Priyanka's foray into the US parallels other success stories of foreign actresses. Penelope Cruz was already an established star in Spain having acted in a range of films, including a few with Pedro Almodovar, which also played in art-house theaters in the US. And then she acted in a few Hollywood productions including *Vanilla Sky* (2001), two films with Woody Allen—*Vicki Christina Barcelona* (2008), for which she won an Oscar, and *To Rome With Love* (2012), and *Pirates of the Caribbean: On Stranger Tides* (2011). But Penelope had an added advantage. When she arrived in the US, she was dating Tom Cruise and all Hollywood doors opened for her.

There is also the case study of the Colombian actress Sofia Vergara, who has seen success on the ABC sitcom *Modern Family*. Both Cruz and Sofia used their strong Spanish-accented English to their advantage, getting roles that required them to be Spanish-speaking and yet living in America. And then there is the Mexican actress Salma Hayek, who, in addition to acting in Hollywood films, has also produced movies and television shows.

Perhaps Priyanka is trying to follow Salma's path. In the summer of 2017, it was announced that she would produce a TV sitcom inspired by the life of Madhuri Dixit, when she lived in the US. The pilot episode of the show was to be written by the Philadelphia-based scriptwriter Sri Rao (*Baar Baar Dekho*). But ABC eventually passed on the project and the idea died.

Now in addition to the Season 3 of *Quantico*, which started on 26 April 2018, Priyanka had two other Hollywood films—*A Kid*

*Like Jake* and *Isn't It Romantic.*

*A Kid Like Jake* premiered in January 2018 at the Sundance Film Festival and Priyanka was present to promote the film along wih her other co-stars. But she played a small supporting role of an Indian mother, Amal, whose son Sanjay is friends with the film's four-year lead actor Jake—a transgender kid—who prefers to dress up in girls' clothes and play with dolls. *The Hollywood Reporter* briefly mentioned Priyanka along with the other supporting cast. 'Director Silas Howard…elicits superb performances not just from the leads but from the crack cast of supports, which includes Octavia Spencer, Priyanka Chopra (and) Ann Dowd,' the *The Hollywood Reporter* critic wrote.[229]

IndieWire's critic was not impressed with the film and gave it a B-review grade. The critic also failed to mention Priyanka.[230] *Variety* did mention Priyanka's Amal, but added that the character has 'a charming presence (but) slips in and out of the movie without having a compelling reason to be in it.'[231]

The film was set to play in theaters in the US in early summer 2018, but given the subject matter and not-so-good trade publication reviews from Sundance, it was expected to have a small art-house opening. It is unclear why after playing a small role in *Baywatch*, Priyanka chose another supporting role in a Hollywood film. At Sundance, *Deadline* reporter asked her what motivated her to act in *A Kid Like Jake*. She responded by saying that what drives her as an artist is fighting for onscreen representation and playing characters that defy societal expectations.

'To fight that fight for the next generation that comes in and breaks that concrete, I think for me that's a huge, huge drive,' Priyanka said.[232] 'To just normalize being who I am, and what I look like.' That's a noble idea, but one wonders if that would actually be the key goal for a big Bollywood star to leave everything behind and play supporting roles in Hollywood.

But before her two American films could be released, ABC announced that it was going to cancel *Quantico* after the end of Season 3. The announcement was made on 11 May 2018, three weeks after the show's third season started. The writing was already on the wall. By cutting down the final season to only thirteen episodes, ABC was giving one last shot to the show. But ABC put in no efforts to promote *Quantico*'s Season 3—there were no billboards, no advertisements in subway stations or buses.

In September 2015, 7.1 million Americans tuned in to watch the first episode of *Quantico*.[233] But the viewership had dropped substantially in Season 2 where the show was averaging a rating of 0.7 or 2.8 million viewers. It was ABC's lowest-rated show renewed for one more season.[234] In the third season, the show was averaging 2.4 million viewers per episode on a rating of 0.5.[235] It obviously did not make sense to continue with a show that had lost its audience.

Priyanka did not say much about the show being cancelled other than posting a story on Instagram, where she was dubbing for *Quantico*. Her comment for the story read: 'The last time I ADR for #alexparrish (with a sad face). I'll miss her!'

In the spring of 2018, there were speculations again that Priyanka was looking at a big Bollywood project. Perhaps she already knew that *Quantico* was about to be cancelled. Finally, it was announced that she would act opposite Salman Khan in *Bharat*, which was to be directed by Ali Abbas Zafar. The director's previous works include *Gunday* (2014), and two films with Salman Khan—*Sultan* (2016) *and Tiger Zinda Hai* (2017). *Bharat* is scheduled to open on Eid 2019. Salman and Priyanka have worked on three films together, but not since *God Tussi Great Ho* in 2008.

They seem to have a friendly relationship. Salman used Twitter to announce the project. And he wrote:

*#Bharat ... welcomes u back home @priyankachopra. See u soon ... By the way humari film Hindi hai;)*

And to that, Priyanka responded:

*UP Bareilly* की पली बड़ी हूँ जनाब*... #DesiGirl forever. Very happy to be a part of #Bharat and see all of u on set!!*

Speaking to *Hindustan Times,* Director Ali Abbas Zaffar said that Priyanka was the right choice for the role. 'What's really important is that the character of the girl in the film is very strong and we wanted to cast a very strong actor, who can do justice to that role,' he said. He added, 'This is the homecoming film for Priyanka Chopra. Honestly, she was always my first choice for the film and she readily came on board.'

There was one more possible Indian project in development for Priyanka. Reports indicate, and her mother Dr Madhu Chopra confirmed, that once Priyanka finished her *Quantico* Season 3 shooting obligations, she would act in a joint production of Viacom 18 Motion Pictures and Purple Pebble Pictures—a film based on the life the Indian-American astronaut Kalpana Chawla. The film was to be an Indian production, but since Chawla lived in the US, it was expected to be set there.

But now the Kalpana Chawla film has been shelved or perhaps placed on the back-burner. It was reported that the late astronaut's husband Jean-Pierre Harrison has not agreed to grant the rights to the story to a film production company.[236]

The *Bharat* project announcement means that Priyanka has not closed all her options in India. But her chances of getting ahead in the US depend largely on how well her two new Hollywood films work. And beyond that, will Priyanka look for another TV show in the US? It would certainly be in ABC's interest to develop something else for her, so they can keep her in their family.

Will Priyanka get a serious role like *Barfi!* or DDD in Hollywood where the audience can see her beyond her beauty and sex appeal, and where her acting talent can be tapped? Can Priyanka get the kind of work that goes to A-list stars like Nicole Kidman and Julia Roberts? Could she get the kind of films that Penelope Cruz got when she started her Hollywood career? After all, when Priyanka left India, she was at the same stage in her career as Penelope was in Spain in the mid to late 1990s, when she entered Hollywood.

'I think someone would have to write that part for her and it probably might be an Indian woman writer,' journalist Sheila Marikar says. 'I don't know if people who have written roles for Meryl Streep, Nicole Kidman or Julia Roberts are going to be the ones who will write big roles for Priyanka. It's matter of finding the material. She is probably looking for an opportunity like that, but it has to be the right part.'

I ask Karan Johar the same question. 'It's tough I know, but then who thought she would be here? So I don't know what to say. Today the sky could be her limit.'

But this much is clear. Given the way *Quantico* was promoted with Priyanka's face as the main selling point for the show, the strategy will always be for her to get big projects on big networks, as opposed to smaller niche-market projects on Netflix, Amazon or Hulu.

Her approach has been to reach the most number of people with the things she is doing, including the television appearances and big budget movies such as *Baywatch*. She was in the Pantene campaign, with billboards all over California and New York, and even in TV commercials during prime time entertainment shows. The strategy seems to be—the bigger the company, the bigger the network, the bigger the franchise, the better for her.

Priyanka Chopra's story does not end here. It is an ongoing journey that she is certainly enjoying. She is exploring new avenues, projects and challenging roles. And she continues to define herself, even surprising herself at times.

In May 2017, at the time of the release of *Baywatch*, *Vogue* magazine asked her seventy-three questions, including what she carries in her bag (a small Hindu temple with idols of a couple of Gods, to a bottle of Tabasco sauce). The interview is available on YouTube. Priyanka was animated, seemingly excited about the interview that was shot in one take as the star moved around in what appears to be her apartment in Manhattan.

And then she was asked, 'If your life were a book what would the title be?' Without batting her eyes, she said, 'Unfinished!'[237]

# FILMOGRAPHY

## AS AN ACTOR:

### MOVIES

**THAMIZHAN (2002)**
**Banner/Producer:** G. Venkateswaran
**Director:** A. Majid
**Music Composer:** D. Imman
**Cast:** Priyanka Chopra, Joseph Vijay Chandrasekhar, Nassar, Revathy

**THE HERO: LOVE STORY OF A SPY (2003)**
**Banner/Producer:** Dhirajlal Shah, Hasmukh Shah,
Pravin Shah
**Director:** Anil Sharma
**Music Composer:** Uttam Singh
**Cast:** Priyanka Chopra, Sunny Deol, Preity Zinta, Amrish Puri

**ANDAAZ (2003)**
**Banner/Producer:** Suneel Darshan
**Director:** Raj Kanwar
**Music Composer:** Nadeem-Shravan, Naresh Sharma
**Cast:** Priyanka Chopra, Akshay Kumar, Lara Dutta, Rajeev Verma

**PLAN (2004)**
**Banner/Producer:** Sanjay Gupta
**Director:** Hriday Shetty
**Music Composer:** Anand Raj Anand, Vishal-Shekhar,
Sandeep Shriodkar
**Cast:** Priyanka Chopra, Sanjay Dutt, Dino Morea, Sanjay Suri

**KISMAT (2004)**
**Banner/Producer:** Dhirajlal Shah, Hasmukh Shah, Pravin Shah
**Director:** Guddu Dhanoa
**Music Composer:** Anand Raj Anand
**Cast:** Priyanka Chopra, Bobby Deol, Kabir Bedi, Sanjay Narvekar

**ASAMBHAV (2004)**
**Banner/Producer:** Gulshan Rai
**Director:** Rajiv Rai
**Music Composer:** Viju Shah
**Cast:** Priyanka Chopra, Naseeruddin Shah, Arjun Rampal,
Yashpal Sharma

**MUJHSE SHAADI KAROGI (2004)**
**Banner/Producer:** Sajid Nadiadwala
**Director:** David Dhawan
**Music Composer:** Sajid Ali, Salim-Sulaiman
**Cast:** Priyanka Chopra, Salman Khan, Akshay Kumar, Satish Shah,
Amrish Puri

**AITRAAZ (2004)**
**Banner/Producer:** Subhash Ghai
**Director:** Abbas-Mustan
**Music Composer:** Salim-Sulaiman, Himesh Reshammiya
**Cast:** Priyanka Chopra, Akshay Kumar, Kareena Kapoor, Amrish Puri

**BLACKMAIL (2005)**
**Banner/Producer:** Narendra Bajaj, Shyam Bajaj

**Director:** Sanjay Gupta
**Music Composer:** Anand Raj Anand, Anu Malik, Harmeet Singh, Mustafa Zahid
**Cast:** Priyanka Chopra, Anil Kapoor, John Abraham, Manoj Bajpayee, Tusshar Kapoor

**PLANES (2013) (Voice-over)**
**Banner/Producer:** Tracy Balthazor
**Director:** Klay Hall
**Music Composer:** Mark Mancina
**Cast:** Priyanka Chopra, Dane Cook, Stacy Keach, Brad Garrett, Teri Hatcher

**ZANJEER (TOOFAN in Telugu) (2013)**
**Banner/Producer:** Shabbir Ahluwalia, Anil V. Kumar, Puneet Prakash Mehra, Sumeet Prakash Mehra
**Director:** Apoorva Lakhia
**Music Composer:** Anand Raj Anand, Harmeet Singh
**Cast:** Priyanka Chopra, Ram Charan, Sanjay Dutt, Prakash Jha

**KRRISH 3 (2013)**
**Banner/Producer:** Rakesh Roshan
**Director:** Rakesh Roshan
**Music Composer:** Rajesh Roshan, Salim-Sulaiman
**Cast:** Priyanka Chopra, Hrithik Roshan, Kangana Ranaut, Amitabh Bachchan, Vivek Oberoi

**GOLIYON KI RASLEELA RAM-LEELA (2013)**
**Banner/Producer:** Sanjay Leela Bhansali, Kishore Lulla
**Director:** Sanjay Leela Bhansali
**Music Composer:** Sanjay Leela Bhansali, Monty Sharma
**Cast:** Priyanka Chopra, Ranveer Singh, Deepika Padukone, Supriya Pathak

**GUNDAY (2014)**
**Banner/Producer:** Aditya Chopra

**Director:** Ali Abbas Zafar
**Music Composer:** Julius Packiam, Sohail Sen
**Cast:** Priyanka Chopra, Ranveer Singh, Arjun Kapoor, Irrfan Khan

**MARY KOM (2014)**
**Banner/Producer:** Sanjay Leela Bhansali
**Director:** Omung Kumar
**Music Composer:** Rohit Kulkarni, Shashi Shivamm
**Cast:** Priyanka Chopra, Zachary Coffin, Robin Das, Rajni Basumatary

**DIL DHADAKNE DO (2015)**
**Banner/Producer:** Farhan Akhtar, Ritesh Sidhwani
**Director:** Zoya Akhtar
**Music Composer:** Shankar-Ehsaan-Loy
**Cast:** Priyanka Chopra, Anil Kapoor, Shefali Shah, Anushka Sharma, Farhan Akhtar, Rahul Bose, Ranveer Singh

**BAJIRAO MASTANI (2015)**
**Banner/Producer:** Sanjay Leela Bhansali, Kishore Lulla
**Director:** Sanjay Leela Bhansali
**Music Composer:** Sanchit Balhara, Sanjay Leela Bhansali
**Cast:** Priyanka Chopra, Ranveer Singh, Deepika Padukone, Tanvi Azmi, Mahesh Manjrekar

**VENTILATOR (2016)**
**Banner/Producer:** Madhu Chopra, Priyanka Chopra, Ishan Dutta
**Director:** Rajesh Mapuskar
**Music Composer:** Rohan-Rohan
**Cast:** Priyanka Chopra, Ashutosh Gowariker, Jitendra Joshi, Sulabha Arya, Sukanya Kulkarni Mone

**JAI GANGAAJAL (2016)**
**Banner/Producer:** Prakash Jha, Milind Dabke
**Director:** Prakash Jha, Milind Dabke
**Music Composer:** Salim-Sulaiman
**Cast:** Priyanka Chopra, Prakash Jha, Manav Kaul, Ninad Kamat

**SARVANN (2017)**
**Banner/Producer:** Madhu Chopra, Priyanka Chopra,
Deepshikha Deshmukh
**Director:** Karann Guliani
**Music Composer:** Jatinder Shah
**Cast:** Priyanka Chopra, Amrinder Gill, Simi Chahal, Ranjit Bawa, Sardar
Sohi, Dilnoor Kaur

**BAYWATCH (2017)**
**Banner/Producer:** Dwayne Johnson, Ivan Reitman, Beau Flynn,
Michael Berk, Douglas Schwartz
**Director:** Seth Gordon
**Music Composer:** Christopher Lennertz
**Cast:** Priyanka Chopra, Zac Efron, Dwayne Johnson,
Alexandria Daddario, David Hasselhoff

**A KID LIKE JAKE (2018)**
**Banner/Producer:** Bankside Films, Burn Later Productions, Double
Nickel Entertainment, Paul Bernon, Eric Norsoph, Jim Parsons, Rachel
Xiaowen Song, Todd Speikwak
**Director:** Silas Howard
**Music Composer:** Roger Neill
**Cast:** Priyanka Chopra, Claire Danes, Jim Parsons, Octavia Spencer,
Ann Dowd

**BHARAT (2019)**
**Banner/Producer:** Atul Agnihotri, Alvira Khan, Nikhil Namit
**Director:** Ali Abbas Zafar
**Music Composer:** Vishal Dadlani, Shekhar Ravjiani
**Cast:** Priyanka Chopra, Salman Khan, Disha Patani

**ISN'T IT ROMANTIC? (2019)**
**Banner/Producer:** New Line Cinema, Tod Garner, Grant Scharbo,
Gina Matthews
**Director:** Todd Strauss-Schulson
**Music Composer:** Theodore Shapiro

**Cast:** Priyanka Chopra, Liam Hemsworth, Adam DeVine, Rebel Wilson

## TV SHOW

**QUANTICO (2015–18)**
**Banner:** American Broadcasting Company (ABC)
**Creator:** Joshua Safran
**Cast:** Priyanka Chopra, Jake McLaughlin, Johanna Braddy

# AS PRODUCER

**GIRL RISING (2013) (Documentary)**
**Banner/Producer:** Priyanka Chopra, Martha Adams, Richard Robbins
**Language:** English
**Director:** Richard Robbins
**Music Composer:** Lorne Balfe
**Cast:** Amina, Azmera, Arindol Bagchi, Rekha Banerjee

**BAM BAM BOL RAHA HAI KASHI (2016)**
**Banner/Producer:** Priyanka Chopra, Madhu Chopra
**Language:** Bhojpuri
**Director:** Santosh Mishra
**Music Composer:** Rajesh Rajnish, Madhukar Anand
**Cast:** Amrapali Dubey, Ravi Shankar Jaiswal,
Dinesh Lal Yadav 'Nirauha'

**VENTILATOR (2016)**
**Banner/Producer:** Priyanka Chopra, Madhu Chopra,
Ishan Dutta
**Language:** Marathi
**Director:** Rajesh Mapuskar
**Music Composer:** Rohan-Rohan
**Cast:** Priyanka Chopra, Ashutosh Gowariker, Jitendra Joshi,
Sulabha Arya, Sukanya Kulkarni Mone

## KASHI AMARNATH (2017)
**Banner/Producer:** Priyanka Chopra, Madhu Chopra
**Language:** Bhojpuri
**Director:** Santosh Mishra
**Music Composer:** Madhukar Anand
**Cast:** Anoop Arora, Amrapali Dubey, Sapna Gill, Ravi Kishan

## PAHUNA: THE LITTLE VISITORS (2017)
**Banner/Producer:** Priyanka Chopra, Madhu Chopra
**Language:** Nepali
**Director:** Paakhi A. Tyrewala
**Music Composer:** Sagar Desai
**Cast:** Ishika Gurung, Anmol Limbu, Sujoy Rai, Rupa Tamang

## KAAY RE RASCALAA (2017)
**Banner/Producer:** Priyanka Chopra
**Language:** Marathi
**Director:** Giridharan Swamy
**Music Composer:** Sonu Nigam, Rohan-Rohan, Shaan
**Cast:** Gaurav Ghatnekar, Nihar Gite, Supriya Pathare, Nikhil Ratnaparkhi

## SARVAAN (2017)
**Banner/Producer:** Priyanka Chopra, Madhu Chopra, Deepshika Deshmukh
**Language:** Punjabi
**Director:** Karaan Guliani
**Music Composer:** Jatinder Shah
**Cast:** Priyanka Chopra, Amrinder Gill, Simi Chahal, Ranjit Bawa

# ENDNOTES

1. '2017 Celebrity 100', *Forbes India* (http://www.forbesindia.com/lists/2017-celebrity-100/1665/all)

2. 'Priyanka Chopra Wants to Give Voice to the Voiceless With UNICEF', *Variety*, October 2017 (http://variety.com/2017/tv/news/priyanka-chopra-unicef-goodwill-ambassador-1202583243/)

3. 'The World's 100 Most Powerful Women', *Forbes.com* (https://www.forbes.com/power-women/list/)

4. 'The Power of Priyanka', MarieClaire.com, 13 March 2017 (http://www.marieclaire.com/celebrity/a25804/priyanka-chopra-april-2017-cover/)

5. 'How Bollywood Crossover Star Priyanka Chopra Made $10 Million Last Year', Forbes.com, 30 August 2017 (https://www.forbes.com/sites/maddieberg/2017/08/30/how-bollywood-crossover-priyanka-chopra-made-10-million-last-year/#735e55401dc4)

6. 'The Hunger For More', *Complex*, June/July 2016 (http://www.complex.com/pop-culture/priyanka-chopra-interview-2016-cover-story)

7. 'The Power of Priyanka', MarieClaire.com, 13 March 2017 (http://www.marieclaire.com/celebrity/a25804/priyanka-chopra-april-2017-cover/)

8. 'The Power of Priyanka', MarieClaire.com, 13 March 2017 (http://www.marieclaire.com/celebrity/a25804/priyanka-chopra-april-2017-cover/)

9. 'The Power of Priyanka', MarieClaire.com, 13 March 2017 (http://www.marieclaire.com/celebrity/a25804/priyanka-chopra-april-2017-cover/.)

10. 'The Priyanka Chopra You Didn't Know', Rediff.com, 6 November 2016 (http://www.rediff.com/movies/report/the-priyanka-chopra-you-didnt-know/20161104.htm)

11. 'Diwali is always a fun time: Priyanka Chopra', DNAIndia.com, 25 October 2008 (http://www.dnaindia.com/lifestyle/inner-spaces-diwali-is-always-a-fun-time-priyanka-chopra-1201128)

12. 'Cloudburst flattened the Leh of memories: Priyanka Chopra', Mid-day.com, 13 August 2010 (http://archive.mid-day.com/entertainment/2010/aug/130810-priyanka-chopra-cloudburst.htm)

13. *The Anupam Kher Show: Kuch Bhi Ho Sakta Hai*, 2 August 2015 (https://www.voot.com/shows/the-anupam-kher-show-s02/2/383623/being-candid-with-priyanka-chopra/381705)

14. 'Diwali is always a fun time: Priyanka Chopra', DNAIndia.com, 25 October 2008 (http://www.dnaindia.com/lifestyle/inner-spaces-diwali-is-always-a-fun-time-priyanka-chopra-1201128)

15. 'Priyanka Chopra shares her childhood Christmas memories', *India Forum*, 25 December 2015 (http://www.india-forums.com/bollywood/hot-n-happening/59842-priyanka-chopra-shares-her-childhood-christmas-memories.htm)

16. 'Priyanka Chopra on being called Mimi', Anupama Chopra, *Face Time*, 1 September 2014 (https://www.youtube.com/watch?v=oo5T_iyyQLI)

17. 'Priyanka Chopra *Live With Kelly and Michael*', 4 March 2016 (https://www.youtube.com/watch?v=CmixCz3es3g)

18. 'Priyanka Chopra *Live With Kelly and Michael*' (https://www.youtube.com/watch?v=AfoSXkN-9NY)

19. 'Priyanka Chopra and Jimmy Have Wing Eating Contest', *The Tonight Show Starring Jimmy Fallon*, 4 March 2016 (https://www.youtube.com/watch?v=BkyhFJ6QADU)

20. 'Priyanka Chopra *Live With Kelly and Michael*', 4 March 2016 (https://www.youtube.com/watch?v=CmixCz3es3g)

21. 'Priyanka Chopra is Living in America on a Visa', *The Late Show*

*With Stephen Colbert*, 4 February 2017 (https://www.youtube.com/watch?v=4vMCbXdWEnw)

22. 'The Hunger For More', *Complex*, June/ July 2016 (http://www.complex.com/pop-culture/priyanka-chopra-interview-2016-cover-story)

23. 'I have not regretted any film I have done', RajivMasand.com (http://www.rajeevmasand.com/uncategorized/i-have-not-regretted-any-film-i-have-done/)

24. 'Priyanka Chopra: ' I'm not arrogant, I'm self assured', *The Guardian*, 27 February 2016 (https://www.theguardian.com/film/2016/feb/28/priyanka-chopra-interview-bollywood-us-tv)

25. '73 Questions With Priyanka Chopra', *Vogue*, 24 May 2017 (https://www.youtube.com/watch?v=dOUV2rwMr1g)

26. 'Priyanka Chopra is destiny's child', *Business Standard,* 2 October 2015 (http://www.business-standard.com/article/beyond-business/priyanka-chopra-destiny-s-child-115100200822_1.html)

27. 'Priyanka Chopra on fame and being lonely', *Friday*, 24 December 2013 (https://fridaymagazine.ae/life-culture/people-profiles/priyanka-chopra-on-fame-and-being-lonely-1.1270302)

28. '10 Things You Didn't Know About Quantico's Priyanka Chopra', *Glamour*, 25 September 2015 (https://www.glamour.com/story/quantico-priyanka-chopra-facts)

29. *The Anupam Kher Show: Kuch Bhi Ho Sakta Hai,* 2 August 2015 (https://www.voot.com/shows/the-anupam-kher-show-s02/2/383623/being-candid-with-priyanka-chopra/381705)

30. 'The Priyanka Chopra you didn't know', Rediff.com, 6 November 2016 (http://www.rediff.com/movies/report/the-priyanka-chopra-you-didnt-know/20161104.htm)

31. *The Anupam Kher Show: Kuch Bhi Ho Sakta Hai,* 2 August 2015 (https://www.voot.com/shows/the-anupam-kher-show-s02/2/383623/being-candid-with-priyanka-chopra/381705)

32. 'In "Quantico" Bollywood's Priyanka Chopra Seeks an American Foothold', *The New York Times*, 18 September 2015 (https://www.nytimes.com/2015/09/20/arts/television/in-quantico-bollywoods-priyanka-chopra-seeks-an-american-foothold.html)

33. *The Anupam Kher Show: Kuch Bhi Ho Sakta Hai,* 2 August

2015 (https://www.voot.com/shows/the-anupam-kher-show-s02/2/383623/being-candid-with-priyanka-chopra/381705)

34. *The Anupam Kher Show: Kuch Bhi Ho Sakta Hai*, 2 August 2015 (https://www.voot.com/shows/the-anupam-kher-show-s02/2/383623/being-candid-with-priyanka-chopra/381705)

35. 'Priyanka lost big films as she said no to harassment: mother Madhu Chopra', *Deccan Chronicle*, 11 November 2017 (https://www.deccanchronicle.com/entertainment/bollywood/111117/priyanka-lost-films-as-she-said-no-to-harassment-says-mother-madhu-chopra.html)

36. 'The Barracks and the Beautiful', *Verve*, 10 April 2014 (http://www.vervemagazine.in/people/the-barracks-and-the-beautiful)

37. 'India, Beauty Superpower, is Becoming Jaded', *The New York Times*, 13 December 2000 (http://www.nytimes.com/2000/12/13/world/india-beauty-superpower-is-becoming-jaded.html)

38. 'India, Beauty Superpower, is Becoming Jaded', *The New York Times*, 13 December 2000. (http://www.nytimes.com/2000/12/13/world/india-beauty-superpower-is-becoming-jaded.html)

39. 'The Rediff Diary,'' Rediff.com, 24 January 2000 (http://www.rediff.com/news/2000/jan/24diary.htm)

40. Priyanka Chopra Miss India 2000 Final Question Round by Shah Rukh Khan (https://www.youtube.com/watch?v=BYBZgdfV7dE)

41. 'Exclusive pictures of Shah Rukh Khan and Priyanka Chopra's 3 a.m. friendship', FirstPost.com, 18 January 2012 (http://www.firstpost.com/entertainment/srk-and-priyanka-chopras-3am-friendship-186761.html)

42. 'Priyanka Chopra is very close to my heart: Shah Rukh Khan', FirstPost.com, 30 November 2012 (http://www.firstpost.com/politics/priyanka-chopra-is-very-close-to-my-heart-shah-rukh-khan-538189.html)

43. '*Don 3:* New Actress to replace Priyanka Chopra opposite Shah Rukh Khan', *The Times of India*, 5 April 2018 (https://timesofindia.indiatimes.com/entertainment/hindi/bollywood/photo-features/movies-to-look-forward-to/Don-3-New-actress-to-replace-Priyanka-Chopra-opposite-Shah-Rukh-Khan/photostory/63212831.cms)

44. 'Shah Rukh Khan gets Priyanka Chopra replaced by Deepika Padukone in Don 3?' *India Today*, 23 November 2017 (http://indiatoday.intoday.in/story/shah-rukh-khan-priyanka-chopra-deepika-padukone-don-3/1/1095480.html)

45. 'The Priyanka Chopra you didn't know', Rediff.com, 6 November 2016 (http://www.rediff.com/movies/report/the-priyanka-chopra-you-didnt-know/20161104.htm)

46. 'Miss World Beauty queen, inspired by Mother Teresa', *The Guardian*, 20 November 2000 (https://www.theguardian.com/uk/2000/dec/01/2)

47. 'Smalltown girl conquers world', *The Hindu*, 2 December 2000 (http://www.thehindu.com/2000/12/02/stories/02020004.htm)

48. 'India, Beauty Superpower, Is Becoming Jaded', *The New York Times*, 13 December 2000 (https://www.nytimes.com/2000/12/13/world/india-beauty-superpower-is-becoming-jaded.html)

49. 'Priyanka Chopra: The girl who leapt through time', *Hindustan Times*, 10 October 2015 (http://www.hindustantimes.com/brunch/priyanka-chopra-the-girl-who-leapt-through-time/story-Rt4Vwx9Nb8c9z0Damv9N6K.html)

50. 'UP CM favours ban on beauty contests', Rediff.com, 13 December 2000 (http://www.rediff.com/news/2000/dec/13up1.htm)

51. 'Woman accuses Miss World's father of sexual abuse', *Gulf News*, 23 January 2001 (http://gulfnews.com/news/uae/general/woman-accuses-miss-world-s-father-of-sexual-abuse-1.408377)

52. 'Miss World's Father Faces Abuse Case', *The Telegraph*, 15 January 2000 (https://www.telegraphindia.com/1010116/front_pa.htm)

52. 'Miss World's father says sexual abuse charges bizarre', *Gulf News*, 18 February 2001 (http://gulfnews.com/news/uae/general/miss-world-s-father-says-sexual-abuse-charges-bizarre-1.415547)

54. 'Priyanka does world of good', Rediff.com, 3 July 2002 (http://www.rediff.com/entertai/2002/jul/03priyan.htm)

55. 'Priyanka does world of good', Rediff.com, 3 July 2002 (http://www.rediff.com/entertai/2002/jul/03priyan.htm)

56. 'Priyanka does a world of good', Vivek Fernandes, Rediff.com, 3 July 2002 (http://www.rediff.com/entertai/2002/jul/03priyan.htm)

57. 'I don't see myself as "sexy": Priyanka', RajeevMasand.com (http://www.rajeevmasand.com/uncategorized/i-dont-see-myself-as-sexy-priyanka/)

58. 'I don't see myself as "sexy": Priyanka', RajeevMasand.com, (http://www.rajeevmasand.com/uncategorized/i-dont-see-myself-as-sexy-priyanka/)

59. 'Hrithik, Priyanka are at top of their art form', *Bombay Times*, 30 October 2013 (http://www.knkactinginstitute.com/pdf/Kishore-Namit-Kapoor-FP-30-10-2013.pdf)

60. '*Humraaz* will not go bust', Rediff.com, 5 July 2002 (http://www.rediff.com/entertai/2002/jul/05abbas.htm)

61. '*Thamizhan*', *The Hindu*, 19 April 2002 (http://www.thehindu.com/thehindu/fr/2002/04/19/stories/2002041900820203.htm)

62. 'From beauty pageant to celluloid', *The Hindu*, 14 December 2001 (https://web.archive.org/web/20131207145033/http://www.hindu.com/thehindu/fr/2001/12/14/stories/2001121400720200.htm)

63. 'I don't see myself as "sexy": Priyanka', RajeevMasand.com (http://www.rajeevmasand.com/uncategorized/i-dont-see-myself-as-sexy-priyanka/)

64. '*The Hero: Love Story of a Spy*', *Variety*, 16 April 2003 (http://variety.com/2003/film/reviews/the-hero-love-story-of-a-spy-1200542160/)

65. 'A comicbook spy movie', Rediff.com, 11 April 2003 (http://www.rediff.com/movies/2003/apr/11hero.htm)

66. '*Andaaz:* Flight to boredom', Rediff.com, 24 May 2003 (http://www.rediff.com/movies/2003/may/23andaaz.htm)

67. '*Mujhse Shaadi Karogi* is another *Main Hoon Na*, "Rediff.com, 30 July 2004 (http://www.rediff.com/movies/2004/jul/30mujhse.htm)

68. '*Mujhse Shaadi Karogi*', *The Hindu*, 6 August 2004, (http://www.thehindu.com/thehindu/fr/2004/08/06/stories/2004080602740301.htm)

69. '*Mujhse Shaadi Karogi*', *The Times of India*, 2 August 2004, (https://timesofindia.indiatimes.com/bollywood/Mujhse-Shaadi-Karoge/articleshow/799491.cms)

70. 'Film review: Abbas-Mustan's *Aitraaz* starring Akshay Kumar, Priyanka Chopra', *India Today*, 29 November 2004 (https://www.indiatoday.in/magazine/your-week/story/20041129-film-review-of-aitraaz-by-abbas-mustan-starring-akshay-kumar-priyanka-chopra-789172-2004-11-29)

71. '*Aitraaz* (film review)', Sify.com, 15 November 2004 (https://web.archive.org/web/20161231204336/http:/www.sify.com/movies/aitraaz-news-review-kkfvEtbifhgsi.html)

72. 'To Catch a Star: Priyanka on her best role', RajivMasand.com (http://www.rajeevmasand.com/uncategorized/to-catch-a-star-priyanka-on-her-best-role/)

73. '*Koffee with Karan*: Season 1', Episode 17, 26 March 2005 (http://www.hotstar.com/tv/koffee-with-karan/1525/priyanka-chopra-and-arjun-rampal/1000004958)

74. 'Akshay Kumar's alleged love affairs', *The Times of India*, 8 June 2014, (https://timesofindia.indiatimes.com/entertainment/hindi/bollywood/photo-features/akshay-kumars-alleged-love-affairs/akshay-kumars-alleged-love-affairs/photostory/36250580.cms)

75. 'Did you know? *Barsaat* would have been Priyanka Chopra and Akshay Kumar's 6th last film together', DNAIndia.com, 8 October 2017 (http://www.dnaindia.com/bollywood/report-did-you-know-barsaat-would-have-been-priyanka-chopra-and-akshay-kumar-s-6th-last-film-together-2551216)

76. 'Akki-Twinkle pair set to split?' *The Times of India*, 29 September 2004 (https://timesofindia.indiatimes.com/entertainment/hindi/bollywood/news/Akki-Twinkle-pair-set-to-split/articleshow/868270.cms)

77. 'Akshay Kumar on his "tiff" with Priyanka Chopra: "Let's call Priyanka and find out the truth"', *The Indian Express*, 3 February 2017 (http://indianexpress.com/article/entertainment/bollywood/akshay-kumar-on-his-tiff-with-priyanka-chopra-lets-call-priyanka-and-find-out-the-truth-4506126/)

78. '*Koffee With Karan*: Season 2, Episode 2', 17 February 2007 (http://www.hotstar.com/tv/koffee-with-karan/1525/hrithik-and-priyanka-chopra/1000004207)

79.  'Priyanka's ex-secretary Prakash Jaju arrested', WebIndia123.com, 26 August 2008 (https://news.webindia123.com/news/articles/India/20080826/1037084.html)

80.  'PeeCee Sends Legal Notice To Former Boyfriend And Manager', *Mumbai Mirror*, 2 June 2014 (https://mumbaimirror.indiatimes.com/entertainment/bollywood/PeeCee-sends-legal-notice-to-former-boyfriend-and-manager/articleshow/35937696.cms)

81.  'Priyanka Chopra's mother Madhu calls Prakash Jaju "a liar" over suicide claims', *The Indian Express*, 4 April 2016 (http://indianexpress.com/article/entertainment/bollywood/priyanka-chopras-mother-madhu-slams-prakash-jaju-for-daughters-suicide-claims/)

82.  'Koffee With Karan: Season 3, Episode 7', 19 December 2010 (http://www.hotstar.com/tv/koffee-with-karan/1525/priyanka-chopra-and-shahid-kapoor/1000004237)

83.  'Priyanka replaces Ash in Sippy's *Bluffmaster!*', *Hindustan Times* (http://www.hindustantimes.com/india/priyanka-replaces-ash-in-sippy-s-bluff-master/story-2cA7Anfo8w07IZDLLheSlM.html)

84.  'Chatting with the real bluffmaster', Rediff.com, 22 December 2005 (http://www.rediff.com/movies/report/rohan/20051222.htm)

85.  '*Bluffmaster*: A timepass blast', Rediff.com, 16 December 2005 (http://www.rediff.com/movies/2005/dec/16bluff.htm)

86.  'Movie review of *Bluffmaster*, starring Abhishek Bachchan, Priyanka Chopra', *India Today*, 2 January 2006 (http://indiatoday.intoday.in/story/movie-review-of-bluffmaster-starring-abhishek-bachchan-priyanka-chopra/1/182157.html)

87.  'I don't see myself as "sexy": Priyanka', RajeevMasand.com, (http://www.rajeevmasand.com/uncategorized/i-dont-see-myself-as-sexy-priyanka/)

88.  '*Krrish* Tells the Further Adventures of a Bollywood Superhero', *The New York Times*, 30 June 2006 (http://www.nytimes.com/2006/06/30/movies/30krri.html)

89.  'Hrithik makes Krrish work', Rediff.com, 23 June 2006 (http://www.rediff.com/movies/2006/jun/23krrish.htm)

90.  '*Krrish*: Old tricks, new trappings', *Hindustan Times*, 26 June 2006

(https://web.archive.org/web/20140607122038/http://www.hindustantimes.com/News-Feed/NM12/Krrish-Old-tricks-new-trappings/Article1-113686.aspx)

91. 'Priyanka replaces Ash in Sippy's *Bluffmaster*', *Hindustan Times*, 29 June 2005 (http://www.hindustantimes.com/india/priyanka-replaces-ash-in-sippy-s-bluff-master/story-2cA7Anfo8w07IZDLLheSlM.html)

92. 'Hrithik makes *Krrish* work', Rediff.com, 23 June 2006 (http://www.rediff.com/movies/2006/jun/23krrish.htm)

93. '*Krrish 3* review: Krrash landing for Hrithik, Vivek, Priyanka and Kangana', FirstPost.com, 1 November 2013 (http://www.firstpost.com/entertainment/krrish-3-review-krraash-landing-for-hrithik-vivek-priyanka-and-kangana-1205619.html).

94. '*Krrish 3* is a colossal waste', Rediff.com, 1 November 2013 (http://www.rediff.com/movies/report/review-krrish-3-is-a-colossal-waste/20131101.htm)

95. 'Priyanka Chopra declares herself heroine of *Krrissh 3*. Is she insecure of Kangana?' *India Today*, 18 October 2013 (http://indiatoday.intoday.in/story/priyanka-chopra-says-i-am-the-heroine-of-krrish-3/1/316871.html).

96. 'Sultry Kangana has the last laugh', *India Today*, 7 November 2013 (http://indiatoday.intoday.in/story/kangana-has-the-last-laugh-after-the-release-of-krrish-3/1/322033.html)

97. 'Kangana not insecure about acting with Priyanka', DNAIndia.com, 28 October 2007 (http://www.dnaindia.com/entertainment/report-kangana-not-insecure-about-acting-with-priyanka-1130342)

98. 'Masand's verdit: Fashion is all masala, no reality', RajeevMasand.com (http://www.rajeevmasand.com/uncategorized/masands-verdict-fashion-is-all-masala-no-reality/).

99. 'Fashion does not touch you', Rediff.com, 29 October 2008 (http://www.rediff.com/movies/2008/oct/29fashion.htm)

100. 'When Hritikh Roshan made headlines', *The Times of India*, 21 February 2018 (https://timesofindia.indiatimes.com/entertainment/hindi/bollywood/when-hrithik-roshan-made-headlines/photostory/45790830.cms)

101. 'Dostana is injuriously entertaining', Rediff.com, 14 November

2008    (http://www.rediff.com/movies/2008/nov/14dostana-is-injuriously-entertaining.htm)

102. 'Masand's verdict: *Dostana* | Dasvidaniya', RajeevMasand. com (http://www.rajeevmasand.com/uncategorized/masands-verdict-dostana-dasvidaniya/)

103. 'Movie review: *Kaminey*', The Indian Express, 14 August 2009, (http://archive.indianexpress.com/news/movie-review-kaminey/502164/2)

104. '*Kaminey* review: Very, very fexy', Rediff.com, 12 August 2009 (http://movies.rediff.com/report/2009/aug/12/kaminey-review.htm)

105. 'What Happened When Kareena and Shahid Kapoor Broke-Up While Shooting For *Jab We Met*', Cosmopolitan.in, 24 October 2017 (https://www.cosmopolitan.in/celebrity/news/a12030/heres-what-happened-when-kareena-and-shahid-kapoor-broke-up-while-shooting-for-jab-we-met)

106. '*Koffee With Karan*: Season 3, Episode 7', 19 December 2010 (http://www.hotstar.com/tv/koffee-with-karan/1525/priyanka-chopra-and-shahid-kapoor/1000004237)

107. 'Shahid Kapoor was at my apartment admits Priyanka Chopra', DNAIndia.com, 2 February 2011 (http://www.dnaindia.com/entertainment/report-shahid-kapur-was-at-my-apartment-admits-priyanka-chopra-1502096)

108. '*Koffee With Karan*: Season 4, Episode 6, 5 January 2014 (http://www.hotstar.com/tv/koffee-with-karan/1525/priyanka-chopra-and-deepika-padukone/1000004258)

109. 'Priyanka Chopra on *The Late Show With Colbert*', 4 February 2017 (https://www.youtube.com/watch?v=4vMCbXdWEnw&t=251s)

110. Robert De Niro, imdb.com (http://www.imdb.com/name/nm0000134/?ref_=fn_al_nm_2)

111. 'Priyanka—I don't think I can match up to Zeenat', Sify.com, 18 October 2006 (http://www.sify.com/movies/priyanka-i-don-t-think-i-can-match-up-to-zeenat-news-bollywood-kkfvhNjcdaesi.html)

112. 'I want Priyanka Chopra to do my biopic: Zeenat Aman',

*Deccan Chronicle*, 5 May 2017 (http://www.deccanchronicle. com/entertainment/bollywood/050517/i-want-priyanka-chopra-to-do-my-biopic-zeenat-aman.html)

113. 'SRK pays just tribute to Big B's Don', Rediff.com, 20 October 2006 (http://www.rediff.com/movies/2006/oct/20don.htm)

114. 'Shah Rukh's "Sexy Twisted" Don Triumphs Over A Loose Plot And Languid Pace To Make It Worth A Watch', *The Telegraph*, 24 December 2011 (https://www.telegraphindia.com/1111224/ jsp/entertainment/story_14921919.jsp)

115. 'Anupama Chopra's review: *Barfi*', *Hindustan Times*, 15 September 2011 (http://www.hindustantimes.com/ movie-reviews/anupama-chopra-s-review-barfi/story-8rCfZkjHqQrOIiNKDvycJM.html)

116. 'In *Barfi* Priyanka is like a cute puppy: Ranbir Kapoor', FirstPost.com, 3 June 2012 (http://www.firstpost.com/ entertainment/in-barfi-priyanka-is-like-a-cute-puppy-ranbir-kapoor-364918.html)

117. '*Koffee with Karan*: Season 4, Episode 6', 5 January 2014 (http:// www.hotstar.com/tv/koffee-with-karan/1525/priyanka-chopra-and-deepika-padukone/1000004258)

118. 'Priyanka Chopra redeems herself in latest item song "Ram Chahe Leela" from *Ramleela*', DNAIndia.com, 25 October 2013 (http://www.dnaindia.com/entertainment/report-priyanka-chopra-redeems-herself-in-latest-item-song-ram-chahe-leela-from-ramleela-1908751)

119. '*Koffee With Karan*: Season 4, Episode 6', 5 January 2014 (http:// www.hotstar.com/tv/koffee-with-karan/1525/priyanka-chopra-and-deepika-padukone/1000004258)

120. '*Gunday* is utter garbage', Rediff.com, 14 February 2014 (http://www.rediff.com/movies/review/review-gunday-is-utter-garbage/20140214.htm)

121. 'Film Review: *Gunday*', *Variety*, 16 February 2014 (http://variety. com/2014/film/reviews/film-review-gunday-1201103256/)

122. 'Bollywood's thinking is boxed in', *Mumbai Mirror*, 16 April 2013.

123. '*Mary Kom* review: This Priyanka Chopra film is a disservice to the boxer', FirstPost.com, 6 September 2014 (https://www.

firstpost.com/entertainment/mary-kom-review-this-priyanka-chopra-film-is-a-disservice-to-the-boxer-1696517.html)

124. 'Film review: *Mary Kom*', LiveMint.com, 5 September 2015 (https://www.livemint.com/Leisure/LsAWZGZiMuRgCKLHK38GaK/Film-Review--Mary-Kom.html)

125. 'I have the highest regard for Priyanka Chopra's talent: Farhan Akhtar', *The Indian Express*, 13 January 2016 (http://indianexpress.com/article/entertainment/bollywood/i-have-highest-regard-for-priyanka-chopras-talent-farhan-akhtar/)

126. 'Priyanka Chopra and Ranveer Singh on the bittersweet comedy *Dil Dhadakne Do*', *The National*, 2 June 2015 (https://www.thenational.ae/arts-culture/priyanka-chopra-and-ranveer-singh-on-the-bittersweet-comedy-dil-dhadakne-do-1.98438 )

127. 'Priyanka Chopra did not want to be Kashibai in *Bajirao Mastani*', DNAIndia.com, 21 November 2015 (http://www.dnaindia.com/entertainment/report-priyanka-chopra-did-not-want-to-be-kashibai-in-bajirao-mastani-2147518)

128. 'What made Priyanka Chopra do *Bajirao Mastani*? This, and 6 more questions answered', *Catch News*, 14 February 2017 (http://www.catchnews.com/bollywood-news/priyanka-chopra-finally-revealed-that-why-did-work-in-sanjay-leela-bhansali-bajirao-mastani-despite-the-fact-that-it-is-all-about-ranveer-singh-and-deepika-padukone-6-interesting-answers-priyanka-chopra-gave-1450349217.html)

129. 'Creating Kashibai', *The Hindu*, 18 December 2015 (http://www.thehindu.com/news/cities/mumbai/creating-kashibai/article8003512.ece)

130. '*Bajirao Mastani*, A Bollywood Forbidden Romance', *The New York Times*, 17 December 2015 (https://www.nytimes.com/2015/12/18/movies/review-bajirao-mastani-a-bollywood-forbidden-romance.html?_r=0)

131. '*Bajirao Mastani* review—lusty yet progressive historical love triangle', *The Guardian*, 23 December 2015 (https://www.theguardian.com/film/2015/dec/23/bajirao-mastani-review-historical-love-triangle-deepika-padukone-ranveer-singh-priyanka-chopra)

132. '*Bajirao Mastani* review by Anupama Chopra: Soaring, searing,

sumptuous', *Hindustan Times*, 22 December 2015 (http://www.hindustantimes.com/movie-reviews/bajirao-mastani-review-by-anupama-chopra-soaring-searing-sumptuous/story-gZmskukJnTmbRtcS15D3XK.html)

133. 'Priyanka, Ranveer are terrific in *Bajirao Mastani*', Rediff.com, 18 December 2015 (http://www.rediff.com/movies/report/review-priyanka-ranveer-are-terrific-in-bajirao-mastani/20151218.htm

134. 'Jai Gangaajal movie review: Priyanka Chopra's too-sophisticated unmade-up-make-up is very distracting', *The Indian Express*, 6 March 2016 (http://indianexpress.com/article/entertainment/movie-review/jai-gangaajal-movie-review-priyanka-chopra-jai-gangaajal-review-stars/)

135. 'Jai Gangaajal: Copping the drama', *The Hindu*, 5 March 2016 (http://www.thehindu.com/features/cinema/cinema-reviews/jai-gangaajal-review-priyanka-chopra-prakash-jha/article8316012.ece)

136. 'It's PeeCee the Producer', *Mumbai Mirror*, 21 May 2014 (https://mumbaimirror.indiatimes.com/entertainment/bollywood//articleshow/35405185.cms?)

137. 'Madamji: Priyanka Chopra ropes in Madhur Bhandarkar for maiden production venture', *The Times of India*, 20 August 2014 (http://timesofindia.indiatimes.com/entertainment/hindi/bollywood/news/Madamji-Priyanka-Chopra-ropes-in-Madhur-Bhandarkar-for-maiden-production-venture/articleshow/40408114.cms)

138. 'Priyanka Chopra wants to promote new talent', DNAIndia.com, 14 January 2016 (http://www.dnaindia.com/entertainment/report-priyanka-chopra-wants-to-promote-new-talent-2165696)

139. 'Priyanka Chopra on *BBC Asian Radio* Sarvann Interview', 29 January 2017 (https://www.youtube.com/watch?v=SFarrLCAr0I)

140. 'The Priyanka Chopra you didn't know', Rediff.com, 6 November 2016 (http://www.rediff.com/movies/report/the-priyanka-chopra-you-didnt-know/20161104.htm)

141. 'Priyanka Chopra's Banner in a Spot of Bother', Mid-day.com,

8 January 2016, (http://www.mid-day.com/articles/priyanka-chopras-production-banner-in-a-spot-of-bother/16842198)

142. 'Marathi-Punjabi films that made the mark', *The Hindu*, 26 December 2016 (http://www.thehindu.com/entertainment/movies/Marathi-Punjabi-films-that-made-a-mark-in-2016/article16944908.ece1)

143. 'Priyanka Chopra and her mom Madhu Chopra disappointed with "Newton" being India's official entry to Oscars?', DNAIndia.com, 26 September 2017 (http://www.dnaindia.com/bollywood/report-priyanka-chopra-and-her-mom-madhu-chopra-disappointed-with-newton-being-nominated-for-oscars-2548344)

144. 'Priyanka Chopra on *BBC Asian Radio* Sarvann Interview', 29 January 2017 (https://www.youtube.com/watch?v=SFarrLCAr0I)

145. 'Priyanka Chopra Wants To Kick Down The Door Of Racism, *ET Canada*, YouTube, 7 September 2017 (https://www.youtube.com/watch?v=JUHM2cWei9c)

146. 'You dense, ignorant imbecile': Priyanka Chopra faces online backlash for "inaccurate" Sikkim comments', *Hindustan Times*, 14 September 2017 (https://www.hindustantimes.com/bollywood/priyanka-chopra-faces-backlash-for-calling-sikkim-troubled-with-insurgency-pahuna-first-film-from-region/story-GBXX9wWEBkBcX3IHTf3DKL.html)

147. 'Priyanka Chopra apologizes after being attacked for calling Sikkim insurgency-hit', *India Today*, 14 September 2017 (http://indiatoday.intoday.in/story/priyanka-chopra-attacked-sikkim-insurgency-tiff/1/1047589.html)

148. 'Never meant to imply that Sikkim has insurgency: Priyanka Chopra', *Khaleej Times*, 15 September 2017 (https://www.khaleejtimes.com/citytimes/bollywood/never-meant-to-imply-sikkim-has-insurgency-priyanka-chopra)

149. 'Trolled, Priyanka Chopra Apologises For Calling Sikkim "Trouble By Insurgency"', NDTV.com, 14 September 2017 (https://www.ndtv.com/entertainment/priyanka-chopra-made-people-very-angry-by-calling-sikkim-insurgency-troubled-1750119)

150. 'Priyanka Deletes Holocaust Memorial Selfies After Online

Backlash', TheQuint.com, 1 June 2017 (https://www.thequint. com/entertainment/priyanka-chopra-deletes-holocaust-memorial-selfies)

151. 'Indian Baywatch star criticised for Berlin "Holocaust selfies"', TheQuint.com, 1 June 2017 (https://www.thequint.com/ entertainment/priyanka-chopra-deletes-holocaust-memorial-selfies)

152. 'Bollywood star Priyanka Chopra apologises over "insensitive" refugee T-shirt', Reuters, 18 October 2016 (https://www. theguardian.com/world/2016/oct/18/bollywood-star-priyanka-chopra-apologises-over-insensitive-refugee-t-shirt)

153. 'Immigrant, Refugee T-Shirt: Feel Horrible, Says Priyanka Chopra', NDTV, 18 October 2016 (https://www.youtube.com/ watch?v=dMRTeYvlYaY)

154. 'Anjula Acharia-Bath: The angel investor propelling Priyanka Chopra's American dream', LiveMint.com, 4 October 2015 (http://www.livemint.com/Sundayapp/3fOentBqW1R01IznNXJ PkJ/Anjula-AchariaBath-The-angel-investor-propelling-Priyanka. html)

155. 'New Trinity Ventures Partner Anjula Achaira Bath Connects Tech and Tinseltown, East and West', Forbes.com, 26 October 2015 (https://www.forbes.com/sites/anushayhossain/2015/10/26/ new-trinity-ventures-partner-anjula-acharia-bath-connects-tech-and-tinseltown-east-and-west/#3e62765932b7).

156. 'Anjula Acharia-Bath: The angel investor propelling Priyanka Chopra's American dream', LiveMint.com, 4 October 2015 (http://www.livemint.com/Sundayapp/3fOentBqW1R01IznNXJ PkJ/Anjula-AchariaBath-The-angel-investor-propelling-Priyanka. html)

157. 'Music label aims to put pop in India', *Variety*, 3 March 2014 (http://variety.com/2012/music/news/music-label-aims-to-put-pop-in-india-1118050969/)

158. 'The Reluctant Singer', *The Indian Express*, 27 October 2012 (http:// archive.indianexpress.com/news/the-reluctant-singer/1022671/)

159. 'Bollywood's Priyanka Chopra as pioneering pop act in U.S.', *Los Angeles Times*, 20 November 2012 (http://articles.latimes.

com/2012/nov/20/entertainment/la-et-ms-1120-bollywood-pop-20121120)

160. 'Priyanka Chopra & Anjula Acharia Bath, HuffPost Live (https://www.youtube.com/watch?v=u4-M8v1wMR0)

161. 'Bollywood's Priyanka Chopra as pioneering pop act in U.S.', *Los Angeles Times*, 20 November 2012 (http://articles.latimes.com/2012/nov/20/entertainment/la-et-ms-1120-bollywood-pop-20121120)

162. 'Priyanka Chopra records 45 new songs after In My City success', DigitalSpy.com, 22 January 2013 (http://www.digitalspy.com/bollywood/news/a404941/priyanka-chopra-music-was-a-big-influence-in-my-life/)

163. 'Gordon-Levitt to add Priyanka Chopra's song to his iPod list', FirstPost.com, 4 October 2012 (http://www.firstpost.com/entertainment/gordon-levitt-to-add-priyanka-chopras-song-to-his-ipod-list-479514.html)

164. 'Joseph Gordon-Levitt: 'Priyanka Chopra's In My City going on iPod', Digital Spy, 4 October 2012 (http://www.digitalspy.com/bollywood/news/a410243/joseph-gordon-levitt-priyanka-chopras-in-my-city-going-on-my-ipod/)

165. 'Bollywood's Priyanka Chopra as pioneering pop act in U.S.', *Los Angeles Times*, 20 November 2012 (http://articles.latimes.com/2012/nov/20/entertainment/la-et-ms-1120-bollywood-pop-20121120)

166. 'Who Is Priyanka Chopra? Bollywood Beauty Makes a Splash on NFL's "Thursday Night"', Yahoo.com, 13 September 2013 (https://www.yahoo.com/music/blogs/the-new-now/priyanka-chopra-bollywood-beauty-makes-splash-nfl-thursday-175546487.html)

167. 'Priyanka Chopra: I was Called A Terrorist by NFL Fans', WSJ.com, 18 January 2014 (http://www.wsj.com/video/priyanka-chopra-i-was-called-a-terrorist-by-nfl-fans/CCB1844A-F884-45EA-AAC0-47C48F0C0B83.html)

168. 'From Bollywood to will.i.am: Priyanka Chopra's Big Shot', SPIN.com, 12 October 2012 (https://www.spin.com/2012/10/priyanka-chopra-actress-singer-album-william/)

169. 'Priyanka Chopra on *Nightline*', 6 November 2013 (https://www.

youtube.com/watch?v=DMZiGLnUoK0P)

170. 'The musical journey of the exotic Priyanka Chopra', G Khamba, Firstpost.com, 16 July 2013 https://www.firstpost.com/entertainment/the-musical-journey-of-the-exotic-priyanka-chopra-958479.html

171. 'Priyanka Chopra's song is not so Exotic', *Hindustan Times*, 15 July 2013 (http://www.hindustantimes.com/music/priyanka-chopras-song-is-not-so-exotic/story-kxh2J5fIqBI9shNjFKOiGN.html)

172. 'Pitbull Makes Sexy Beach Vid With Exotic Bollywood Queen Priyanka Chopra!', Perezhilton.com, 7 November 2011 (http://perezhilton.com/2013-07-11-priyanka-chopra-pitbull-exotic-music-video-premiere-sexy-beach#.WtiJIYhubIU)

173. 'Priyanka Chopra Visits Millions of Milkshakes, Makes Fans Go Wild', HuffingtonPost.com, 26 July 2013 (http://www.huffingtonpost.ca/2013/07/26/priyanka-chopra-millions-of-milkshakes_n_3658224.html)

174. 'Priyanka Chopra lends her voice for animated film *Planes*', *The Indian Express,* 26 March 2013 (http://indianexpress.com/article/entertainment/entertainment-others/priyanka-chopra-lends-her-voice-for-animated-film-planes/

175. 'For a Crop-Duster, There's More to Life Than Spraying the Fields', *The New York Times,* 8 August 2013 (http://www.nytimes.com/2013/08/09/movies/disneys-planes-follows-in-the-footsteps-of-cars.html?smid=tw-nytmovies&seid=auto)

176. 'Film Review: *Planes*', *Variety*, 6 August 2013 (http://variety.com/2013/film/reviews/film-review-planes-1200575126/)

177. 'The Move From Celebrity to Ubiquity: Priyanka Chopra, a Bollywood Star From India, Becomes a Top Model for Guess', *The New York Times*, 9 February 2014 (https://www.nytimes.com/2014/02/09/fashion/Priyanka-Chopra-Bollywood-India-Guess.html?ref=fashion&_r=0)

178. 'Priyanka Chopra becomes the first Indian Guess girl', *The Telegraph*, 30 October 2013 (http://fashion.telegraph.co.uk/news-features/TMG10411763/Priyanka-Chopra-becomes-the-first-Indian-Guess-girl.html)

179. 'Guess off to a flying start in India', Rediff.com, 17 September

2005 (http://www.rediff.com/money/2005/sep/17spec1.htm)

180. 'The Epic Fall of Guess Jeans And The Marciano Brothers', Forbes.com, 1 July 2015 (https://www.forbes.com/sites/abrambrown/2015/07/01/the-fall-of-guess-jeans-and-the-marciano-brothers/#75e388171469)

181. 'Priyanka Chopra becomes the first Indian Guess girl', *Telegraph*, 30 October 2013 (http://fashion.telegraph.co.uk/news-features/TMG10411763/Priyanka-Chopra-becomes-the-first-Indian-Guess-girl.html)

182. 'Priyanka Chopra Named New Guess Girl, Bryan Adams Shoots Print Campaign', *The Hollywood Reporter*, 4 November 2013 (https://www.hollywoodreporter.com/news/priyanka-chopra-named-new-guess-653244)

183. 'Priyanka Chopra Named New Guess Girl, Bryan Adams Shoots Print Campaign', *The Hollywood Reporter*, 4 November 2013 (https://www.hollywoodreporter.com/news/priyanka-chopra-named-new-guess-653244)

184. 'When Priyanka Chopra met Bryan Adams', *Bollywood Journalist*, 3 December 2013 (https://bollywoodjournalist.com/2013/12/03/when-priyanka-chopra-met-bryan-adams/comment-page-1/)

185. 'Q&A: Priyanka Chopra, the New Guess Girl', WWD.com, 28 October 2013 (http://wwd.com/fashion-news/sportswear/the-new-guess-girl-7250630/)

186. 'Priyanka Chopra on Her New Country Single and Shattering Indian Stereotypes', Elle.com, 29 April 2014 (http://www.elle.com/culture/music/news/a19247/priyanka-chopra-i-cant-make-you-love-me/)

187. 'The Move From Celebrity to Ubiquity: Priyanka Chopra, a Bollywood Star From India, Becomes a Top Model for Guess', *The New York Times*, 9 February 2014 (https://www.nytimes.com/2014/02/09/fashion/Priyanka-Chopra-Bollywood-India-Guess.html?ref=fashion&_r=0)

188. 'India's Priyanka Chopra masters TV's *Quantico*', *Pacific Daily News*, 28 October 2015 (http://www.guampdn.com/story/

life / tv / 2015 / 10 / 27 / priyanka-chopra-india-abc-quantico-star / 74598088 /)

189. 'India's Priyanka Chopra masters TV's *Quantico*', *Pacific Daily News*, 28 October 2015 (http://www.guampdn.com/story/life / tv / 2015 / 10 / 27 / priyanka-chopra-india-abc-quantico-star / 74598088 /)

190. 'Priyanka Chopra: The girl who leapt through time', MSN.com, 12 October 2015 (https://www.msn.com/en-my/entertainment/news/priyanka-chopra-the-girl-who-leapt-through-time/ar-AAfkJlU)

191. 'Priyanka Chopra: The girl who leapt through time', MSN.com, 12 October 2015 (https://www.msn.com/en-my/entertainment/news/priyanka-chopra-the-girl-who-leapt-through-time/ar-AAfkJlU)

192. 'ABC Exec Keli Lee Talks Casting For Diversity In Hollywood', Forbes.com, 17 November 2015 (https://www.forbes.com/sites/anushayhossain/2015/11/17/abc-exec-keli-lee-talks-casting-for-diversity-in-hollywood/2/#6e06b3235e1a)

193. 'ABC Exec Keli Lee Talks Casting For Diversity In Hollywood', Forbes.com, 17 November 2015 (https://www.forbes.com/sites/anushayhossain/2015/11/17/abc-exec-keli-lee-talks-casting-for-diversity-in-hollywood/2/#6e06b3235e1a)

194. 'Meet Priyanka Chopra, the Bollywood Star Who's More than Ready for Prime Time', *Vanity Fair*, 24 September 2015 (https://www.vanityfair.com/hollywood/2015/09/priyanka-chopra-quantico).

195. 'Quantico Premiere Preview: Priyanka Chopra, showrunner Joshua Safran speak', *Entertainment Weekly*, 27 September 2015 (http://ew.com/article/2015/09/27/quantico-season-premiere-preview/)

196. 'In *Quantico*, Bollywood's Priyanka Chopra Seeks an American Foothold', *The New York Times*, 20 September 2015 (https://www.nytimes.com/2015/09/20/arts/television/in-quantico-bollywoods-priyanka-chopra-seeks-an-american-foothold.html)

197. 'Why Priyanka Chopra's *Quantico* Casting Was a Game Changer for EP Joshua Safran', TheWrap.com, 27 September 2015 (https://

www.thewrap.com/why-priyanka-chopras-quantico-casting-was-a-game-changer-for-ep-joshua-safran/)

198. 'In *Quantico*, Bollywood's Priyanka Chopra Seeks an American Foothold', *The New York Times*, 20 September 2015 (https://www.nytimes.com/2015/09/20/arts/television/in-quantico-bollywoods-priyanka-chopra-seeks-an-american-foothold.html)

199. 'In *Quantico*, Bollywood's Priyanka Chopra Seeks an American Foothold', *The New York Times*, 20 September 2015 (https://www.nytimes.com/2015/09/20/arts/television/in-quantico-bollywoods-priyanka-chopra-seeks-an-american-foothold.html)

200. 'From Bollywood to Hollywood: Shattering Stereotypes on the Silver Screen', NPR.org, 10 December 2015 (http://www.npr.org/sections/codeswitch/2015/12/10/459247595/from-bollywood-to-hollywood-shattering-stereotypes-on-the-silver-screen)

201. 'Priyanka Chopra on *Late Night With Seth Myers*', 3 November 2016 (https://www.youtube.com/watch?v=_tvSxExy9TI&t=27s)

202. 'Priyanka Chopra's Accent Is Helping Me Solve My Biggest Identity Crisis', Buzzfeed.com, 13 September 2015 (https://www.buzzfeed.com/regajha/how-do-you-pronounce-quantico?utm_term=.lnG2Ovoge#.ie5Kp4d5a)

203. 'Meet Priyanka Chopra, the Bollywood Star Who's More than Ready for Prime Time', *Vanity Fair*, 24 September 2015 (https://www.vanityfair.com/hollywood/2015/09/priyanka-chopra-quantico)

204. '*Quantico* premiere previews: Priyanka Chopra, showrunner Joshua Safran speak', *Entertainment Weekly*, 27 September 2015 (http://ew.com/article/2015/09/27/quantico-season-premiere-preview/)

205. '*Quantico's* Priyanka Chopra High-Wattage Indian Star, Got TV Bug From Kevin Spacey', *The Hollywood Reporter*, 4 August 2015 (http://www.hollywoodreporter.com/live-feed/quanticos-priyanka-chopra-high-wattage-813098)

206. '*Quantico* TV Review', *The Hollywood Reporter*, 27 September 2015 (http://www.hollywoodreporter.com/review/quantico-tv-review-827460)

207. '*Quantico's* Review: Priyanka Chopra Scores in Silly Spy Drama',

Tim Grierson, TheWrap.com, 27 September 2015 http://www.thewrap.com/quantico-review-priyanka-chopra-scores-in-silly-spy-drama/

208. https://twitter.com/QuanticoTV/media
209. 'Quantico Flips Between Jousting FBI Recruits and a Terrorist Attack', *The New York Times*, 24 September 2015 (http://www.nytimes.com/2015/09/25/arts/television/review-quantico-flips-between-jousting-fbi-recruits-and-a-terrorist-attack.html?_r=0)
210. 'Priyanka Chopra says no to film with Abhishek Bachchan', *The Asian Age*, 3 October 2017 (http://www.asianage.com/entertainment/bollywood/031017/priyanka-chopra-says-abhishek-bachchan-nahi.html)
211. 'Priyanka Chopra explains her "scary" concussion at People's Choice', *USA Today*, 19 January 2017 (https://www.usatoday.com/story/life/entertainthis/2017/01/18/priyanka-chopra-explains-her-scary-concussion-peoples-choice-awards/96750256/)
212. 'Quantico premiere previews: Priyanka Chopra, showrunner Joshua Safran speak', *Entertainment Weekly*, 27 September 2015 (http://ew.com/article/2015/09/27/quantico-season-premiere-preview/)
213. 'Priyanka Chopra on the *Arsenio Hall Show*', 29 October 2013 (https://www.youtube.com/watch?v=bFWql_9yZJA)
214. 'Priyanka Chopra on *Jimmy Kimmel Live*', 20 January 2017 (https://www.youtube.com/watch?v=IlOXxmU_Dng)
215. 'Tom Hiddleston and Priyanka Chopra Spotted Getting Flirty at Emmy's After-Party', *eonline.com*, 18 September 2016 (http://www.eonline.com/news/795772/tom-hiddleston-and-priyanka-chopra-spotted-getting-flirty-at-emmys-after-party)
216. 'Priyanka Chopra Lost a Movie Because of Her Skin Colour', *InStyle*, 10 April 2018 (http://www.instyle.com/news/priyanka-chopra-equal-pay)
217. 'The 100 Most Influential People: Priyanka Chopra', *Time*, 21 April 2016 (http://time.com/collection-post/4299686/priyanka-chopra-2016-time-100/)
218. 'Quantico's' Priyanka Chopra, High-Wattage Indian Star, Got TV Bug From Kevin Spacey', *The Hollywood Reporter*, 4 August

2014 (http://www.hollywoodreporter.com/live-feed/quanticos-priyanka-chopra-high-wattage-813098)

219. 'Priyanka Chopra says *Baywatch* is what the world needs right now', *Metro*, 17 June 2017 (http://metro.co.uk/2017/06/17/priyanka-chopra-says-baywatch-is-what-the-world-needs-right-now-6715115/)

220. '*Baywatch* and Letters From Baghdad', *The New Yorker*, 5 and 12 June 2017 (https://www.newyorker.com/magazine/2017/06/05/baywatch-and-letters-from-baghdad)

221. 'One Day They'll Say the *Baywatch* Movie Was the Day Dwayne Johnson Became the President', *The Village Voice*, 26 May 2017 https://www.villagevoice.com/2017/05/26/one-day-theyll-say-the-baywatch-movie-was-the-day-dwayne-johnson-became-president/)

222. '*Baywatch* Movie Review: Priyanka Chopra Deserves Better Than This', NDTV.com, 2 June 2017 (https://www.ndtv.com/india-news/baywatch-movie-review-priyanka-chopra-deserves-better-than-this-1706906)

223. 'Priyanka Chopra brings the world to Toronto', *The Toronto Star*, 1 September 2017 (https://www.thestar.com/entertainment/tiff/2017/09/01/priyanka-chopra-brings-the-world-to-toronto-govani.html)

224. 'Om Puri: The actor who never got his due', BBC.com, 6 January 2017 (http://www.bbc.co.uk/news/world-asia-india-38527144)

225. 'Academy Awards Acceptance Speech Database: Satyajit Ray', (http://aaspeechesdb.oscars.org/link/064-24/)

226. 'Aishwarya Rai on *The Late Show With David Letterman*', March 2005 (https://www.youtube.com/watch?v=vbCzbjvCCSk)

227. 'The World's Most Beautiful Woman', *60 Minutes* (https://www.youtube.com/watch?v=ZumBp1wXJQc)

228. 'Hot & Handsome: these photos of Fawad Khan will make you drool', Pinkvilla.com, 15 November 2017 (https://www.pinkvilla.com/entertainment/photos/hot-handsome-these-photos-fawad-khan-will-make-you-drool-391307)

229. '*A Kid Like Jake*: Film Review', *The Hollywood Reporter*, 24 January 2018 (https://www.hollywoodreporter.com/review/a-kid-like-

jake-review-1077799)

230. '*A Kid Like Jake* Review: Silad Howard Directs a Simple but Effective Drama About Raising a Non-Binary Child—Sundance 2018', IndieWire.com, 24 January 2018 (http://www.indiewire. com/2018/01/a-kid-like-jake-review-silas-howard-jim-parsons-claire-danes-sundance-2018-1201921477/)

231. 'Sundance Film Review: *A Kid Like Jake*', *Variety* (http://variety. com/2018/film/reviews/a-kid-like-jake-review-1202679732/ )

232. '*A Kid Like Jake*'s Claire Danes on Silad Howard's "Intensely Relatable" Family Drama—Sundance Studio', Deadline.com, 22 January 2018 (http://deadline.com/2018/01/a-kid-like-jake-claire-danes-jim-parsons-sundance-interview-1202265878/)

233. 'Quantico Season 1 Just Got a Lot Bigger', CinemaBlend.com, (https://www.cinemablend.com/television/Quantico-Season-1-Just-Got-Lot-Bigger-92047.html)

234. 'Quantico gets a shorter third season and will get a new showrunner', TV By The Numbers, 15 May 2017 (http:// tvbythenumbers.zap2it.com/more-tv-news/quantico-gets-a-shorter-third-season-and-will-get-a-new-showrunner/)

235. 'ABC cancels Quantico, Designated Survivor', *Entertainment Weekly*, 11 May 2018 (http://ew.com/tv/2018/05/11/abc-cancels-quantico-designated-survivor/)

236. 'Priyanka Chopra's Kalpana Chawla biopic stalled', *DNA India*, 28 April 2018 (http://www.dnaindia.com/bollywood/report-priyanka-chopra-s-kalpana-chawla-biopic-stalled-2609308)

237. 73 Questions With Priyanka Chopra, *Vogue*, 24 May 2017 (https:// www.youtube.com/watch?v=dOUV2rwMr1g)

# ACKNOWLEDGEMENTS

In the fall of 2016, I approached Priyanka Chopra's team in the US, hoping to spend some time with her and interview her for this book. I had interviewed Priyanka a few times in the past, but I wanted to talk to her in depth about her life and her work. After a series of messages and emails and a lengthy phone conversation with her lawyers in New York, I was eventually told that Priyanka would not be available to talk to me for this book.

I was disappointed, but many people were more than happy to speak to me about Priyanka Chopra—the person, the actress, and the star.

This book would not have been possible without the interviews I conducted with the following people (some before I had set out to write this book): Anjula Acharya, Sharbari Zohra Ahmed, Zoya Akhtar, Anurag Basu, Madhur Bhandarkar, Vishal Bhardwaj, Rahul Bose, Subarna Ray Chaudhuri, Madhu Chopra, Vishal Dadlani, Dharmesh Darshan, Suneel Darshan, Eric Deggans, Pradeep Guha, Prakash Jha, Karan Johar, Omung Kumar, Manav Kaul, Tarun Mansukhani, Rajesh Mapuskar, Paul Marciano, Sheila Marikar, Sabira Merchant, Dia Mirza, Samarth Nagarkar, Gitesh Pandya, Sathya Saran, Rohan Sippy, Rajiv Suri and Paakhi Tyerwala.

I am also grateful to the following people who advised me,

sent me research material during the writing of the book, shared images of Priyanka and contact information for people I wanted to interview. So, thank you Farhan Akhtar, Madeline Berg, Rekha Bhardwaj, Rohit Bhatnagar, Amarjeet Chahal, Pratim Das Gupta, Siobhan Egan, Anisha Jhaveri, Shrey Khetarpal, Ronjita Kulkarni, Nikhil Lakshman, Rajeev Masand, Somen Mishra, Ishika Mohan Motwane, Kim Nabozny, Maitreya Padukone, Nisha Pahuja, Sri Rao, Shobha Iyer Sant, Swati Shetty, Aroon Shivdasani, and Aarti Virani.

Special thanks to my editor, Shambhu Sahu. His passion for the book kept me going, even when some of the interviews were not happening. We had healthy arguments during the editing stages. He was patient, listened to my point of view and almost always let me win. Thanks also to my other editor— Aparna Kumar for meticulously reading and editing through the manuscript.

In the fall of 2016, when I was starting to work on this book, I made a life-changing decision—to spend more time in India to care for my ailing mother. I had lived for the past three and a half decades in the US. A large portion of the book was researched, written and edited in 2017, and then in the early months of 2018, when I was living in Noida, India. I must thank my cousins, Rakesh and Sonal Popli, for feeding me during those days, as I lived next to their apartment. Also special thanks to my niece and nephew—Diya and Avi Popli—for their company and excitement in my work, and cousins Radhika and Rajiv Duggal for the number of times they asked me how the book was coming along. Their interest in Priyanka Chopra and excitement about the book kept me motivated.

A special thanks to my New York friends, who, in many ways, are closer to me than my own family. I met many of them during the days we were active members of the South Asian Journalists

Association, but the bonding became stronger over the years, especially after they all followed me and moved to Queens, New York. So thank you S. Mitra Kalita, Nitin Mukul, Arun Venugopal, Meera Nair, Vikas Bajaj, Hari Sreenivasan, Sucheta Sachdev, and Manu and Sree Bhagwan for feeding me on many occasions and letting me stay in their apartments for extended periods of times. Thanks for the long gossip sessions and conversations about books, films and how to survive in the age of Donald Trump. Thanks to many friends in Manhattan, including Sree Sreenivasan and Roopa Unnikrishnan, for supporting me through all these years; to Mallika Dutt for constantly reminding me that I should be writing books; to Geetanjali Misra, my Telluride Film Festival companion for more than a decade, who, on many occasions, pulled me out of my boredom in Delhi and Noida and kept my spirits high over many glasses of wine; and to Megha Bhouraskar for sharing her love for films and movie stars with me.

I am grateful to my friends, Girimohan Coneti and Kruti Suba, who let me stay in their apartment in Brooklyn for weeks, while I visited New York and was working on this book. Thanks Giri da for giving me a home in New York. And thanks to Dev Benegal for keeping me abreast with stories about Bombay's film industry and, well, for laughing at my jokes.

And thank you Priyanka Chopra, for entertaining the fan in me, keeping me enthralled with many amazing characters you have played on screen and for leading a fascinating life. I am honoured to have spent nearly two years of my life—watching your films, reading, thinking and writing about you.

CPSIA information can be obtained
at www.ICGtesting.com
Printed in the USA
LVHW082045220520
656320LV00013B/125/J

9 789353 041168